Anthem of the Unwoke

—Yep! the other lot's gone bonkers

Tony Thomas

Anthem of the Unwoke

—Yep! the other lot's gone bonkers

Tony Thomas

Connor Court Publishing Pty Ltd

CONTENTS

INTRODUCTION

I'd better confess: I'm obsessed with writing. At age 82 I don't have many commitments and I get a buzz working up every new article or essay.

My main pleasure is exposing and mocking the green/Left/feminist crowd known as the "wokerati". This powerful minority now seems to control education, electricity, race politics, our history, the arts, sex and gender discussion, the ABC, the bureaucracy and much of the media.

The wokerati's intolerance of dissent goes against Australians' traditional mindset of "a fair go". Step out of line at the office, workplace, laboratory or school staffroom and your career's in jeopardy. Worse, no-one knows any more where the line is. Someone might decide you've committed a micro-aggression or made them feel "unsafe" or used an expression that is not "inclusive". No grovelling can save you from the pile-on.

Moreover, the wokerati operates a time machine. They crucify you for something you wrote or did 20 years ago, even during your teen student days. I myself should be cancelled: in the Perth newspaper I worked for in the 1960s we wrote as though females were irrelevant – it was a man's world. In another 50 years, today's proclaimed truths for sure will also be viewed with scorn and contempt.

Wokerati's "feelings" are paramount. These people don't respect facts or make things work or provide valued business services. Wokerati waffle has no boundaries or tests. Unlike, for example, the gang of concreters laying in the foundations for a pair of two-storey houses on a block down the road – I walk our pup past there mornings and evenings and enjoy watching their progress.

On one cold and drizzly day they started soon after 6am and were loading stuff back into their utes at 6.30pm, also in the dark. One concreter had worked in nothing but shorts and boots. I got chatting. He was about 30, stocky and well-padded. He had a decisive manner and seemed pleased to be noticed.

"Aren't you freezing?" – "Nah, not on this job all day."

"How do you get the levels so exact?" – "Easy, with these lasers. Come round tomorrow and I'll give you a demo."

"Geez you start early!" – "Look, if we didn't we'd still be here at midnight. It's dark enough now as it is."

"Well I really admire your skills. You really know what you're doing." – "Ha! We get it right some of the time."

I looked at the new stretches of rectangular slabs with quite a few stepped levels and blocked-out shapes, all as smooth as billiard tables and silky enough to eat off. The site was low-lying and around the concrete borders the churned-over mud looked half a metre deep. I wondered how my concreter friend had managed to avoid mud-baths, or did he have ways to clean himself down at knock-off? What did he have for lunch, if anything? He lives in a different world to mine.

It struck me how much teamwork is involved, right from when the old weatherboard cottage on the block was knocked down. The on-site guys had been directing earth-movers for a week. And when these new foundations harden, new teams will take over to complete two fine new houses. There's nothing "woke" about construction guys.

My own less-arduous desk-work that day was googling the earnest activities of green-minded feminists at Sydney and RMIT universities. Here's a sample:

I've been crying myself to sleep a lot lately. And crying at random times too. It's not as though I watch a video about climate change, and I cry during it. I mean sometimes that happens. It's more like, something little happens, like my toast burns, and I have an existential breakdown because I think it's a metaphor for how the world is burning because we aren't paying attention.

Pollsters have found that in the 2022 federal election, electorates with high wealth and high years of education voted for Greens candidates, while battlers' areas were choosing conservatives. The new Greens MPs – nearly all affluent women professionals – won on feel-good slogans about climate policy. I'd love to know the voting trend among my non-woke concreters: would they be interested in electric concrete trucks and electric Komatsu excavators? What size batteries would these machines need anyway? Would the feminist academics' thinking about the climate in 2050 pass these blokes' pub test? I reckon not.

Woke craziness is multiplying. As I write, the Australian Department of Health has finally provided Parliament with an answer to the Question on Notice, "What is a woman?" Running scared, the department's 80-word answer includes,

The Department of Health does not adopt a single definition. Health policies and access to health programs are based on clinical evidence and clinical need for all Australians, regardless of gender identity, biological characteristics, or genetic variations ...

I suspect that not one Australian in 20 subscribes to this sort of woke piety. But the young are going for it, thanks to brainwashing at school. The woke Left has captured the education system to give kids a giant dose of training in wokeness. It starts literally at child-care, kindergarten and pre-school, followed by a decade's worth at primary and secondary schools and several extra years' propaganda for the 60% who go on to university.

In that whole period kids have probably never been exposed to contrary arguments – such as the weaknesses of climate models, the downsides of "Voices" for those identifying as Aborigines, and drawbacks of big government. At most, educators provide kids with straw-man ('straw person?') arguments for kids to easily knock over, while warning them against visiting internet sites displaying data that's non-conforming.

Curriculum writers and educators are frank that they are coaching kids to be activists. It's meant to prepare kids for "citizenship" – to become involved in community affairs. Apart from the bias towards green activism, I'd argue that kids who don't know much about anything are in no position to "reform" society anyway.

The first slab of this book is about climate change or, more correctly, how the anti-emissions crowd has become deranged about it. This material's all factual, but you might think, "Surely he's made that up!"

Part two is more disquieting: what's going on now in class and tutorial rooms. I've drawn their materials from text books and lesson templates and inadvertent disclosures by teachers and kids. My own formative years were marred by adults' politics and I really feel kids should enjoy their childhood free of brainwashing and going on demos for causes beyond their comprehension.

Other sections of the book deal with controversies about Aborigines, the biased state of the media and ABC, and fondness of the wokerati for Karl Marx and his legacies.

Readers are often curious about an author, so I'll mention my 42 years in paid journalism (*The West Australian* and Fairfax) and 20 years post-retirement writing essays for pleasure. This book is my fifth collection since 2016, drawn from more than 500 pieces published in *Quadrant Online* via my excellent editor Roger Franklin.

Finally, thanks and love to my long-suffering wife and best friend Marg, whose labours on the home front and other sacrifices make possible my obsessive writing.

Feel free to send me feedback, good or bad, to tthomas061@gmail.com

PART ONE

CLIMATE CRAZINESS IN FULL CRY

Shut them up, argues the Academy of Science

30 August 2022

In a move unprecedented in the democratic world, the Australian Academy of Science is lobbying the tech giants Meta (Facebook), Twitter, Google, Microsoft, Apple, Adobe and TikTok to censor and harass any Australians who circulate what the Academy insultingly labels "climate denialism misinformation".

The Academy represents 589 leading scientists and operates as funding/political lobby and trade union for the largely university-based science community. When not disrespecting freedom of speech and crying wolf about climate perils, it does good work promoting Australian science in education and the community.

It wants the Big Tech giants to "inoculate" Australians against critics of alarmism by "actively promoting reliable, peer-reviewed and appropriately labelled material from trusted sources," presumably the Academy and its followers. "These positive measures should be in addition to measures to reduce the spread of disinformation."

The Orwellian agenda is in the Academy's public submission to the tech giants' 2022 review of the Australian Code of Practice on Misinformation and Disinformation. The Academy made its submission on August 3 in conjunction with the junior group, the Australian Academy of Technology & Engineering.

The Academies want the tech giants' power brought to bear against news organisations – it specifically names Rupert Murdoch's "Sky News Australia and its media personalities".

Dr Garth Paltridge, who has been a Fellow of the Science Academy for more than 30 years, is shocked that the Academy is turning to Big Tech to shut down climate debate. He says, "The bottom line is that research on climate change is indeed still highly controversial – both in the prediction of the extent of the change and (even more so) in the prediction of the impact of the change on society.

"I just cannot understand how any science academy that is supposed to operate through rational debate can behave like this – that is, to use pure political brute force to prevent one side of the argument from putting its case.

"I can only assume that the Academy is subconsciously 'chasing the money' and is influenced by the vast funding available these days for the support of alarmist climate research. Certainly there is virtually no money to support scientists brave enough to put their heads above the parapet with a contrary view. That might be why the critical scientists seem largely to be retired."

The Academies' submission says,

The Code currently excludes professional news content that is published under a publicly available editorial code, except where a platform determines that specific instances fall within the scope of disinformation. However, some Australian news outlets are havens for climate science misinformation (Lowe, 2018) – so this exclusion undermines the ability of the Code to guard against such denialism.

This exclusion allows climate science denialism and other misinformation to flourish, either through lack of enforcement of the disinformation provision of the Code or failure of news outlets' misinformation to meet the higher bar of being considered disinformation. For example, a UK report recently found that Sky News Australia and its media personalities are a key source of climate science misinformation globally, including during the late 2021 United Nations Climate Change

*Conference (COP26) (King, Janulewicz & Arcostanzo, 2022).
Clearly, the Code was not sufficient to address the traction of
climate misinformation from Sky News Australia during this
time.*

A King et al paper, *Deny, Deceive, Delay*, which the Academies'
submission cites approvingly, refers to "political right-wing … top
influencers" as part of an alleged "intellectual dark web". The authors
name Sky Australia's Rita Panahi and prominent UK, European and
North American sceptics. The authors condemn Ms Panahi as follows:

> *Pahani [sic] is an American-born Iranian refugee who be-
> came a prominent right-wing media personality in Australia.
> Starting her media career at the major News Corp newspaper
> the Herald Sun, Panani [sic] also hosts a show at Sky News
> Australia. She belongs to a set of presenters at the station that
> are promoting the most controversial content and platform
> conspiracy theorists. During COP26, Panahi attacked Prince
> Charles as the "biggest hypocrite and idiot" and claimed he
> bullied a hitherto reluctant Australian PM Scott Morrison
> to attend the summit. Previously, she called climate change
> "scaremongering" that was not "rooted in hard science."*

It's curious that Rita Panahi is the only ornery Australian individual actually named in the Academies' submission and citations.
The major damage to the Academies' catastrophism is being done
by Andrew Bolt on Sky, Chris Kenny in *The Australian*, the *Specta-
tor (Australia)*, Joanne Nova's world-ranked sceptic blog, the Institute of Public Affairs' bulletins and speakers, Tim Blair's blog for
the *Daily Telegraph* (sadly, paywalled), Senators Malcolm Roberts
and Pauline Hanson, the Nationals' ex-Minister Matt Canavan and

ex-PM Tony Abbott, famed for calling climate science "absolute crap" and likening climate scientists – presciently – as "thought police".

All this sceptic output is re-cited and re-published on social media. Clearly the Academies would be delighted to see the tech-media giants slapping "Misinformation!" and "Code Violation!" labels on it, cancelling accounts, as LinkedIn has been doing to US sceptics, and down-ranking the material to oblivion on search engines.

The Science Academy's chief executive is Anna-Maria Arabia, whose early career included a total of five years as an adviser with Anthony Albanese and Kim Beazley. In a subsequent job as chief executive of Science & Technology Australia, she led a march of 200 members to Parliament in 2011 calling for legislation or similar means to silence global warming sceptics. She jumped to the Academy leadership in 2016 after three years part-time as policy director for the Opposition Leader Bill Shorten.

Various members of the alleged " intellectual dark web", according to the Academies' cited King paper, include mega-best-selling psychologist Dr Jordan B. Petersen, Danish climate rationalist (but orthodox warmist) Dr Bjorn Lomborg, US investigative author Dinesh D'Souza, Canadian founder of Rebel Media Ezra Levant, US blogger Tony Heller who daily fact-checks alarmist propaganda, Dr Patrick Moore, who co-founded Greenpeace but quit over its anti-science campaigns, Michael Shellenberger, another sceptic convert from environmentalist lobbies, Prager University which combats left-wing academia's brainwashing, US media personality Sebastian Gorka who has perceptively likened climate policy to Stalinism, artist Scott Adams and his Dilbert cartoons, and American Tom Fitton of *Judicial Watch* and critic of Antifa – justifiably — as a far-Left terror group. The King paper says (p. 32),

While climate issues are not part of their [conservative pundits] main content strategy, they nevertheless engage in frequent criticism of their respective governments' environmental policies, attack or ridicule prominent climate activists, or employ narratives outlined in the previous section of this report. During COP26 in particular, they downplayed the climate emergency and amplified accusations of hypocrisy against politicians and other figures attending the Glasgow summit.

Another paper cited approvingly and quoted by the two Academies is a conspiracy rant *The Toxic Ten — How ten fringe publishers fuel 69% of digital climate change denial.* It is published by a fringe leftist group calling itself Center for Countering Digital Hate. Calling the sceptics "fringe" publishers is odd as the Center then says they have 186 million direct followers. The Center's evil-ten list is *Breitbart News, The Western Journal,* Newsmax, Townhall, *Washington Times* (as distinct from leftist *Washington Post*), *The Federalist,* hugely popular centre-right commentator Ben Shapiro's *Daily Wire, The Patriot Post* and the Media Research Center. And just to smear sceptics by association, "Russian State Media".

I am familiar with the US Media Research Center, a well-resourced and incisive critic of America's Democrat-supporting mainstream media. I read every morning its "Newsbusters" update (damned in the cited paper) which pillories the daily bias in left-liberal print and electronic media. I also tune in regularly to Ben Shapiro's daily podcasts, which involve per month 20 million visitors, 130 million page views and 40 million downloads. Blocking such outlets would be a huge win for the Left.

The Academies' cited *Toxic Ten* paper actually attacks Facebook, Twitter et al for supposed slackness in censoring critics of alarmism, calling them "greedy platforms" sucking in money from fossil fuel interests:

> *It is the greatest crisis ever faced by our species ... We are calling on Facebook and Google to stop promoting and funding climate denial, start labelling it as misinformation, and stop giving the advantages of their enormous platform to lies and misinformation. As long as Facebook and Google carry on doing business with climate deniers, they cannot claim to be 'green.' They owe it to us and the planet we all share, to deliver.*

The two Academies also want a tech-giant crackdown on any "issues advertising" involving criticism of their net-zero CO_2 fantasies and apocalyptic forecasting. A sceptic group called "The Climate Study Group" has paid for about ten ads in *The Australian* exposing flaws in the climate-apocalyse narrative and the harmful impacts of renewables. It could be the Academy's target.

The Academies also want a crackdown on health information with which it disagrees, notwithstanding that health bureaucrats such as America's Dr Fauci, Victoria's Dr Brett Sutton and politicians often change their minds about what COVID science claims are valid. So much for "misinformation".

The Academies also appear stung by the revelation from the Australian Institute of Marine Science that the Barrier Reef's coral extent is the highest on record, notwithstanding the Science Academy harping for decades on the Reef's alleged perilous decline. The Academy now says (my emphasis),

> *Climate denialism is just one example of how misinformation results in societal harm. Disinformation on health matters (such as false and misleading vaccination, sexual and reproductive health information), or ecological and environ-*

mental matters **(such as material misrepresenting studies of coral bleaching on the Great Barrier Reef)** *are a barrier to good policy and a healthy society.*

The Science Academy began life in 1954 as a respected body, but in the past decade has been captured by the green/Left lobby. For example, it displayed its dark-green philosophy and economic illiteracy in 2014 by sponsoring and bankrolling its Fenner conference on an anti-growth theme titled, "Addicted to Growth? How to move to a Steady State Economy in Australia." The show attracted a host of eco-nutters keen to drag Australian living standards down by 50-90%.

About the same year it dumped on high schoolers a supposed "Science by Doing" course, taxpayer-funded, for 10,000 science teachers and around 60,000 students.

It urged the teachers to shame kids into climate activism:

Ask [15-16 years old] students if they have ever taken action or advocated for a cause. Do they know of anyone who has?"... Key vocabulary: advocacy, campaign, champion, environmentalist.

PLUS lesson outcomes: *At the end of this activity students will ... appreciate the need to lobby at all levels of government to ignite and lead change – even if it is unpopular with the voters.*

PLUS: *"If you were concerned about Earth's sustainability, who would you vote for?"*

PLUS: *"Could we do without it [mining]? ... Would you work for a mining company?"*

PLUS: *"Students debate the merits of government spending on science. They research six big-systems experiments and justify their funding proposals. Which big experiment will you fund?"*

PLUS (in an updated 2018 version): *"Scientists let us know all the facts and figures about climate change. They know just how quickly the icebergs are melting, and almost to the day when the Great Barrier Reef will be dead."* [Today, record coral extent]

PLUS: propaganda songs, cartoons of "CO2 elephants" dropping from the sky, featuring of conspiracists like Naomi Oreskes and video rants by alarmists competing with Al Gore to depict the coming apocalypse.

It withdrew the course soon after its public exposure.

The Academy not only fell hook line and sinker for "death threat" nonsense from ANU luvvies some years back, but just last year ran the fauxborigine Bruce Pascoe as its opening plenary speaker at its Future Earth three-day summit called Reimagining Climate Adaptation. Bruce regaled the Academy's science-friendly audience about how his alleged forebears chatted to whales in Bass Strait circa 12,000BC, before joining their peace-loving cousins in Victoria (shields an optional fashion accessory).

The Academies' submission shows influencing from the psychologists Drs John Cook and Stephan Lewandowski playbook on how to deal with "deniers" who continually find support among the public. Those two psychologists spent much of their careers at Monash/Queensland and WA Universities respectively, trying to liken climate sceptics to various sorts of lunatic conspirators. Cook was lead author for the 2013 paper claiming a 97 per cent scientific consensus for the orthodox warming hypothesis – though he defined the hypothesis so broadly that the vast majority of sceptics would also agree with it. Cook's paper on the alleged "97 per cent" was eviscerated in the peer-reviewed science literature by Dr David Legates et al as flawed in every dimension and actually showing only a 0.3% consensus. Another of the Cook-Lewandowsky papers on "deniers" (Recursive Fury) in 2014 was retracted by its hosting journal, Frontiers.

Cook-Lewandowski's 28-page playbook invented the concept of "inoculating" people against "denialism" by getting in first with orthodox claims. The Academies' third recommendation uses the same meme:

Platforms should consider mechanisms for proactive promotion of trusted information to inoculate against misinformation.

The Academies' submission also castigates "anti-scientific" scepticism without any attempt to answer claims by scientists who dispute the orthodoxy – scientists often an order of magnitude more eminent than the Academy executives trying to shut them down.

For example, in mid-2019 ninety leading Italian scientists petitioned the Italian government that the IPCC climate narrative about CO_2 warming from human activity was an unproven hypothesis deduced merely from complex computer models. They said natural variability involving the sun, moon and ocean currents can explain most of the warming, and the suppression of fossil-fuel energy is therefore harmful to society.

The petition's lead authors are below. I am not saying numbers of signatories matter, only disputing the Academy suggestion that sceptics are anti-science nutters:

1. Uberto Crescenti, Emeritus Professor of Applied Geology, University G. D'Annunzio, Chieti-Pescara, formerly Rector and President of the Italian Geological Society.

2. Giuliano Panza, Professor of Seismology, University of Trieste, Academician of the Lincei and of the National Academy of Sciences, awardee of the 2018 International Award of the American Geophysical Union.

3. Alberto Prestininzi, Professor of Applied Geology, La Sapi-

enza University, Rome, formerly Scientific Editor in Chief of the magazine International IJEGE and Director of the Geological Risk Forecasting and Control Research Center.

It's my speculation that the Academies were emboldened to take their brazen anti-debate stance by the success of Twitter and Facebook in swinging the US 2020 election Biden's way. The Academy had been appalled by Trump's disavowal of the Paris 2015 agreement and his rollback of Obama's anti-emissions regime. The digitech giants in the crucial last weeks of the campaign suppressed the corruption revelations from Hunter Biden's laptop. Facebook was encouraged by the politically corrupted FBI and more than 50 ex-intelligence operatives to falsely label the laptop contents as Russian disinformation. The Washington Post and New York Times, six months after Biden's accession, admitted the contents were authentic.

Oh well, the Academy of Science seems happy now to trash its own credibility. Say what you like, I still insist the Academy does some good work in non-alarmist disciplines.#

The strange thoughts of catastrophe lovers

21 September 2021

I was about to plough through the global politicians' summary of the IPCC's sixth report, but then I saw the Australian psychologists' guidelines for reading it safely:

> How you read the IPCC report or climate media reports bears thinking about. It is important to be kind to yourself, and to be in as calm and grounded a state as one can be. Ideally do this with a trusted companion or a group of colleagues. Choose the time of day to read and a pleasant setting, perhaps first walking or meditating in a natural setting. It can be helpful to read slowly, noting your feelings, taking pauses to focus on your breath and checking in with yourself and with others. Try not to take in more than you can digest, and take time out for refreshments.

Their alert includes a twilight pic of a maiden on the end of a jetty, considering a dip pending the planet's fiery demise. The Melbourne-founded group called Psychology for a Safe Climate provides the warning. I laid the IPCC aside and tucked up in bed with psychotherapist member Dr Sally Gillespie's Western Sydney University Ph.D. thesis "*Mapping Myths, Dreams and Conversations in the Era of Global Warming*".

I found another group spokesperson is Melbourne psychiatrist Charles Le Feuvre, who has written:

> In Australia there continues to be Government denial. Our leaders could be seen psychiatrically as deluded and a danger to others and if so certifiable. At worst they can be seen as

guilty of crimes against humanity and nature-homicide and ecocide — and indeed in the future they may be found to be ... What is the nature of [then Prime Minister] Scott Morrison's denial?

Le Feuvre, who sees the unfortunate Greta Thunberg as "an incredible role model" and "highly rational", had his climate motives reinforced by the Wye River (Vic) bushfires: "Our house was completely destroyed apart from a statue of Venus," he wrote piteously.

Here's Sally's dream on Page 1 of her thesis, a dream that turned her into a climate activist:

It's the end of the world through climate change. Whole continents are sinking beneath the sea as water levels rise. Millions of people are attempting to cling to the shore, and to their lives, fruitlessly. At one stage I swing in the air clinging to a rope as land masses shift around beneath me. At another stage I cling to the shore line and a poodle swims up into my arms. I steal biscuits for us, and someone says about the poodle "He's a salesman".

I know billions must die and only tens of thousands will remain ... It's horrifying. Any possibility of distancing myself from climate change reports collapses through this night vision which awakens such intense feelings of vulnerability, for myself and all others on Earth.

She doesn't say whether the poodle is a Royal Standard, Standard, Moyen, Toy, Miniature or Tea-Cup, but it's definitely not a goldendoodle, Labradoodle or Pekapoos. Whichever the peckish paddling poodle might be, I share Dr Sally's intense identification with all other poodles and peoples on Earth.

She writes,

The dream crashed through my justifications and denials, insisting that I live fully in the knowledge of the seriousness of climate change. I closed my psychotherapy practice of twenty five years to focus on research into psychological responses to climate change and its reports ... I start to calm down.

In another dream, Dr Sally is assigned to critique a Doris Lessing novel about climate change. She gets low marks from "a young woman, a smart cultural theorist" who provides comments written on ravioli.

The tantalising image of the 'ravioli marks' stayed with me, strangely apt in its sensual interplay of inner and outer, forms and fillings, offering richly-embodied sustenance and meaning.

She writes that climate denialists are not directly comparable to Nazis. Thanks for that, Sally. But she does "observe some mutual resonances in our responses to them". Sally has her own "dictatorial fantasies", writing

When my self-righteousness flares, dictatorial fantasies appeal, eager to impose my version of right thinking and behaviour in an attempt to bolster ego, constrain anxiety and control 'the other' ... I feel all this in my body as a dullness and heaviness–and a thud in my guts, something like uterine cramps with a bit of nausea. It's hot, I sweat–hot flushes and global warming combined ...

When a hot flush creeps up on me as I read yet another report on melting ice caps, I feel overwhelmed by its slow burn along with my anxiety about living in a hotter world, and the powerlessness of my responses to stop either.

To Sally, we denialists are desperately cowering from "unbearable anxiety or loss", rather than laughing at doom-criers' 50 years of failed predictions.

She created a seven-member group of mainly excitable women, some 50-plus, to share their own climate-apocalypse dreams – "fellow crew members sailing a vessel of inquiry." It's thrilling to discover what makes climate feminists tick. By their second meeting they're fantasising about surviving "systemic collapse." They suspect their present core values might alter. For example, "stories of cannibalism are shared".

Dr Sally: *I wonder what those stories are serving for us at the moment, in teasing us into these questions. Not only the literal question: would I eat someone else or not? [but] what's the value of human life and culture and society?*

If you're on the plump side and walking up Alexandra Parade, Fitzroy, cross the median strip if Sally's team's is coming. You just never know!

She writes in her journal:

This morning I find I have left the iron on for days, while I have been sick – I am horrified and guilty–it's the emissions that I feel so bad about – more than fear of burning the house down or an expensive electricity bill. This cannot be undone. How to compensate? How to be more responsible, conscious? I decide to put the iron away. I hardly ever use it anyway – a relic from when ironing was a part of daily life, no longer necessary or important.

But Sally nonetheless does some planet-unfriendly flying:

I tell our group that "I have to confess" that I will be travelling to conferences overseas in a few months.

16

Some members contemplated their early demise via what we might deem "Darwin's Law". Veronica leads the way by disclosing that she and her husband have decided they will be 'suicide people' in the event of a breakdown of civilisation.

Veronica recounts her involvement in the assisted suicide of a friend with multiple sclerosis years ago. She says:

Because I've done that and ... I have a spiritual belief in the eternality of the soul ... that gives me comfort. So having gone all the way out there to the shit, and said "OK, I've got a plan", it helps me ... because however it goes I am going to be OK. And I don't plan for it, I don't have any suicide pills ... it's not at all crystallised or real ... other than that I have a sense of trust with my husband that we would not be violent.

I can imagine Veronica's next visit to the pharmacy.

Mary X, BPharm (Hons): *Here's the Ventolin for your inhaler and ointment for your bunionectomy. The allergy-free suicide pills are not yet on the approved list so we'll be charging you $37.80. Take two before meals and be sure to finish the whole packet.*

Sally's group melts down over planet-friendly disposal of dead AA batteries. This angst is 'battery incapacitation' – no pun intended — and intrudes into the ladies' dreams.

Veronica: *I have [dead batteries] hidden in one of my kitchen drawers. One day they will take over my kitchen and I'll be like 'Shit! I've got to do something!'*

Sara: *I am not going to spend hours upon hours thinking about where I should put the batteries. I want things to be easy for me ... if I can find an ecological solution to something, fine–but if I can't, then I have to accept I have to put it into the rubbish bin ... because it does my mind in thinking about it.*

Lisa announces that she has just had a dream about this waste problem:

I didn't know where to do it. I was surrounded by people. I surreptitiously just did it in a deckchair [laughter]. And it's about shit. It's exactly what we are talking about ... And I've had this dream before ... I just couldn't bring myself to tell [it]. It's so strong, I couldn't possibly forget it, and I have to say it now because it's so appropriate.

Sara immediately feels the connection between this dream and her feelings about dumping her batteries, prompting Lisa to speak about the lack of functioning toilets in her dream, further adding:

I just had to do it ... everybody was just going on with their lives ... I was just intensely embarrassed and uncomfortable and not knowing what to do ... not knowing how to dispose of it without doing something gross ... The dream was very visceral animal kind of thing. So when I woke up ... my first thought was like I was out of control, and then I thought the way I'm living, we're all living, is out of control. [Pause] It's a mess.

If Sara invites you to lunch, be careful where you sit.

Sally pauses from running her group to dropping in on her local council's environment meetings. Describing her team as "seven brave souls", she thinks their "breadth of expertise and interests was a major strength in this research".

Speaking personally, I found Veronica the most spectacular member, in a car-crash sort of way. She watched the dopey documentary Gasland on television one night and sobbed "huge wailing tears–my parents live right near where fracking is going on, they're having earthquakes for the first time in recorded history."

She and her husband fled to Australia from "their very grief filled time" in the US, "in the hugest bastion of denial". If she didn't believe in the eternal soul, "I would be one angry bitch."

Rather than coveting Zoloft like some of her peers, she says

climate information [makes] me want to go and crawl in a hole with a bottle of vodka–and a big ice bucket … Our awareness and perception of climate change is already taking a toll on our collective mental health.

Sally writes that Veronica

broke into tears on her way to our meeting when she walked past a cat, explaining "I want a cat, but I don't want a cat. And that's climate change in terms of species preservation … I mean the tentacles of this issue are every freaking where!"

Amazingly, Veronica confesses that she used to be a beer lobbyist – "a whore for the beer institute" spinning to play down the risks of foetal alcohol syndrome.

SARA: *But why did you do it?*

VERONICA: *Because I had a husband to support.*

Sara challenges Veronica about her friends' CO2 seriousness.

SARA: *Do they use shampoo?*

VERONICA: *Actually she uses shavings of a special kind of glycerine soap bar that … you put in a pump jar with water and it emulsifies.*

SARA: *Wow! I've gone through this whole process of trying to find shampoo and conditioner that is gentle to the environment but all that happens to me is that I get rashes so I've gone back to the chemical ones … It was really funny because I thought, "Here I am, doing the right thing".*

LINDA: *And you ended up with pustules!*

Here's pen portraits of Sally's brave souls, starting with Sara, who is upset by natural disasters, including the big Japanese tsunami.

Her eyes fill with tears as she speaks: *I'm on this journey. But there is a part of me that just thinks, "Oh my God, Sara! ... you are middle-aged and you've lost the plot!*

Linda is an anxiety-riddled community artist making TV-news friendly puppets for climate demos. Her limited troupe of kids are no comfort.

They're living their lives as if there is no tomorrow. They've kind of given up ... that breaks my heart ... just fills me full of huge sorrow and fury and impotence.

Linda in turn recruited Lisa, "a fellow artist who makes animations in collaboration with climate change scientists." At Lisa's home, Sally admires installations of fish tanks with Perspex messaging, and engraved soft-drink bottles "amongst the long grass in her front yard". The bottles

> *have thermometers sticking out of their tops like straws – a provocative juxtaposition which links climate change with consumerism, endangered species and rising temperatures ...*
> *We start our conversation on a chair and sofa, but Lisa is soon on the floor, and I follow, shedding shoes and formalities.*

Lisa is no lightweight: she gained her doctorate in animation about subjective responses to [non-existent] crises in the Antarctic.

Lisa is a dancer who marries her artist's love of the movement of line with the physical expression of the body. Her great interest lies

in the use of gestures and lines to facilitate dialogues between differ-
ent ways of knowing. Her own ongoing research practice defies easy
categorisation.

I'd have to agree with that, but let us return to what Lisa tells
Sally:

> *When I first started ... someone asked me how I felt about the*
> *Antarctic environment ... I remember feeling this incredible*
> *knot in my gut and my arms flailing, and going "I just don't*
> *know –it's just all over the place", whereas I don't feel that*
> *now ... I still don't understand climate change, but it's sitting*
> *easily now.*

Sally leaves Lisa's grass-overgrown territory

> *buzzing with thoughts and responses to our discussion. Out*
> *of the corner of my eye I spy yet another installation just be-*
> *hind the front fence; a fish tank with a plastic shrimp in it*
> *and a sign that says "Fishy Leaks." I burst out laughing. Lisa's*
> *stimulating and quirky perspectives add to the resilience of*
> *our group in the discussions ahead.*

Zoe, a community policy-maker, is "heartbroken" over drowning Pacific Islands. Actually, the data from 221 Pacific and Indian
Ocean islands show that they're stable or growing. Like myself, Zoe
gets "fire in the belly" from dreams about Nicole Kidman, but with
a different slant (don't tell my wife):

> Nicole Kidman is sitting at a laptop computer by the edge of a
> billabong which is filling with rubbishy *"consumer goods, and cars,*
> *and all of the stuff that is made from petrol."* [Not much stuff is made
> from petrol but let's not quibble].

Zoe does not seem to be a Tony Abbott fan:

> *There's a tone of voice that he uses that absolutely triggers*

21

something in me ... like a snake wanting to strike, it's an instinctive reaction.

Member Simon (30) got disillusioned on a Climate Camp march against a coal-fired power plant:

The march was right through a small town where most of the people worked at this plant, and so it was very confrontational to them ... I just wasn't sure that was the most productive thing to be doing, to be upsetting people that much.

Surprisingly, Simon is impressed by climate-sceptics' science, including links to hundreds of peer-reviewed sceptic papers. He found sceptic science embarrassingly credible, confessing: *Oh OK maybe some of the things that sceptics are saying aren't completely, completely crazy.*

I like Simon!

The other male, Sam, works in the energy sector, I assume in an environmental capacity. His friends talk on camping trips about how humans are pests, just "a virus with shoes" which Gaia is keen to get rid of. As the meetings progressed, Sally says the group's

fears and our dreams became less apocalyptic ... Hysteria markedly lowered as our discussions became more able to observe and reflect upon paradoxes and contradictions.

How I love such happy endings! #

Compost that corpse. It's for the planet

27 May 2021

I've been preening for years since I donated my body to Melbourne University anatomy students. What a fine citizen I am! You can picture the students crowding around, with me as the centre of attention:

Student Mary-Lou: *"Such remarkably flat feet. I do look forward to dissecting them."*

Student Trent: *"Yes, and I'm seeing enough titanium here to build a small aeroplane."*

But five academics at the University of Technology Sydney (UTS) have pricked my bubble of virtue. Their research at the UTS Institute for Sustainable Futures (ISF) shows my corporeal donation is a threat to the planet via climate-changing CO2 emissions. I might only generate half a tonne post-life, compared with, say, China's 12 billion annual tonnes. But as a world citizen I should "tackle" (I love that word) climate change to preserve the planet and civilisation. According to the Climate Council's Professor Will Steffen, our excess emissions threaten even homo sapiens per se:

The ultimate drivers of the Anthropocene if they continue unabated through this century, may well threaten the viability of contemporary civilization and perhaps even the future existence of Homo sapiens.

Ever constructive, the UTS Five offer a planet-friendlier option than my body donation – I should turn myself into high-quality compost. Climate-friendly human compost is already legal in Washington State, Colorado and Oregon, priced at about $US7000 per person.

To sketch the background, a chorus of every UTS academic, student and staffer believes 100 per cent in the heat-exaggerating forecasts of climate scientists' models. It's doom for everybody without zero net emissions by 2030, 2035 or 2050 (take your pick).

As UTS trumpets,

Our society faces a climate emergency. UTS believes climate change requires urgent and transformative action. Inspired by the 2019 Global Climate Strike, UTS signed a climate declaration, pledging to take greater climate action. UTS aims to commit more resources to climate change research and skills creation, increase (sic) sustainability education across our curriculum, campus and community programs. By continuing to bring communities, industry and government together to debate the contested themes around the climate emergency [but no skeptic themes welcome] we can argue the need for a climate consensus; and work towards carbon neutrality on campus.

Coal miners' losing their jobs? UTS has that covered. As a research director Chris Briggs puts it,

We've been doing research on jobs in renewable energy and how we might transition workers in coal regions into new industries. There's not a lot of information on renewable energy jobs ... and so we've been seeking to fill that gap and help these regions transition across to clean energy.

I wonder if well-paid and productive coal, gas and oil workers actually want to be transitioned by UTS into jobs like collecting the dead wedgetails under bird-mincing wind turbines and dusting hectares of solar panels in the outback?

The five academics' Sustainable Futures home looks like a sister body to Melbourne University's Sustainable Society Institute (MSSI) which Pro Vice-Chancellor Mark Hargreaves plopped into the university's green bin last year. Heaven forbid that UTS Vice-Chancellor Andrew Parfitt is impelled by loss of revenue from China to emulate Hargreaves, especially as 2022 is the ISF's 25th anniversary.

Anyway, the UTS Five, who long for carbon taxes, have done a 100-page report to Cemeteries & Crematoria NSW which regulates the private operators. The report promotes environmental sustainability and aims *"to spark conversations across the sector, and among consumers and families, and promote best practice sustainability by looking at what is currently occurring both globally and in Australia."*

On body donations, the authors say

From a sustainability perspective, evaluating donations of bodies to science is not straightforward. While prolonging the 'useful' life of the body, donation to science still holds sustainability implications. Firstly, the body is embalmed, usually using formalin, a toxic substance. Secondly, the body is kept in refrigeration for up to four years, with a resulting energy footprint relating to electricity use. Finally, at the cessation of its use in anatomy labs, the body is then cremated in a conventional cremator or buried – meaning that its overall environmental impact is generally not less than that of a body disposed of immediately after death – and may, in fact, be higher.

However, the 'usefulness' of the body to medical knowledge and education cannot be easily weighed in an assessment of environmental impact ... [D]onation of bodies to science does not present a solution to environmental impacts, but presents a means by which individuals can feel that they will be 'useful' after death and can contribute to medical knowledge and education.

In its discussion of "emerging alternatives" the report foresees a small market in NSW for composting, although regulatory bans would first have to be lifted.

The composting of human remains is a new innovation (sic) emerging in response to demand for gentler and more environmentally friendly options. The method emerges from the livestock industry, where composting has long been considered the best way to manage animal remains ...

According to US studies composting is cheaper and less emissions-intense than burials and cremations. The world leader in the human composting business is called Recompose, based near Seattle. Its 24 female and five male staff and advisers "approach this work with energy, tenacity, and joy" as they "use the principles of nature to transform our dead into soil."

It took Recompose's founder, the aptly-named Katrina Spade, a decade's pioneering to start operations, in a light-industrial suburb and behind big roll-up warehouse doors. A visiting reporter called it

an environmentalist's version of a sleek, futuristic spaceship: spare, calm, utilitarian, with silvery ductwork above, a few soil-working tools (shovels, rakes, pitchforks) on racks, bags of tightly packaged straw neatly stacked on shelves, fern-green walls, potted plants of various sizes.

One immense object dominates the space, looking like an enormous fragment of white honeycomb. These are Recom-

pose's 10 "vessels," each a hexagon enclosing a steel cylinder full of soil. One day in mid-January [2021], eight decedents were already inside eight vessels, undergoing the process of natural organic reduction (NOR) or, more colloquially, human composting.

Using the Recompose formula under the heading Healing the Climate, I'd be stacked inside a steel rotatable cylinder for 30 days with three cubic metres of alfalfa, woodchips and straw, and then taken out for several weeks further curing. As a final product I'd become one metre of "nutrient-rich soil amendment" and save the planet from 0.84 and 1.4 tonnes of CO_2. As Recompose says,

Human compost can be used on trees, yards, house plants, and flower gardens, just like any other type of compost (such as compost created by food scraps or garden prunings).

Recompose charges $US7000 per composting, the same as the median US cost of cremation ($US6970) and a good discount to burial at $US7848. Ms Spade says, "We have transformed over 100 bodies into soil and have over 1000 Precompose members. That means we have already saved the emissions equivalent of 10 million miles driven, 480 homes powered for one year, or 450,000 gallons of gasoline."

As for routine interments, the UTS Five give conventional styles a bad rap for hurting the climate. It laments the "significant emissions" from fossil-fuel-powered cremation – cremation is used for two-thirds of Australian disposals. The combustion is better created from solar or biogas-powered operation, they say.

Many consumers hold a perception of cremation as 'cleaner' than other body disposal options – an interesting perception given cremation's high energy consumption and resultant pol-

lutant release … Each cremation emits around 160kg of carbon dioxide into the atmosphere (Potter, 2019) … Adelaide Cemeteries Authority research indicates that the total greenhouse impact, taking into account electricity, transport and resources inputs as well as natural gas, of a single cremation is around 430kg of CO2 equivalent.

The authors also give low climate marks to burials, unless in coffins made of seagrass, willow, bamboo, cork, wicker, cardboard or wool. A standard burial involves 780kg or nearly a tonne of greenhouse emissions, they grumble.

They seem to like a US company offering $US1500 mushroom-suit shrouds for burials, made from organic cotton and a bio-mix of mushrooms. Another promising technology is cryomation, using liquid nitrogen to freeze the body to make it crystalline and brittle. It is then shattered into 1mm pieces through ultrasonic vibration, which turn into mulch when buried. *"It is expected to have a significantly lower carbon footprint than conventional cremation, as it avoids the need for fossil fuel inputs, however studies on [cryomation's] energy footprint do not appear to be available currently."* Their focus groups weren't impressed by it.

Leaving no stone unturned in their research, the UTS people discovered a Swiss company, Algordanza, that will synthesise 500 grams of your ashes into a diamond, a pricey option taking half a year.

Given that the method involves conventional cremation, international transport of remains, high-tech treatment of synthesised remains and then return international transport, it is difficult to imagine that this method of memorialisation offers any environmental benefits over other methods, the report concludes.

I'm sure you think "Algordanza" is a play on Al Gore dancing, but it's actually an old Swiss Rhaeto-Romanic word for "remembrance". To my surprise I've found that Algordanza now has a specific Australian operation for the very well-heeled.

As you can now see, I have heaps of options if I cancel my personal donation to Melbourne University. I'm rather torn between composting and unleashing the "exceptional sparkling" of myself as a radiant-cut Al Gore diamond.#

Sooking and snivelling for climate justice

1 September 2021

As we all know, universities' tutorial and staff rooms are awash in climate-doom hysterics. But academics are not just horrifying their late-teen paying customers, they're also traumatising each other. Here's a real-life local example:

> Another educator that my co-researchers and I surveyed mentioned that after their [sic] class one day they [sic] 'had a long cry on my commute home, and wound up cancelling plans I had to meet friends that evening.' Such experiences demonstrate that trying to support others to engage with and navigate their own ecological distress often leads to feelings of inadequacy and despair becoming contagious.

We can be grateful to Dr Blanche Verlie of the Sydney University's Environment Institute for this glimpse of mortar-board mayhem. She ran climate courses for five years and did her Monash PhD on climate education. She's followed up with peer-reviewed papers and last week, launched a whole book on the traumas of climate educators and their students. It's called *Learning to Live with Climate Change* (free to good homes) and I took part in the Zoom launch, one of the few males present.

No male other than myself posted a question on Chat. Mine, unanswered, was *"How can we persuade China to stop planning and building so many coal-fired power stations?"*

Verlie's book "draws on and contributes to eco-feminist, posthuman, multispecies and affect studies." Her particular villains causing global warming are – surprise! – white Western heterosexual settler-colonial male managerial capitalists.

She warns that everything is connected and "leaving the lights on in Australia may mean death for polar bears". I must have inadvertently slain thousands of the beasts.

As a tutor Dr Verlie taught 45 Melbourne students at RMIT University for three months on 'climate justice'. She describes the shimmering "cloudy collective" that evolved in her classes. In my own young days of hormone-clouded tutes, my focus ranged from skirts to staying awake, rather than shimmering cloudy collectives. In those years the looming threat of global cooling was keeping climate scientists in a tizz.

Verlie's book *"is written with climate change 'educators' in mind: teachers, activists, communicators, young people, parents, researchers, policy makers, community members, artists, politicans ..."* She describes herself as "a white settler-Australian" determined on "decolonial climate action". Her co-authored papers include *Becoming Researchers: Making Academic Kin in the Chthulucene.*

Whatever "the Chthulucene" might be, it's dynamite on the Scrabble board – even if the concept remains thickly opaque about its

> *form of refuge from academic stressors, creating spaces for 'composting together' through processes of 'decomposing' and 'recomposing'. Our rejection of neoliberal norms has gifted us experiences of joyful collective pleasures. We share our experiences here in the hope of supporting and inspiring other emerging and established researchers to 'make kin' and challenge the potentially isolating processes of becoming researchers.*

Dr Verlie's book does help normal sane people understand why universities need safe spaces for their tribes. As Dr Verlie writes,

It is worth noting that these vignettes include stories of distress; I encourage you to approach them in a mode that cares for yourself and is responsive to your own ability to engage with the pain of climate change at the moment. As this book documents, climate change is deeply traumatic and while I believe we need to avoid the pitfalls of an individualistic approach to emotional resilience, this is not to say that practices of mindful self-care or professional counselling services have no value.

Dr Verlie provides dramatic quotes from her undergrad students. I suspect that before the kids had even hit RMIT, teachers groomed them through 12 long years of wallowing in climate hysteria, not to mention cravings for socialist world governance. There is so much insanity in the student's excerpts below that I've bolded the most extreme symptoms of derangement to make them stand out from the pack:

I've been crying myself to sleep a lot lately. And crying at random times too. It's not as though I watch a video about climate change, and I cry during it. I mean sometimes that happens. It's more like, something little happens, **like my toast burns**, and I have an **existential breakdown because I think it's a metaphor for how the world is burning because we aren't paying attention.**

I found myself dry retching in the shower for over an hour one evening. The contractions of my stomach muscles, sense of my throat exploding, and my whole body convulsing, felt like I was trying to **spew up some kind of demon**, a wretchedness, a loneliness and desperation, a sense of loss for all that could have been but probably won't, for that which is but will no longer be.

I feel bitter towards individuals and systems and fail to understand why people are **not being charged for climate crimes.**

It [climate] is a constant reminder that the Earth is f****d.

The future, for me, is **dark, cloudy, a black hole of uncertainty.** I don't know how it will play out.

Our knowledges and ignorances about climate change will impact who will live and who will die.

I am constantly butting heads with sceptics and non-believers (particularly my father-in-law) regarding climate change. It is so frustrating that fellow inhabitants don't understand the magnitude of the situation, and worse still, they don't care to learn more about it.

It's like, on warm, sunny winter and early spring days, with the light glistening through young green leaves. Everyone is happy due to the nice weather. But knowing about climate change, you know it means someone somewhere is not getting the rain they need. [Actually warming promotes rain, check with Prof. Andy Pitman at UNSW]. So it's sort of, you can't enjoy it, it's **an uneasiness amongst the glory** that everyone else seems to be celebrating.

I was thinking of the dark, foreboding nature of climate change, its **creeping horror masked by invisibility in the here-and-now of hyperconsumptive capitalism.** Sometimes I see climate change as a chasm opening up before me, and I stand on a precipice overlooking the deep ravine, **teetering on the edge.**

My totally cynical view is that non-fossil-fuel-based energy production will only become the norm once the renewable-energy corporations can provide more money than fossil fuel corporations in bribes to political interests.

Against these morbid undertows, others of Verlie's students were uplifted.

\# I'm so glad I changed into this class – it's more of a climate change therapy group than a university subject.

\# This class has given me hope as … I feel everyone is so **smart, powerful and brilliant.**

\# One day after class, I felt like I was floating on the way home. **Maybe I was deliriou**s because this subject matter is so exhausting. But I really felt buoyed by the energy everyone brings to class.

\# I have been overwhelmed by joy, fear, and passion.

\# But it's [climate apathy] disheartening. You look around, and it's like, where'd everyone go? And they're running away … It's like, (sigh), Jesus guys!

\# I really valued the **ferocious intensity of information** that was shared with us.

No student expresses the least scepticism about the horrowshow material: *I remember a unanimous feeling of frustration shared by the whole class.* The groupthink sadly reflects today's "monoversity" culture. The class also needed a renewables-powered spa retreat after class. Verlie writes:

> As students and I discuss the systems that expose society's most marginalised to lethal heat stress, our bodily reactions such as sweaty armpits, flushed cheeks and croaky voices belie the 'thermal monotony' of our air-conditioned comfort.

Outside the universities, climate derangement has been spreading like COVID, as Verlie's examples suggest:

\# A marine biologist vomits because of her distress about coral bleaching, mimicking her beloved polyps who purge themselves of their symbiotic algae in warming water. [Hey marine biologist! Barrier Reef coral cover is actually at record heights].

Gender expert Rebecca Huntley, a frequent guest luvvie on the ABC, recounts a sensation that 'actually felt physical, as if vital organs had moved inside my body' when watching youth climate activists implore adults to 'do something.'

(Classicists will perhaps hear echoes of St Theresa: *The pain was so great, that it made me moan; and yet so surpassing was the sweetness of this excessive pain, that I could not wish to be rid of it.*)

Verlie confided to her own diary:

Sometimes when I think of climate change, I see this dark, vague, tsunami towering behind me, a frothing wall of utter destruction of which we have felt tremors, but by turning our backs, have not fully comprehended. I catch glimpses of it over my shoulder, about to crash down upon me, obliterating everything, but in front of me, life goes about its daily flow, oblivious to the imminent disaster.

Here's her summation regarding climate undergrads:

In one semester my students stated that climate change made them feel anxious, frustrated, confused, uncertain, cynical, scared, overwhelmed, emotional, devastated, depressed, frightened, angry, gloomy, resentful, challenged, isolated, desperate, disheartened, shocked, concerned, confronted, unsettled, bitter, sad, sick, upset, perplexed, guilty, stressed, amazed, daunted, defeated, dismayed, pessimistic, uneasy, tired, appalled and terrified. Given the incomprehensibly rapid and traumatic changes being wrought upon our planet's climate, it is unsurprising that many of us are overwhelmed with climate anxiety.

Actually, recent measured global temperature is no higher than it was 20 years ago. Blanche, can this be *"incomprehensibly rapid"* climate change?

More seriously, Verlie and her feminist educators are concerned their proteges' fanaticism might gravitate to eco-fascism. At Verlie's Zoom book launch last week, Dr Sarah Jaquette Ray (Humboldt University, California) said she was "very nervous" about climate anxiety creating big emotions leading acolytes to aggressive eco-fascism. She praised Verlie for offering "an alternative path".

Ray wrote in *Scientific American* (of all journals!) just last March:

> *It is a surprisingly short step from 'chronic fear of environmental doom' to xenophobia and fascism ... Early environmentalists in the U.S. were anti-immigrant eugenicists whose ideas were later adopted by Nazis to implement their 'blood and soil' ideology. In a recent, dramatic example, the gunman of the 2019 El Paso shooting [22 people murdered] was motivated by despair about the ecological fate of the planet: 'My whole life I have been preparing for a future that currently doesn't exist.' Intense emotions mobilize people, but not always for the good of all life on this planet.*
>
> *I recently gave a college lecture about climate anxiety. One of the students e-mailed me to say she was so distressed that she'd be willing to submit to a green dictator if they would address climate change. It would be tragic and dangerous if this generation of climate advocates becomes willing to sacrifice democracy and human rights in the name of climate change.*

The Christchurch mosque mass murderer (51 people slaughtered) also described himself as an "eco-fascist".

Verlie gives similar warning in her book. She writes, *Throughout and following the fire season, approaches calling for a 'war-like' response to the climate crisis, including the suppression of democracy, increased in volume and frequency.* Her footnote points to one-time federal Labor Climate Minister (and later School Education Minister) Peter Garrett's speech last year wanting to put Australia back into a 1939-style footing for war on the (non-existent) climate emergency.

Getting back to the RMIT kids, Verlie's tutes had high turnover:

In one of my tutorials there were a lot of student absences in the first few weeks of semester, but it was not the same students missing class each week. Some would show up one week, then not again for a while, then suddenly arrive energised and passionate …

Accompanying our discussions about such disconcertment, people sigh; smile; sweat; frown; pause; laugh; cry; lean back in their chairs; wriggle in their chairs; close their eyes; rub their eyes; roll their eyes; wipe tears from their eyes; establish, maintain or avert eye contact; hug each other; turn away from each other; listen or talk over each other; get up and leave; put their head in their hands, or on the table; stare at the ceiling; shrug their shoulders; slump their shoulders.

In an odd way she feels climate fanatics' bodies reflect the gassy air:

We are not just 'like' clouds. As breathing, sweating, radiating bags of gas and liquid that metabolise and reconfigure carbon, hydrogen and oxygen, human bodies are 'only precariously contained in a skin sac.'

… These moody menageries emerge through, and in turn stimulate, our breathy practices of collectively storying cli-

mate change. Cloudy collectives are composed as our voices crack when we verbalise the violences of climate injustice; as we groan with exasperation at governments approving new fossil fuel projects; as we whisper our fears in climate grief workshops; as we shout 'climate action now' at rally after rally, after rally...

Don't ask her students if they can unblock toilets or program a combine harvester's sat-nav:

Some students took up roles facilitating environmental community building; others wrote and shared poetry; some made documentary films. Another organised a music festival and invited some of us to speak to the punters about climate change; as part of this we made a banner which read 'loving low carbon life' and took it to the People's Climate March in the lead up to the Paris Climate Summit.

Verlie writes: "Climate protests are always atmospheric ... chanting 'climate action now' when corralled under a baking sun leaves you feeling both exhausted and justified."

Conversely, would sleet leave her feeling unjustified? She doesn't say whether she actually joined Extinction Rebellion bourgeois types "playing 'dead fish' in public places to symbolise the possibility of human extinction." Those who did, she says, often experienced emotional burnout needing therapy from XR's 'regenerative culture' specialists.

Last week's book launch learned that Verlie sees her task as bringing people face to face with the most incomprehensible unfathomable injustices, which had led to spaces *where people are in tears and can't speak, and it is really hard work. You always run the risk of just being traumatic and it is immensely difficult.*

38

She agreed that it was better to work with schoolkids about climate rather than the small privileged caste studying at tertiary level: "It will require transformation of what education is and how it works and that alone is a pretty big slog."

She conceded students could be "grumpy from arguments with their parents" and from "how do we live on this planet that many economic systems are bent on destroying". Questioned about how kids can ever learn to dream happily again, she replied that climate change is more about their nightmares and how one in five British kids had reported bad dreams about climate.

For myself, I'm having bad dreams about university education. #

Green doctors: suitable cases for treatment

16 June 2022

On climate, a lot of medicos are out there on the nuttiest end of the doom spectrum. But I had no idea their hysteria could even out-do and embarrass Greenpeace, *The Guardian* and Tim Flannery's Climate Council.

Last month three anaesthetists published a peer-reviewed paper in *Australasian Anaesthesia* discouraging birthing mothers from using nitrous oxide for pain relief. The trio warn, *"While it may be innocuous for the pregnant woman and unborn baby, that is certainly not the case for the environment."*

About 200,000 Australian pregnant women per year choose the help of nitrous oxide. The learned paper wants them to use more climate-friendly pain-killers, and/or epidurals, hypnobirthing, massage, acupuncture, and Tens – elaborate equipment called "Transcutaneous electric nerve stimulator". They're all costlier, but hang the expense.

I hasten to add that two of the trio of authors are females, albeit gung-ho for purported planetary healing. Dr Alice Gynther is from Western Health Melbourne and Fiona Pearson from Sunderland Royal Hospital UK. The lone male Forbes McGain of Western Health is a stalwart of Doctors for the Environment Australia (DEA). I'll chart DEA's extremism later in the course of my obstetric odyssey.[1]

---

[1] The following seven colleges have declared their ridiculous "climate emergencies", along with 2300 individual medicos:

* Royal Australian College of General Practitioners (RACGP)
* Royal Australian College of Physicians (RACP)
* Australian College of Emergency Medicine (ACEM)
* Royal Australian and New Zealand College of Psychiatrists (RANZCP)
* Australian College of Rural and Remote Medicine (ACRRM)

These three mothers' helpers write

By educating medical staff and pregnant women about the carbon impact of N2O, ensuring that it is delivered and used as efficiently as possible and considering the use of more carbon-friendly alternatives, we can reduce GHG emissions from the labour ward and help to mitigate the effects of climate change. Ensuring that midwifery, obstetric and anaesthetic staff are aware of the environmental impact of N2O is crucial ...

In order to support women's autonomy and help them make informed choices regarding their labour analgesia [pain reduction], we have a duty to explain the risks and benefits of the different analgesic options. As climate change is a threat to public health, the carbon footprint of [nitrous oxide] is arguably a 'risk' worthy of inclusion in such discussions. Ideally such discussions would occur during antenatal classes, that is, well prior to childbirth itself. This knowledge, coupled with the lack of good evidence for nitrous oxide's analgesic efficacy, may reduce the number of women choosing to use it for labour.

I can picture the scene at the doctor's.

Woke medico: *Good morning Alice! How about saving some greenhouse warming via an epidural?*

Mother-to-be Alice: *Dr Wittgenstein, I actually came here to talk about the risk of pre-eclampsia to my baby. How self-centred of me! What do the climate scientists models' predict for 2050-2100? What can I and my baby do personally to offset China's 12 billion annual tonnes of emissions, which I understand are accelerating?*

---

* College of Intensive Care Medicine (CICM)

* Australian & New Zealand College of Anaesthetists (ANZCA)

Woke medico: *No pain, no gain. You go, girl!*

The reports' authors say nitrous oxide is only 7 per cent of all "long-lived" greenhouse gases, and only 1 per cent of that 7 per cent is from women reducing their distress in labour. But being sciencey types, the authors work out how much global warming is created by Victorian women in labour using nitrous oxide. Their model involves a 70kg woman starting with 4cm cervical dilation. First-timers average 5.5 hours and others 4.5 hours. They suck nitrous oxide for 60 seconds per contraction and have three contractions each 10 minutes, hence 18 minutes on the gas per hour.

Then the authors add the extra greenhouse damage like

Coal-fired Victorian electricity (75% of output) used to power the medical pumps

Making of mouthpiece, needles, syringes, tubing and contents, sterile single-use drapes, gown and gloves and

Incineration of clinical waste products

Their dreadful conclusion is that emissions-wise, Mrs 70kg might as well have driven an average-polluting car almost 1500km. An epidural equated with just six kilometres breezing along the boulevard in an econobox Barina.

Not all medicos are obsessed about global warming. The green/ Left *Guardian* quotes Gino Pecoraro, president of the Association of Specialist Obstetricians and Gynaecologists:

> *During childbirth, some women wouldn't care how many coal-fired power stations are needed to reduce their pain. If pregnant women in labour were denied a proven safe and effective pain relieving method, I'd think we'd be going down the wrong path.*

The *Guardian* quotes Greenpeace types (of all people):

Rapid phase out of coal and gas, by far the biggest climate culprits, is the fastest and most effective way to tackle the climate crisis, rather than focusing on the relatively low emissions from obstetric medicine.

Flannery's Climate Council also prefers banning coal, oil and gas first before chasing down emissions from behind the drapes in labour wards. In a flash of sanity, the Council says, "No individual mother should be made to feel guilty about her choice of pain relief." But it continued, "Parents could do more to protect their child's health, their wallets and the climate by doing simple things like getting gas out of their homes." I didn't realise swapping out gas heaters for electrics was a "simple thing" and a friend down the road says it cost him $6500.

The Guardian piece by journalist Isabelle Oderberg finished,

I don't see anyone asking men queuing up from colonoscopies or transurethral resections of the prostate to give a Tens machine or massage a go. They're knocked out quicker than you can say 'Bob's your uncle'.

While the report in itself may not be "incorrect" in any way [all climate propaganda is good propaganda. TT], it feels like the lowest hanging, cheap-as-chips fruit. Context is everything and, in a world where people who aren't men [I think she means "women"] are fighting for their right to be treated with care, equality and compassion, the release of this report in this way was deeply ill-advised and made for painful reading.

While our anaesthetist trio finds innumerable fringe studies about alleged health impacts of global warming, they haven't caught up with a report last February by Britain's Office for National Statistics that warming in England and Wales alone in the past 20 years can be credited with a net 550,000-plus lives saved. That's because mortality from cold outweighs by around ten-fold any mortality from heat. (Even in India, cold deaths outweigh heat deaths by 7-to-1). Extrapolate the England/Wales result to northern Europe, Asia and America and global warming is a giant health benefit to humanity, even without considering the boon to agriculture.

Noted climate blogger Joanne Nova sums up all this fuss, a little unkindly, as "Junk models meets junk research, junk journals, and junk reporting." Her commenters also show some robust common-sense. Like Annie, for instance:

Carrying a growing baby and giving birth is perhaps the most rewarding and frightening and triumphant moment in the lives of many women and I feel that using that to score points about Greenhouse gases is sick.

It is evil to suggest denying pain relief at what can be an extremely frightening and painful time for women. How can this ugliness be allowed to continue in a supposedly civil society?

And another:

What? No information on how much Nitrous the MEN will need when they give birth? It'll be a LOT!

I've mentioned that the paper's co-author Dr McGain is a stalwart of the Doctors for the Environment Australia (DEA). Of all the global-warming groups among medicos, DEA seems the loopiest about "preventing catastrophic climate change" and the alleged perils of "the current market society".[2]

---

[2] From the 2019 DEA media kit: *"Interview and photo opportunities – Doctors in scrubs, surgical masks and stethoscopes will gather to issue the Climate Emergency declaration on Saturday, 6 April, at the Menzies Research Institute, 17 Liverpool Street, Hobart at 10:20 am."*

DEA teams flung their weight behind the Teal candidates in five electorates to oust Morrison's conservatives last month, putting "Climate Action Now" signs on their Teslas in Wentworth "at their own cost to raise awareness" and running a "picnic party for our planet" in Boothby (Adelaide). They've been advised by a "Scientific Committee" featuring Nobelist Peter Doherty at one end and the ABC's once-was-medico Dr Norman Swan at the other.

Back in 2019 DEA was already

\# declaring a climate "health emergency"

\# demanding a ban on new oil, gas and coal-seam fields and

\# pronouncing that "Climate change is killing people".

In today's real world, PM Albanese's Resources Minister Madeleine King vows never to put a limit on how much coal Australia will export, with Australia possibly still exporting coal to Asian trading partners past 2050, and Labor is scrambling to protect two big aluminium smelters from grid crises.

The climate-crazed medicos campaigned for the demolition of the Port Augusta coal-fired power station, which happened, but DEA's pipedream of substituting solar thermal energy fell to bits after failing to secure finance. DEA has also striven to lock coal-seam gas in the ground. It gave 100 per cent credence to a report, "Lethal Power", by Greenpeace activists that coal-fired power plant emissions are killing 373-1310 citizens a year. In a revealing aside, Greenpeace added that the health damage equated to $15.40 per megawatt hour, or about a quarter of the value of electricity's then-cost. Oh boy, that means that only three years ago our electricity was costing $60 per megawatt hour, compared with $300 this month – and that $300 involves officially capped pricing.

One DEA enthusiast, a Dr Kimberley Humphrey, bewails that

"the rate of suicide among young people is also increasing with the threat of global warming and this needs to be prevented by young people able to see we are doing something to save the planet." If activists would cease scaring the daylights out of little Billy and Sally, the kids might have less incentive to self-harm.

DEA now expresses some *Schadenfreude* that our health sector "is responsible for a whopping 7 per cent of Australia's carbon emissions." Maybe we should dispense with health services by 2030, along with fossil fuels, to save our perspiring planet. #

What green academics do instead of work

12 July 2022

Excitement is building at Sydney University as each day brings its 8000 academics and 75,000 students one sleep closer to their two-day climate-crisis spectacular, namely *"Nature Feelz (sic) Symposium: Perspectives and Reflections on Ecological Emotions"*. The symposium, from 5-7 December, is convened by the university's Dr. Blanche Verlie, Dr. James Dunk, Professor Danielle Celermajer, Associate Professor Paul Rhodes and Associate Professor Rosanne Quinnell.

This symposium is part of the university's massive *Ecological Emotions, Feelings and Affects* research project. Academics globally can submit symposium papers and proposals for talks to Sydney University by 31 July. That's in just a few weeks so, scholars, get your skates on! Your guidelines (emphasis added):

> *As interconnected biodiversity, climate, water and related socio-ecological crises intensify around the world, experiences of ecological distress are proliferating. Variously termed solastalgia, climate anxiety, or ecological grief, these multifaceted experiences of loss are becoming more common, and are being articulated and shared, but they are also significantly differentiated.*
>
> *This is particularly the case for many young people who, from early on, have been conscious of the insecurity of their ecosystems, the transience of other species, and their own profound vulnerability.*
>
> *All of this would be almost prosaic by now – a well-known narrative – were it not so visceral, and so wrenching ...*

*... Affective ties with other beings have always been a core part of human experiences, **despite colonial-capitalist-patriarchal extractivism** which has denied, denigrated and punished emotional engagements with the environment ... Surviving and resisting the violence of colonial forces, Indigenous peoples have developed powerful languages of ecological grief and practices of survivance.*

*But extractive cultures are not unemotional either. They prioritise and normalise certain emotions which benefit particular stakeholders, **as systemic climate denial exemplifies.***

Assuming you're not a climate denialist, you'll be delighted to learn that the convenors are fully inclusive, saying,

15-minute presentations are the standard. Alternative formats, including poetry, flashtalks, walk-shops [sic] and roundtable discussions, are encouraged and we will do our best to accommodate them (including through longer time slots as required).

The convenors spell out the symposium theme:

*Different emotions and affects, mobilised in different ways by different people, will play critical roles in whether this moment of planetary change leads towards 'the Anthropocene,' or **somewhere more promising (the 'Symbiocene,' 'Planthropocene,' 'Chthulucene' or otherwise).** As scholars, activists, citizens and community members, we want to take stock of how diverse humans are creating, experiencing, suppressing, making sense of, managing, preventing, intensifying, and resisting ecological distress. We are also interested in what it would mean to consider the ecological emotions of **beings other than human.***

48

The "ecological emotions" of koalas, eels and huntsmen spiders, for instance?

First things first. Unless you are Sydney University-educated, you must surely be wondering about the 'Symbiocene', 'Planthropocene', and 'Chthulucene'. My research suggests some aspects may cause you distress or are Not Safe For Work.

The Symbiocene

This is a concept pioneered by the internationally-famed Dr Glenn Albrecht, along with his term "solastalgia" meaning inconsolable pre-traumatic stress over the imminent climate apocalypse. Dr Albrecht retired from sustainability pieties at Murdoch University in 2014 and, according to wiki, is an honorary fellow in Sydney University's School of Geosciences. He has footnoted himself as "freelance environmental philosopher and farmosopher and has pioneered the domain of psychoterratic or psyche – earth relationships [earth related mental health conditions]…"

Dr Albrecht has won an impressive array of taxpayer-funded grants for his transdisciplinary research into things like climate change and "social and ethical aspects of the thoroughbred horse industry worldwide."

As for his 'Symbioscene', he wrote in 2019 that this is to be led by the teenage followers of Greta Thunberg who comprise his "Generation Z". The "Z" teens

> are characterised as having a broad global outlook, no current investment or employment chains and a highly nuanced, critical perspective on the use of social media and the role of information dissemination within it.

I assume Glenn means that the teens are still sponging off mum and pop and are spending the parental largesse on iPhone 13s rather than saving for a house deposit.

Dr Albrecht continues,

> *It is no exaggeration to say that within Gen Z there is now the vanguard of a global movement challenging all the forces that are causing humans to commit climacide and ecocide. In addition, our wise teenagers now know that the climate crisis is an integral part of a much bigger crisis.*

I would have thought "wise teenagers" an oxymoron, but not Dr Albrecht, who writes that we oldies are to unite with those post-puberty pandits "to form Generation S – a force to combat corporate gigantism and to shape cultural and social revolutions." Generation S in turn "will lead the rest of humanity into the Symbiocene ... While the Anthropocene is generating despair and desolation, the Symbiocene gives generously of hope and optimism". The Symbiocene involves "a new epoch" to achieve

> *a complete change of the biophysical and emotional foundations of society... The momentum created by Gen Z is now unstoppable ... In addition, marginalized groups within the Anthropocene, including LGBTQIA, indigenous groups and subsistent people in the so-called developing world, have every reason to join this movement...*
>
> *The most urgent tasks for Gen S will be to protest and fight against gigantism. By gigantism, I mean the dictatorial governments of nation states and corporate rulers that exercise authoritarian and totalitarian control over almost all aspects of our lives. The globalised system of production, transport and consumption is run by a powerful elite of wealthy indi-*

viduals at the head of the command economies, monopolies and oligopolies that rule the world.

It is these powerful, gigantic bodies that are in control of the Anthropocene and the way it is evolving as a psychopathic juggernaut ... To achieve this end, the Symbiocene will have to be initiated by protesters, activists and hacktivists. Every-thing, from how we conduct politics to how we eat and live, will have to be disrupted ... As Gen S dismantles gigantism, at the same time they need to be furiously building a new economy ... Gen S will become technological "terroirists" [sic] and sumbiofacts will replace artifacts.

I hope you're staying with me so far.

Human reproduction will be voluntarily tailored to the limits of place and productivity.

That is not the Not Safe For Work bit I mentioned earlier, if you've been reading out of prurient interest.

The gender sharing of the socialisation of children will be-come the norm and symbio-literate children will play a vi-tal role in the further development of the Symbiocene ... The Baby Boomers have set up and now enforce dependency on centralised energy-systems. For safe, just and pollution-free energy, Gen S will dismantle the current form of energy pro-vision and the power structures that operate and own it ... Many of these renewable energy systems are already in exis-tence with an energy delivery cost structure lower than that of finite, high-risk polluting alternatives such as coal ...

Regenerating soil by rebuilding symbiotic, living soil commu-nities will be labour intensive but immensely satisfying. Bees will flourish and their buzzing will be a sign for all that food production without the 'cides' is once again life-affirming. Gen S will ensure there is no insectageddon.

In joining Gen S, as their last act of generosity on Earth, the Boomers will achieve a degree of clemency ... The acolytes of the Anthropocene will be "on the run" by the 2070s and the Symbiocene on the rise.

To sum up the promising Symbiocene element of Sydney University's forthcoming symposium, I'd just say the above sort of deep thinking is what makes the $14,630 a year fees of a Sydney University arts student worth paying for. And now for my research on ...

The Plantropocene (NSFW)

My first googled hit on "Plantropocene" was an article in an Italian arts magazine, *Nomad Lampoon*. The article by Bianca Lee Vasquez is titled "Nudity: the flesh, the body, and the divine in the character of Planthropocene [it seems to have at least three spellings including Planthroposcene]." I had to look away hastily as the piece is illustrated by three ladies including Ms Vasquez in their birthday suits. A less confronting illustration of the Plantropocene involves a single prone unclothed lady, maybe Ms Vasquez, who is covered (mostly) with moss. She writes,

Body is sacred, nudity is art, and nature is a living being. Bianca Lee Vasquez seeks the veracity and the reverence nature holds with living beings: We need to see divinity in one another.

Miami-born and Paris-based, Ms Vasquez practices Mesoamerican and Inca rituals derived from her Cuban-Ecuadorian roots. She grew up in a practising Christian family who gave her full-on Biblical readings and exegesis. She then "left the job that firmed up her income" to artistically tackle *the thousands of years our society has put up with patriarchy. The female body has been suppressed and measured to a scale of how it weighs value, bears desirability, and can be of use to men.*

In 2015 she embarked on a career as a nude performance artiste, and after six years plucked up the courage to "come out" to her parents. She doesn't tell us how they reacted, but after in-depth study of the Anthropocene and the Plantropocene, Ms Vasquez

takes part in her photographs as a woman who decorates her body with tendrils while she lies down on a wooden bench with her eyes closed or as she looks at the camera with her hands grazing on the leaves.

There's plenty more like that. If I were still an undergraduate, I'd sign up for Sydney University's Plantropocene theorising in a flash.

Don't get me wrong, the Plantropocene is a serious branch of the university world's taxpayer-funded contribution to human betterment. The movement, as reverenced during Sydney University symposiums, was founded by Associate Professor Dr. Natasha Myers, of York University, who cultivates a wild head of hair and a roguish grin:

Natasha leads us to a world where magic happens through our active collaboration with plant kin. Beyond appreciation for plants, Natasha shares the importance of experimenting with the playful work of plant embodiment and seeding "plant-people conspiracies." How can these connective practices provide diverse ways of knowing through a boundary-breaking experience?

[Her] current ethnographic projects speculate on the contours of the Planthroposcene, with investigations spanning the arts and sciences of vegetal sensing and sentience, the politics of gardens, and the enduring colonial violence of restoration ecology. Since 2015 she has been working with dancer and filmmaker Ayelen Liberona on Becoming Sensor, a research creation project to invent protocols for an ungridable ecology of the happenings taking shape across ancient and urban lands in Toronto.

The Chthulucene

The Chthulucene, since you asked, is a new epoch,

where refugees from environmental disaster (both human and non-human) will come together. This is a time when humans will try to live in balance and harmony with nature (or what's left of it) in 'mixed assemblages'.

That's the definition provided by some entity called "Southern Fried Science". We learn via symposium co-convenor Dr Verlie's peer-reviewed scholarship – Becoming Researchers: Making Academic Kin in the Chthulucene that researchers covet

a form of refuge from academic stressors, creating spaces for 'composting together' [no misprint] through processes of 'decomposing' and 'recomposing'. Our rejection of neoliberal norms has gifted us experiences of joyful collective pleasures.

I hope your curiosity about these three promising eras of the 2070s (as viewed by Sydney University) is fully satisfied. As a proud graduate of UWA (poetry major, 1964), why don't I myself submit a paper to this important symposium in their suggested poetic format? Here goes:

WHAT IS TO BE DONE*

We're done for in the Anthropocene

I don't want a scene

But Dr James Dunk

Is in a funk.

That's two rhymes out of the way.

What rhymes with Chthulucene?

I'll work it out another day.

*Acknowledgement to Mr V.I. Lenin.

PART TWO

THE BARE-FACED BRAINWASHING OF OUR
YOUNGSTERS

Australians all let us deplore ...

17 September 2021

What! I wouldn't believe it, except I have the print-out sitting in my hand. Australian schoolkids in their thousands in the classrooms are being coached to disrespect the national anthem by sitting down through it. The coaching is via the green/Left crowd Cool Australia, founded by Jason Kimberley of the Just Jeans multi-millionaire family. By rich, know that last November Christine and Roger Kimberley sold their Sorrento mansion for $25 million.

Cool Australia is aware its anti-Australian claptrap might make some kids uneasy or upset. I'd put more than half kids in that category – i.e. kids coming from conservative homes – so Cool warns teachers (my emphasis):

> It is important that teachers subtly monitor the welfare and wellbeing of students during this lesson [specifically, on "Invasion Day/Survival Day"] and for a couple of weeks afterward to make sure they are feeling safe and able to cope with the content raised in this lesson. (Paywalled and for teachers only).

First I'll give some background on Cool, then I'll quote its Teacher Guide to getting kids to sit down during the national anthem.

Cool boasts that its overall goal is "active empowered young people", or for short, kid activists, and certainly not activist for conservative causes like free speech and small government. Here's more (my emphases):

> Our resources embed environmental, social and economic

issues into core subject areas. Cool resources address inequality and the precarious state of our natural world. [The planet and humanity has never been in better shape, absent COVID-19]. Our lessons cover climate change, social justice issues, creativity in STEM ... and much more. Our action-based pedagogical approach means that kids are enabled to take action on issues that are important to them.

Education departments, abetted by Labor and the Greens' militant teachers' unions, in effect have contracted out a good slice of primary and secondary education to the leftist curriculum experts at Cool. These experts create free, ready-to-go lessons with all the trimmings, neatly collated and referenced to state and federal curricula. Teachers love to download and use the lessons, since this is a damn sight easier than concocting them themselves about topics they know little/nothing about. (Cool says that 76 per cent of teachers find their workload unmanageable, and 45 per cent teach outside their expertise). Cool quotes primary teacher Shannon Ruskin (NSW) saying that when students act upon the lessons, they "contribute to making our world a better place." According to Shannon, anyway.

The usage of Cool's lessons is staggering – a word I was trained not to use lightly. At least 8400 of Australia's total 9000 schools use their lessons, as do 52 per cent of all teachers. Cool says it reached 3.6 million students last year, with lesson downloads more than trebling since 2015. Cool claims 9 million hours of teacher prep time saved, and $252 million worth of teacher time saved since inception in 2008. To give the devil his due, 90 per cent of Cool's material seems positive and valuable. This makes its 10% of propaganda material so much more effective.

Cool's material is pushing against an open classroom door. The annual costs of distributing its material nationwide to schools is a piddling $1.65 million including Cool's staff ($0.9 million), IT, offices and overheads. The bulk of funding is from "grants", particularly left-wing charitable foundations. Cool must be running the most cost-effective mass political campaign in Australian history.

Possibly in homage to last year's Black Lives Matter riots and looting, Cool has swung its resources into racist indoctrination, by which I mean teaching kids of pink skin to acknowledge and jettison their unwitting "white privilege" and defer socially, culturally and especially politically to the Aboriginal Industry. Cool's previous obsession with asylum seekers as a stick to beat conservative politicians appears to have lost traction these days.

Cool's race weapon of choice is the propaganda documentary *The Final Quarter* by Ian Darling, about the alleged race-inspired booing and alleged persecution of Sydney Swans' Aboriginal star Adam Goodes. The 52 lessons stretch from school years 5 to 12. As if that were not enough, the ABC's unaccountable education TV service (currently slobbering over fauxboriginal scribbler Bruce Pascoe) offers a comparable array of lessons involving Stan Grant's lookalike documentary on Goodes, *Australian Dream*.

In my previous research into Cool and Adam Goodes, I didn't notice them bringing the term "White Privilege" into play. But now in a single edition of Cool's "Teacher Preparation" notes (paywalled) I count more than 50 uses of the term "Privilege".

The national anthem is supposedly a manifestation of white privilege. This sit-down lesson starts

Learning intentions: Students...

#... understand that privilege can hide within recognised institutions as well as individuals.

#… understand the impact that symbols can have on those who don't experience privilege

#… develop the capacity to analyse symbols of oppression and privilege in the world around them

#… consider opportunities for challenging privilege at the systemic/symbolic level.

Success criteria: Students can…

#… identify how symbols, texts or events include and exclude different voices/perspectives.

#… explain the impact of symbols, texts or events on audiences.

#… collaborate to problem-solve and consider alternatives to the status quo.

This document of 3600 words coaches teachers to coach kids to "deconstruct" three of Australia's most important symbols – the Australian flag, Australia Day and the National Anthem. In each case, Cool provides a loaded case, with a token nod to conservative values for the "pro" case. Cool's "anti" case packs an emotional wallop and there is no way that kids get, or could properly examine, the conservative position. (Of course, one might wonder why the flag etc need reconstructing in the first place, any more than motherhood, the Enlightenment, or the rule of law).

Anyway, I'll skip to page 10 of Cool's 12-page teachers' guide, dubbed Part C: *Evaluating Alternatives.*

Step 1. How can people challenge symbols of white privilege?

Step 2. Show students this clip as an example of a response and complete the SWOT (strengths, weaknesses, opportunities and threats) analysis below as a class on this response [a video]:

The clip is worth the click. It shows the Queensland nine-year-old girl who refused to stand for the National Anthem at her school and was sent home/suspended. The kid declaims all the woke mantras down pat and good luck to her – I was pretty obnoxious myself at age 9 (and thereafter). Her parents must be delighted to see their little darling on the front line of the culture wars.

Cool then pretends to run SWOT analyses (Strengths, Weaknesses, Opportunities and Threats) on the 9-year-old's sit-down strike/protest, which is just another excuse to indoctrinate. Cool's printed table for teachers is headed,

"Response 1: Seated protest of (sic) national anthem".

1. Strengths:

 # Anyone who witnesses the national anthem can do it.

 # Easy – doesn't cost money or require organisation

 # Non-violent [that's a relief!]

Weaknesses:

 # May not get a chance to share reasons for sitting down [what a woke tragedy that would be!].

 # Doesn't necessarily change any other people's behaviour

Opportunities – ways you could build upon the response –

 # Post about it on social media to gain media attention [thus putting kids in the firing line of being trolled and abused online, nice work Cool Australia!]

 # Get other students to partake (sic – do these sub-standard writers mean 'participate'?).

Threats (ways the response may be impacted)

 # Students could receive penalties for partaking (sic)

 # Backlash against Aboriginal and Torres Strait Islander students and community members may occur.

That last point is preposterous. If a kid sits during the National Anthem, why would anyone set about attacking Aborigines?

Alongside this Soviet-style miseducation, Cool offers blank SWOT boxes for the kids to fill in. Teachers are referred back to "Step 1 – How can people [kids] challenge symbols of white privilege?" The elaboration of "Step 1" involves kids absorbing the whole panoply of leftist attacks on Australian nationhood as embodied in the 3600-word teachers' guide. They lay out their favourite attacks on white privilege and the teacher writes these memes on the blackboard. Then, as "Step 3", kids select any of these blackboard memes for a SWOT exercise. My suggested example: "The national flag is racist and should be taken down from the school flagpole and ceremonially burnt outside the principal's office".

Cool Australia isn't done yet. We move on to "Step 4: Ask students to discuss on (sic) their tables"

 # How might the race of the person challenging white privilege affect their actions?

 # How might the race of the person challenging white privilege affect the reactions they experience from others?

 # Which options resonated with you? Why/why not?

 # Would you consider pursuing any of these options? Why/why not?

And there's more. The Teachers' Guide finishes the section with "Reflection". Cool tells teachers to show their kids yet another propaganda documentary clip for the Aboriginal industry, namely the Indigenous rapper Adam Briggs on the ABC's left-drenched Q&A whining about "Indigenous Disadvantage and Racism on Social Media".

Cool's point is that some kids have doubtless become uncomfortable during the previous indoctrination session. I judge that the new clip teaches them that their discomfort is their own problem rather than an imposition from the teacher or Cool Australia.

Ask students to reflect on this statement, using the following prompts:

 # When did you feel comfortable or uncomfortable in today's class? Why?

 # What types of experiences make people uncomfortable?

*# **What are some positive outcomes of discomfort?***

 # Do you think there is value in leaning into discomfort?

These SWOT examples only scratch the surface of the Cool onslaught on conservative values. To deal fully with their "Teachers' Guides" would be like wading through a rancid soup of the Left's causes *du jour*, so I'll just pick out a few highlights.

1. Cool's offered photo of an Australian who is proud of the flag depicts a redneck swigging a beer and covered with Union Jacks and stars.

2. Cool wants kids to study a girl's "heartfelt" scrawled letter in felt-tip about Australia Day. It starts, "Dear govmint". This kid wants the January 26 celebration scrapped because *"it's the day we stole Australia from the Aboriginal people ... It's like celebrating because we killed lots and lots of Aboriginal people."*

3. In pushing the "racism" angle on booing of Adam Goodes, the material makes no mention of Goodes verbally attacking a 13-year-old country girl who in an excess of Collingwood-supporting zeal

called him an "ape". The girl said she just shouted the insult as a joke, and was unaware of its racist possibility. Goodes said of the identified 13 year-old: "Racism had a face last night". She was separated by police from her grandparent and interrogated solo for two hours, and forced to apologise. (Goodes conceded it was the first racial abuse he'd heard as a footballer for the previous eight years). Even teenage murderers are not publicly identified, brow-beaten and shamed in such fashion. This, plus Goodes' ersatz war-dance at Carlton supporters, was responsible for much of the booing (a Daily Mail poll showed 60 per cent rejecting any racist motive). Cool however says the booing "revealed an undercurrent of racism that still exists in Australia today."

4. *"White privilege is structural and as such may not be recognised by those who hold it."*

5. *"Talking about white privilege can be uncomfortable because it is unfamiliar to many Australians. This is because, as Dr Tim Soutphommasane, the former Race Discrimination Commissioner, argues, 'conversations about discrimination tend to focus on those who are disadvantaged by prejudice. It isn't always the case that we consider the other side of the coin: what it says about those who do not experience discrimination.' For a comprehensive description of white privilege and how the concept came to be articulated, read his speech in full."*

6. Cool even raises the ogre of heterosexual privilege – "White privilege does not discount other disadvantages that people may have experienced, for example, they may not hold socioeconomic privilege, religious privilege, heterosexual privilege."

7. On the national flag – *"Suggested answers – Union Jack is a symbol of the colonisers ... Celebrates colonisation and erases the*

*colonisers' violent history towards Aboriginal and Torres Strait Is-
lander peoples … may offend/upset those Aboriginal and Torres
Strait Islander people who see the Union Jack as a constant reminder
of the genocide and oppression of their people by the colonisers."*

8. "Conclusion: Whose experiences, views and contributions
do Australian symbols reflect, celebrate or include?" [a typically
loaded question].

I haven't included other-than-race Cool propaganda here, but
there's plenty of it.

Somehow in recent decades, education bureaucrats and their
enabling politicians have swapped the purpose of education from
teaching kids about the world to turning them into horrid little
know-nothing woke activists. That goal is now coded into Australian education's DNA.

I'll head off now to wash my hands after touching Cool Australia's anthem sit-down coaching for teachers and their pupils.

Raising a generation of junior jackbooters

13 July 2021

Australian schoolkids get multiple forms of green/Left indoctrination. Conservative state and federal governments do nothing about this and even promote it. But how well are kids actually absorbing the green/Left narrative? Very well indeed, is my guess. Judging from copious material I've been sifting, schools are training a generation of horrid little eco-tyrants hot to embark on the mightiest state planning and control makeover since Stalin destroyed private agriculture and re-introduced mass slavery.

"Young Australians' Plans for the Planet" – an astounding trove – involves myriad pages of kids' takes on social issues. They were organised by local climate zealots to support the United Nation's 17 "Sustainable Development Goals" (SDGs) for 2030. The UN's eight "Millennium Development Goals" for 2000-15 did great work reducing indicators like childbirth mortality and extreme poverty. But the 17 SDGs are a joke on "inclusiveness", involving 169 sub-targets and no prioritisations ("End poverty, protect the planet, and ensure prosperity for all"). Indeed the UN's original SDG draft involved 1400 indiscriminate goals proposed by 120 organisations.

If you imagine the UN is a noble organisation, keep in mind that the China is taking over key committees; the founder of the UN Environmental Program Maurice Strong got sprung with a corrupt cheque for $US988,000; the 2013-14 President of the General Assembly John Ashe (Antigua) enjoyed the proceeds of at least $US1.3 million in bribes; and UN peace-keeping forces have been hotbeds of child sex abuse. *The Age* reported in 2006 that two Jordanian soldiers with the UN Peacekeeping Force in East

Timor were evacuated home with injured penises after attempting intercourse with goats.

Our UN-loving locals organised about 240 kids from Year 10, drawn from 20 high schools nationally, to flesh out kids' own plans for Australia out to 2050. The kids and supervising teachers did the eight months' extra-curricular work during 2016-19, stopping when COVID-19 intervened. The superstructure was bigger than Ben Hur. The exercise went international with kids from Mauritius (10 schools, 120 kids) and Singapore endorsing the template. Asia, Africa and North America wait in the wings.

The local organisers were: Questacon and Inspiring Australia (the National Science and Technology Centre run within the Department of Industry), the green-Left Academy of Science and its affiliate Future Earth, UN Youth Australia, six universities led by the ANU's woke vice-chancellor and Nobelist Brian Schmidt, and green fanatics such as Beyond Zero Emissions and OnePlanet Partnership.

The 240 kid volunteers are probably a green-biased sample (if you know of any free-market warming-sceptic school groups out there somewhere, please let me know). Actually some of the kids taking part occasionally went off-message: an outlier even urged debate and polling on nuclear power, and some others were gung-ho for a gas pipeline from PNG and a gas-powered electricity plant to help North Queensland's industry – climate Armageddon be damned. The mainstream want a green socialist nirvana where governments dictate how we live and work, and ensure we think only proper thoughts about renewables.

I'm not blaming kids for what teachers have dinned into them; I'm sure kids' hearts are in the right place. But here goes, fasten your seat-belts, because here is what the junior jackbooters think is needed to confront the "climate emergency" we're always hearing about.

\# "Stop the debate as climate change is real."

\# Kids want their parents to be slugged with a carbon tax, plus 50 per cent hikes in both petrol prices and car insurance. (Mum and Dad to kid: "Gee thanks, Fiona, that's just what our family needs.")

\# WA kids: "Go to the federal government and ask them to put through a law saying all vehicle owners need to drive an electric vehicle by 2030." (Even the uber-progressive Canberra kids want only an 80 per cent cut in normal cars by 2040).

\# New coal mines are banned and coal and petroleum replaced "with a job-rich, clean energy economy." The kids say that our green jobs can grow by 28 per cent per annum, which on my calculations suggests nearly 60 million green jobs by 2050.

\# Central planners are to decrease fossil fuel exports (the lifeblood of the Australian economy) and increase exports of "sustainably farmed crops and livestock."

\# Federal and state legislation for mandatory use of biofuels in vehicles, aircraft and off-grid electricity production.

\# "Increase fuel excise on non-biofuels with all funds invested back into biofuels technology and development."

\# WA kids: "We aim to stop live export by any means completely. We want live exports to be completely illegal and those who will break this law **will get a reasonable punishment.**"

\# "Legislation/guidelines as to where a shop can import from, based on their location." (This is to support local production, never mind any advantages of trade).

The kids want the government to snuff out "infamously" water-intensive crops like cotton and rice, "while providing viable alternatives". I assume the NSW Premier sets up a Ministry of Artichokes & Pineapples.

WA kids want farmers to be levied "4 per cent of their output or $2 billion a year" to stock "community fridges" available to anyone wanting a feed. (Fat chance that teachers would know that WA farm output isn't $50 billion, it's $11 billion).

"New laws" should place quotas of women in high-paid male-dominated sectors. Workplaces should run compulsory courses against sexism. (Comparable, I assume, to current compulsory safety courses.)

A steadily increasing tax on sugar-laced foods, while subsidising fruit and veges for the poor. The sugar tax to be followed by something called a "trans-fat tax".

Kids want to teach farmers how to run their farms, imagining that profligate farmers are over-spraying fertilisers and pesticides, heedless of cost. Farm problems can, of course, be 'solved' by government funding for increased farmer wages, the kids explain. "It would make sense that we all pay for agriculture through tax."

Australians were once famed as rugged individualists. But today's snowflake kids want a taxpayer-funded program for free beach umbrellas to combat sunburn, and taxpayer-paid seaside sunscreen dispensers. Students from households on less than $80,000 a year should get taxpayer-paid lunches.

The NSW kids, who have been familiarised with green politics, write:

Australia previously had a carbon tax under the Gillard government that lasted from 2011-14. Unfortunately there was

*extreme backlash towards this and it was repealed in July
2014 ... The introduction of a Carbon Tax could be a potentially viable way of reducing the state's dependence on coal
and fossil fuels as it becomes more expensive to use them.*

The NSW kids have got the climate-catastrophe panic prose
down pat:

*We have 18 months to reduce impact of climate change until
irreversible damage including unadaptable changes for animals according to the UN.*

The 18 months are now up, kids, and global temperatures actually fell in June to a range last seen 20 years ago.

Schoolkids, who've learnt so much engineering from their
teachers, envisage

*teaching the community the benefits of renewable energy and
dissipating the myths surrounding solar/wind farms (that
they are too loud, look unattractive in the countryside).*

A reminder, kids: they're also intermittent.

The union movement has tumbled from 51 per cent of the
workforce in 1976 to a under 14 per cent today, with the education
sector probably the most strongly unionised. It appears that union
supporters have invaded the classrooms to shore up future membership. Here's kids' reflections, with "third party" a euphemism
for "union":

*Creating jobs in the renewable energy sector that are attrac-
tive, high salary and have good unions ... All organisations
should have equal pay policies and employee access to third
party pay negotiators. Funding from government to allow
people to have access to a third party negotiator ... Organise*

various third party negotiators for the government/businesses
to readily supply for employers and employees ... By commu-
nicating with their government prior to a job interview, an
employee will be able to access a third party to negotiate pay.

Combatting unemployment is seen as the job of "schools unions and unemployment benefit centres" – employers don't rate a mention.

On Clean Energy goals — the need for baseload power is typically overlooked – coal miners are seen deftly transitioning to solar energy jobs and "the price of electricity will drop to more affordable prices for all communities." Actually, kids, studies show that the more solar/wind wattage a country has, the dearer its electricity. In NSW, electricity is to be 100 per cent renewable by 2030. Heaven help fridge-owners during wind droughts.

The kids' push for electric cars would be aided by taxpayer grants to buyers and free access to bus lanes, toll roads and ferries. Since the kids want electric cars to swamp the roads, bus drivers and ferry operators will be cursing. Buses and trams would have sensors to dob in traffic violators, and the public transport system would get 25% of the fines – bounty-hunting by behemoths

As to CO2 in the atmosphere, currently 416 parts per million, the kids believe it can be sucked down legislatively or by technology to 366ppm in 2030 and to 330ppm in 2050. It was previously at 330ppm in 1975, an era when Asian and African peasants were starving from lack of mechanisation.

The nadir of the kids' teacher-supervised output comes from a Perth high school. Its 31 planet-savers aim to re-shape human society and revise the Western Enlightenment, but they first need more instruction on grammar and spelling. For example, *"This an extra income a little bit more unrestricted."* I wouldn't normally care but shouldn't teachers correct kids' grammar in a public document for clients like the Prime Minister and the Academy of Science? Perhaps the teachers' command of basic grammar and coherence is no better than that of their indoctrinated charges.

These kids, in their plan for quality education, say,

> *Also to improve the staff work ethic so we can (sic) quality teachers over a quantity of average teachers (sic) … More important Topics come first an aren't just restricted to being taught by one person yelling out information expecting others to take notes.*

Understandably, they want the school budget to finance a therapist. These kids lobby for "Quality teachers … performance management salary based incentives" – a good thing but sounds odd coming from the mouths of babes.

During the planning exercise WA had some drought so the kids' plan reads,

> *The amount of drought is reduced by at least 35% in the heavily drought affected areas.*

Almost as ambitious as planning the weather is halting WA coral bleaching for the first time in about 26 million years.

> *Reduce the temperature of sea water by trying to reduce the amount of carbon emissions in the atmosphere that lead to global warming that lead to coral bleaching.*

The budding civil engineers want to turn Argyle, Australia's second-largest dam, into a Malcolm Turnbull-style Snowy 2.0: *Get a huge pump to pump water up pipes. Power the pump by a nearby solar farm that has to be made.*

Kids nationally bemoan water scarcity but seem unaware of green bans on vital new dams and catchments. Some are also clueless but zealous about construction materials, claiming that inter-city water pipes should be converted to copper because copper is the "most affordable" material (recent price $A13,000 per tonne). They know better than water boards how to prevent leaks – boards must apply anti-rust coatings "for all pipes made of a Ferris (sic) metal."

The ACT kids are demanding the honouring of the 2015 Paris climate pledges – notwithstanding that all pledges are discretionary. They urge their fellow young to lobby the Australian curriculum authority to include climate change teaching "in collaboration with students" who clearly know what's what. Like the WA kids, the ACT kids lobby, curiously, for higher teacher pay, more teacher support, benefits and longer annual leave (six weeks' Christmas leave plus term breaks are apparently not enough). Need one be corroded by cynicism to guess who has been planting in kids' heads the notion that teachers need more pay and fewer hours?

Kids meanwhile should be able to change their legal sex identity without the inconvenience of gender assignment surgery, according to the NSW kids. This looks a bit esoteric for Year 10s but nothing in today's education surprises me.

In other kids' miscellany, violent Aboriginals are incarcerated because they're victimised: "We need to uproot biased judges and make sure all trials are fair." And in what must be news to NSW loggers, kids inform us that "The NSW Government also needs to stop subsidising the native forests logging industry with the people's tax money."

My first recommendation is that woke teachers and green do-gooders stop shoving their perverse and naive pet causes down kids' throats. Second, jettison this whole idea that we'll get any wisdom from teenagers' hormone-fevered brains. The kids are in school to learn stuff and acquire some worldly knowhow. When they've flown the parental coop, paid their own way and experienced the real world's rigors, their views might be worth a listen.

Until then, kids can ponder Greta Thunberg's latest message: "The audience has grown weary. This show is over. Thank you." #

Damon Gameau's futuristic fantasies for kiddies

9 May 2021

In the run-up to the federal election, teachers and third-party groups inveigled schoolkids with propaganda about the green/ Left independent candidates. In this essay I'll take a look one such tool of sly persuasion, dark green climate activist Damon Gameau's latest film, *Regenerating Australia*. It's heading for authorised mainstream usage in classrooms and spruiks nameless green/Left independents. Then I'll document half a dozen class-lesson templates about the film, created by Cool Australia which is a Leftist online platform used by 52 per cent of Australian teachers with their reach to 3.2 million students.

Cool Australia brags that Teachers Health insurance fund, with its 300,000 clients, is "Our Coolest Partner". Other funders include various Rich-Listers' foundations (e.g. the Fox family, Purves, Fairfax, Smorgons), billionaire-run Atlassian, Google and Cisco, plus odds and sods such as the Lord Mayors Charitable Foundation.

Two minutes into Gameau's film, a fictitious planet-saving independent, "Lucy Jameson", gets a surprise election win to rapturous acclaim. "The message from the voting public could not be clearer," says the newsreader, claiming "frustrations with leadership and politics had boiled over". Set in the future, the film fantasises that demonstrations by two million people led to a referendum of 12 million Australians, with 82 per cent wanting net zero emissions by 2040.

So how is the flick being received? Let's start with Melbourne's upmarket Brighton Primary School. The principal, Steve Meade, organised a screening for 3 May. There are starring roles for Kerry

O'Brien, the leftist ex-ABC pundit and icon; the Climate Council's Tim "Wonthaggi" Flannery (of course), and greenish independent MHR Zali Steggall. She hails the film's new federal law protecting "30 per cent of Australian native forest and bushland".

Principal Meade invited along ersatz independent candidate for Goldstein, Zoe Daniel (also ex-ABC) and Climate 200's Svengali, Simon Holmes a Court, for the event's question-and-answer session. Conservative parents mutinied and the school deleted the invitation and rescheduled the event with no mention of the Daniels/ Holmes à Court's Q&A.

Principal Meade justified his stance with the time-honoured nonsense about less than ten years to save "our kids and the planet."

The *Herald Sun* quoted one parent, "Political activism has no place in the classroom. I don't think children in primary school need to be politicised in any way." Brighton's Liberal MLA James Newbury quoted outraged Bayside parents, summing up their objections thus: "Our public primary schools should be places of learning not a shopfront for political activism. State Labor is taking advantage of young kids by politicising our schoolyards." Several other schools in the Goldstein zone had previously featured Zoe Daniels.

Departmental anti-indoctrination rules vary by state (and are usually ignored. For example, SA Education Department policy is, "Members of parliament and candidates are welcome at schools and preschools within their electorates when it will not disrupt normal activities. School and preschool visits must not be for political or campaign purposes." I doubt the guideline endorses candidate visits a mere fortnight pre-election.

Gameau's 17-minute *Regenerating* "documentary" is heavily supported by WWF-Australia and philanthropist Ian Darling's Shark

Island Foundation. Gameau claims Regenerating is based on a thousand interviews in 2020 with people of diverse views – though the film involves not one iota of doubt about green cure-alls. Set at end of 2029, it's a prequel to his full-scale futuristic epic *2040* and fantasises that every green gimmick has worked like a charm. *2040* was seized on by teachers who force-fed it to 1.5 million students and downloaded two million copies of the notes.

All this planet-saving has taken its toll on Gameau, as *The Guardian* reports:

[Gameau] says that in the wake of the first Lismore floods, he was on a plane when he heard the news about the record heatwave in Antarctica – with temperatures nearly 40 degrees above average – and he "just burst into tears".

Dry your tears, Damon, momentary spikes in Antarctic temperatures are insignificant and the icy continent hasn't warmed for 70 years.

I suppose some Gameau emotion is understandable as he couldn't get back to his home town of Broken Head (Northern Rivers) when the floods hit, and his two daughters had to be rescued by a friend on a longboard. This has zero relevance to CO_2 emissions, a fact emphasised by omission. His film doesn't mention the planet hasn't warmed for the past seven years and six months, according to the UAH satellite monitoring, and Australia has not warmed since end-2012.

Instead, in a rather sadistic (or sentimental) touch, the film shows in 2029 our last coal-fired power station's stack, likely to be blown up, but with coal workers' names first inscribed on it. It's also rather sadistic for Gameau, circa 2029, to plant mini-forests on what looks like Melbourne's Rod Laver Arena. A lot of balls will get lost in the trees. The scariest scene in the film shows Melbourne's Luna Park headed for at least 3m of sea rise by 2100 – that's 4cm a year from now on. Even the alarmist IPCC expects well under a one-metre rise by 2100.

Gameau modestly likens his climate pitch to that of slavery abolitionists and the human rights movements. He finds Australian traditional democracy dissatisfying, and his film introduces some Swiss-style decision-making via on-line voting, restrictions on political donations and "citizen juries". He claims that the masses are disillusioned with politicians who won't recognise "the Code Red for humanity, the window is closing, now or never" and their alleged capture by the fossil fuel industry and the (Murdoch) media. (Stanford University has just received a $US1b donation for an alarmist climate institute. Sceptic bloggers live off tip jars).

Hence the film's urging for more direct local power for climate activists. Gameau says he has no political ambitions.

Naturally the film reaches a "clear consensus on First Nation's Sovereignty", but a kicker is that we also create a "Youth Parliamentary Advisory Council" with teenagers – Heaven help us! – advising parliament. Youthful woman speaks: "We hope to see climate change on the forefront of their (politicians') minds and really pushing the fight for climate justice."

Gameau's shtick is to only terrify schoolkids a little, while claiming they can run around "taking action" to save the planet. "If you're going to sound the fire alarm, you've got to show people where the exits are," he explains. Kids come up to him crying with relief that the planet can be saved after all. There's no mention in the film of China and India, with their vast expansions of coal-fired power that will swamp every emission cut by the West.

For the scary stuff he depicts the 2020 bushfires as (bogus) demonstrations of climate change. He has a firefighter saying, "We could hear the screams of people" and a distraught housewife thinking of setting fire to her own house because of her stress. Gameau fantasises that devastating fires later in the 2020s leave "hundreds of Australians dead, and saw any doubts about climate change finally put to rest." So much for not scaring kids.

But on the plus side, future-Australia has no trouble putting in a three-hour Melbourne-Sydney rail link, implying top speeds of circa 400kph, with an extension to Brisbane in 2032. Clever electricians install a sub-sea power line to Singapore turning us into a renewable energy export superpower, in the fantasy of Nicky Ison of WWF (curiously labelled as with AMEO – Australian Energy Market Operator). A dozen actors in a conference room – many in jeans and sneakers — see Singapore on a screen lighting up with Australia's green electrons. They leap to their feet waving arms and exchanging high-fives. The price of renewables and batteries has of course "plummeted" and the country runs solely on renewable energy for an entire month. (After which the wind drops and we have blackouts?)

In Gameau's imagination, we send off hydrogen-powered ships laden with "ammonia and green steel made from our iron ore and renewable energy." We revel in a billion-dollar seaweed industry and offshore wind farms, while the feds pass a law banning single-use plastics and the Murray-Darling is granted "Rights of Nature" (whatever that might be). Every green triumph creates "thousands of new jobs". Bikie gangs are so happy with roof gardens and extra street greenery that there is "reduced crime and reduced anti-social behaviour, because we can deal better with the world when we are getting to nature."

Melbourne's dark-green Mayor Sally Capp shares filmic fantasies that her electric bus fleet cuts emissions and boosts jobs. Don't tell her that in Paris in the past month, two electric bus fires caused 150 of them to be taken out of service as a precaution.

Gameau is now winding up an Australia-wide tour of about 70 screenings. The scheduling during the federal election campaign was not intentional, he says.

The screening in Batemans Bay, NSW, seemed more like a revivalist meeting with attendees calling out "yeeeew!" and "boom!" *The Guardian* enthuses:

> *A dance troupe from the local Walbunja people of the Yuin nation perform, and when they greet the audience in Dhurga, a blonde-headed girl licking a choc-top yells back "Wallawani" and pumps her hand in the air. As the event ends, one woman walks out of the cinema and stretches her arms up into the night sky. "My God, I so needed that."*

So now to the "curriculum". Schools have jumped aboard via Cool Australia, the third-party provider of free downloadable prefabricated lessons. The packs are described by Cool as "the Regenerating Australia curriculum". Cool is adulatory in tone about the cast who "shared their hopes and dreams for the country's future." The class brainwashing campaign got under way last February with this spiel:

> *Calling all teachers in Australia!*
>
> *You're invited to a free virtual teacher preview screening of our new short film, Regenerating Australia, ahead of the national release in March!*
>
> *Join us for a live Q+A with Director Damon Gameau, Cool Australia's Head of Education, Mark Drummond, and*

WWF-Australia's Earth Hour Coordinator, Jasmin Ledger, to learn about the free educational resources we are developing and how schools can get involved in Regenerating Australia!

Cool says,

The Regenerating Australia curriculum has been designed to tune your students into the concepts covered in the film, and deep dive into the solutions presented. The lessons in this unit can be used in isolation or mixed and matched in any sequence that suits your curriculum planning. We recommend that you start the investigation of regeneration with the 'Watching the Film' lesson for your year level.

Cool tells teachers to take their classes to cinema screenings (there goes a morning's real education) or get their own licensed copy and "School Action Toolkit" and "Fact Sheet".

Here are a few specific lessons of the Gameau curriculum (paywalled, my emphases).

Sample One:

Subjects: Civics and Citizenship

Year Levels: 9 & 10

Topics: Democracy and politics.

Teaching Time: 180 mins (best taught over two lessons). [Yikes!]

Quick summary:

*Have you ever wondered what it might take to rejuvenate Australia's democracy and get you (sic) adults involved throughout the process? In this lesson, students watch a section of "Regenerating Australia" that explores a rejuvenated and transparent democracy system **and begin to unravel truths**. Students will research their local MP and find out* *how they vote on issues, then become active participants in the democratic system by communicating with their local MP about a topic that is important to them. Finally, students will return to the questions asked in the barometer activity to reflect on whether their understanding has changed.*

Learning intentions:

* *Students will understand how and why individuals and groups participate in, and contribute to, the democratic process*

* *Students will recognise some of the challenges to sustaining a resilient democracy*

Students will become familiar with **ways that the resiliency of the Australian democratic system can be improved.**

A characteristic of Australian school education is that kids learn how things "should" be before they learn what they are.

Sample 2:

Regenerating Australia – Watching The Film – English, Science and Civics and Citizenship – Years 7 & 8

Topics: Sustainability, Regenerating Australia

Teaching Time: 120 minutes. [That's half a day's schooling up the spout].

Quick summary:

The teacher will activate children's prior knowledge on the topic in a vocabulary matching game, prompt their critical thinking skills using the 5Ws, and invite students to develop questions about the concept of regeneration. They will view "Regenerating Australia", then return to their questions and summarise the key themes. Students will be invited to explore their school with an open mind and capture spaces that could benefit from regeneration.

Learning intentions:

* *Students will understand the concept of 'regeneration'*

* *Students will understand that regeneration is something that we can implement in our communities and ecosystems.*

Sample 3:

Regenerating Australia – Film And Production Analysis – English – Years 9 & 10

Teaching Time: 180 mins (this lesson could be split over a number of teaching periods).

Quick summary:

In this lesson, students will view the film "Regenerating Australia" and then watch a video interview with the Writer and Director, Damon Gameau. They will respond to a set of questions that will prompt them to consider the intended impact of the film and the structural and/or visual choices that were made in order to create this impact. Students will use their knowledge on regeneration to create a news report about a real or imagined example of regeneration.

Learning intentions:

* *Understand how cultural perspectives and other texts can influence the construction and interpretation of news reports*

* *Be aware of how people, cultures, places, events, objects and concepts are represented in texts, including media texts, through language, structural and/or visual choices*

* *Know how to create informative texts that present a point of view and advance or illustrate arguments.*

Sample 4:

Activity: Regenerating Australia – Regenerate Your Community – Design and Technology – Years 7 & 8

Topics: Critical and Creative Thinking, Regenerating Australia, design, environment.

Teaching Time: 95 mins.

Quick summary:

*After watching Regenerating Australia, students will work through an investigation of **creative and critical thinking tasks** to gain an in-depth understanding of what regeneration and sustainability mean in the context of their local communities and areas.*

Teachers say the curriculum is too crowded – but they can always squeeze in some more net-zero propaganda.#

A teachers' guide to miseducating the young

28 June 2021

The national primary-school English teachers' association has launched a climate propaganda blitz on the 5 to 14-year-olds placed in their care. The teachers' just-released manual spruiks intermittent wind and solar and demands an end to coal-fired electricity and fossil fuels. As notes to the manual say, *"Chapter 9 is a call for action. Without students taking personal action to mitigate climate change, there is no point to this book."*

It's an error-ridden 174-page blueprint that quarantines kids from any acknowledgement that costly wind and solar farms must be backed up by 24-7 baseload power.

The blueprint would have kids chanting North Korean-style *"an Earth-focused school or class 'anthem' at assemblies. (This) is a great way to build emotional attachment to the planet"*. The authors suggest such lyrics as

> *Earth is getting warmer, oceans rising higher*
> *Storms are growing stronger, floods and fire*
> *We know about the dangers, know there must be changes*
> *The future is in our hands*

The blueprint is called *Teaching the language of climate change science*, and is issued by the Primary English Teaching Association of Australia (PETAA) for its 3500 members and teachers generally. One author is Julie Hayes, retired principal of Cowandilla Primary School, SA, which has been "a Climate Change Focus School" for the past 20 years. The co-author is Dr Bronwyn Parkin, a literacy-linguistics specialist at Adelaide University. Both are listed as PETAA directors.

The indoctrination was poorly vetted by a 20-person academic panel. Its only card-carrying climate scientist was Professor Chris Turney of UNSW. Turney's wife, Annette, a tutor and PhD student at Wollongong University, was a co-panellist, which seems a bit in-group. Turney is famous for leading the "ship of fools" expedition to the Antarctic in 2013 to spruik global warming there. The ship got stuck in the ice that wasn't supposed to be there and the climate scientists and alarmist joy-riders had to be extricated by a series of rescue vessels at huge expense and disruption to real science down there.

The authors excuse their simplified claims on the ground that kids are too young for hard science. But they are happy to indoctrinate kids with nonsense about climate-caused starving polar bears (see below), the (non) warming and (non) melting Antarctic, the (non) drowning Pacific Islands, and (not) worse droughts and (not) worse tornados. The book even includes earthquakes on the roll-call of warming-caused extreme weather.

The authors' view is that training little pre-schoolers as climate activists is somewhat premature, but they can at least be taught that climate scientists are beyond reproach. And kids can be softened up for the coming indoctrination in primary school:

Action at Preschool level: The book doesn't suggest developing a class action plan for young children. Instead, at this influential stage, educators have the opportunity to model care for the environment, conservation of resources and respect for the work of [alarmist] scientists.

Spheres of influence: In the middle and upper years of primary school, the spheres of influence widen … Older students can influence others in the school, from younger students, to staff and the governing council. They can also involve parents and family in their actions. The highest year levels extend their spheres of influence to the wider community, to local shopping centres and the local council.

By Years 4-6, kids are trained to write persuasive texts to parents/carers against using petrol, a paradox in light of parents' chauffeuring kids to and from schools. This indulgence creates ghastly morning and afternoon traffic jams. *"Teachers' involvement and enthusiasm signals to students that acting on climate change is important and that we are all in this together."*

Other supplied book notes re 9 to 10-year-olds:

Parents become an important audience for students as they begin to take on the scientific mantle, with growing attachment to the scientific community.

It's another question whether parents, including power-station workers and coal miners, appreciate lectures from their teacher-indoctrinated sub-Greta offspring.

For kids 11-12yo notes say, *"They begin communication with students in other parts of the world who are also advocating for the Earth."*

I wonder, who are those? Greta's acolytes or Extinction Rebellion teens?

At Year 7-8,

They can take leadership roles in their school, working with students, staff and governing council to audit and reduce reduce energy use ... They may advocate for and support changes from peers, the local community, local businesses and the local council. Their voices can be shared with our political leaders.

The book provides a template letter for 13- to 14-year-olds to pester and wedge their school principals, the notional "Ms Ashwin":

> *We are worried about the future and how climate change is going to impact on our lives. We see documentaries and news items [especially on the ABC – TT] that paint a bleak picture of Australia in the coming decades. It's hard not to feel overwhelmed. Instead we are determined to use Greta Thunberg as our inspiration and get together with other students to do things that really make a difference. Could we please make an appointment to speak with you about our ideas? Your support is important to us.*

Presumably they will ape Greta and decamp on school strikes.

These same kids are to write *"pro-renewable tracts, make videos, write songs, report at assemblies, create works of art or engage in discussion with decision makers".* This includes inviting local, state or federal politicians to explain their energy policies, after which students and teachers combine to write "a follow-up letter with recommendations to the politicians" – and doubtless chiding them for any wrongthink. While the authors are careful not to name their favoured political party, only hard-line Greens politicians and the likes of Extinction Rebellion could ever make a favourable impression on PETAA-led classes.

The book's big theme is warming causing "extreme weather", which kids are to be harangued about from age 7. The authors then write curious material like, *"When the weather forecast is extreme, the teacher can introduce that word to students, 'Today we are having extreme weather.'"*

Teachers are to rally the class with extra water bottles and dog bowls, by shading the vege patch, watering the plants and promoting suitable clothing. This has been common-sense since first settlement, if not Neolithic times, but kids are now warned that CO2 emissions are the real culprit.

The authors hew to this line despite the IPCC's 2013 report (fine print sections) playing down climate-change attribution to weather disasters. Taking the most obvious aspect – heat waves – the IPCC said mildly, referring to the US, "Medium confidence: increases in more regions than decreases, but 1930s [dust bowl] dominates longer-term trends in the USA."

The manual's theoretical underpinning is cited as Canadian professor Maria Ojala on "hopeful transgressive learning". Consulting that study, one finds among the academic gobbledegook that "transgressive" means exactly what it says. "People can transgress or disrupt deeply held and taken-for-granted norms, norms that are at the roots of oppression and unsustainability, by acting in surprising, creative and boundary-crossing ways." Climate hope, Ojala quotes, requires a "disruption of the stubborn neoliberal worldview that we live in the best of societies, a society that furthermore has no alternative and thereby can't be changed."

PETAA author Julie Hayes claims to have "closely followed the science of climate change since the mid-1990s". The booklet's fruits include pages of yet-more nonsense about polar bear peril from climate change, disseminated by the activist group Polar Bears International. Even the International Union for Conservation of Nature put the bears' population in 2015 at 22,000 to 31,000 when warmists' earlier had forecast them expiring from lack of ice to prowl en route to their prey. (A bear perched on an ice floe was poster-boy for Al Gore's *Inconvenient Truth*).[3]

---

[3] Researcher Professor Susan Crockford was fired by her university after debunking polar bear scares.

The book harps to kids that human-caused global warming is responsible for worse drought and bushfire intensity. The CSIRO, grilled in Parliament by Senator Matt Canavan, admitted 18 months ago that "No studies explicitly attributing the Australian increase in fire weather to climate change have been performed at this time." Even warmist icon Professor Andy Pitman has agreed there is no link between climate change and drought.

The PETAA authors actually score an own-goal, recommending to kids a series of weather-disaster books by Jackie French and Bruce Whatley (fun reading, kids!). The book *Drought* subverts PETAA's narrative by saying, "There is no malice in a drought. It is perhaps the way the Australian bush prunes itself down to the toughest and hardiest, recycling nutrients for new growth." Although there is material on the needs of plants, in the entire PETAA tract there is no mention that CO_2 is a life-giving gas for plants, let alone that it is greening the planet.

I noticed only one mention of China, and certainly not its vastly increasing emissions nullifying all costly cuts of the West. This single fact illustrates why the complex, heavily politicised and uncertain field of climate science is inappropriate for small kids' classrooms.

The political nature of the "education" shows via its total silence about (green) nuclear power. Actually there is one mention in a graphic – a 13 to 14-year-old lists nuclear fuel as "non-renewable" along with coal, oil and gas in his notes. The book makes no suggestion that the kid's got it wrong. He/she also puts in "iron ore" as a non-renewable, which is true but no less silly than listing "sand" as a finite resource. Teachers should get out more. They might also discover, via energy expert Alan Moran, that our trek to net zero CO_2 already involves $10 billion a year installing wind and solar, plus subsidies of $7 billion a year, plus $17 billion (total) for new transmission connectors, plus vast bills to consumers for stabilising the grids against intermittency. Moran estimates a total cost of $40,000 per Australian household. In the entire tract I could find only one mention of the intermittency of wind and solar, kids being falsely assured that batteries will solve the problem.

The authors leave no chink for doubt about the warmist narrative. For example, *"Work with students to jointly construct first the 'risk from climate change' paragraph with the words negotiated with the students, but the teacher doing the writing."*

The authors claim to 9 to 10-year-olds that oil, gas and coal will run out "and are not easily or quickly replaced". Getting on for half-century ago, in 1974, I sat in the Press Gallery and heard Labor's energy minister, Rex Connor, forecast that Australia's oil and gas would run out in 1984. I see no reason why kids today should be alarmed by PETAA fanatics about possible problems arising in 2200 or 2300.

The book proudly cites kids' work following trials of the program. Here's a 9-year-old's "assessment task" on plastics, one of the basics of modern civilisation, not to mention kids' smartphones:

> *When plastic is made gases are released into the atmosphere. When plastic is thrown away another layer of gas is thrown onto earth. This extra heat can harm plants people and animals and maybe kill them.*

Although the kids are given no information about the downsides of renewables or flaws/uncertainties in the catastrophic warming hypothesis, the book tells them to challenge misinformation. *"Investigate climate myths. Students write an argument de-*

bunking the main myths about climate change (see Earth Org 2020). Students engage in debate about climate facts."

Earth Org is a green-Left pressure group which has set up straw-man arguments for kids to knock down, while ignoring the real case against renewables and computer-modelled future catastrophes. *"Begin to collect a class list of trustworthy websites that might help with further research. Discuss why these are trustworthy and others are not."* This scuppers any intrusion against the green narrative.

Typical references cited by the book include "Denchak, M., 2018: *Fossil Fuels: The dirty facts.* Natural Resources Defence Council New York." As is obvious, the Council is a politically partisan green lobby, using headlines like "GOP's [Republicans'] Climate Deniers Feeling the Heat." Talking of myths, the manual touts Damon Gameau's idiotic futuristic climate-virtue film *2040*, which is pure propaganda targeting little kids.

The book constantly cites NASA, but not of course for NASA's notorious revising of historic temperature data to convert flat trends to rising trends. The only conservative source I could find among pages of sources was the Queensland Resources Council, cited merely on energy conversion principles.

Throughout, the booklet takes the extremist position that the entire 1degC warming of the past century is human-caused through emissions with no room for natural drivers such as multi-decade oceanic cycles. The text says reassuringly, *"The emphasis is not being alarmist and creating fear, but on reinforcing our interdependence and responsibility to help each other."* But then teachers are referred to doozies from the ABC like "Heatwaves may mean Sydney is too hot for people to live in 'within decades' and from *The Guardian*, January 2013, *"Global food crisis will worsen as heatwaves damage crops, research finds"*. Fact: food output is well outpacing population growth. And there is this, *"Scientists estimate that the total collapse of Thwaites glacier would add half a metre to the sea level."* The actual time frame there is 200-1000 years hence, if ever.

A big theme is "trusting scientists" – do they deserve it? check out Climate-gate 2009. The book says of 11 to-12-year-olds: "They have begun to describe and explain phenomena ... aligning themselves with the world of scientists, and understanding that we have to listen to scientists and act on their advice if we are to slow down climate change." The authors even urge kids to donate money to activists at the Polar Bears International green lobby. Teachers also rattle the cash can: "In Years 3-4, students continue their local advocacy ... They might be involved in raising money for an environmental cause."

Here's the kids being brainwashed to support the killing of coal-fired power:

> *Coal-fired power stations have been essential for life in Australia for decades. However, generating electricity in this way has released huge amounts of additional greenhouse gases into the atmosphere, leading to significant climate change, which is affecting weather in all parts of the globe. Because of the impact of the enhanced greenhouse effect and because of Australia's commitment to reducing greenhouse emissions (Dalzell 2020), coal-fired power plants need to be phased out. We can no longer afford to use coal for generating power. Although the costs of renewables have been prohibitive, they are becoming cheaper and more efficient (Australian Ethical 2018, Kharecha and Hansen 2013).*

My take on the above: the source, Australian Ethical, is conflicted because it's a green energy fund manager, and the Hansen referred to is the fanatical "father of global warming", James Hansen, who compared coal trains to boxcars taking victims to the crematoria and enjoys getting arrested at demos. The Dalzell quoted is ABC reporter Stephanie Dalzell, doing an ABC hit job on the Prime Minister.

Here's the climax of the brainwashing:

Add to the class notes with a brainstorm of arguments for why Australia needs to reduce its dependence on fossil fuels. This is an important discussion and should be given due time. Different groups in Australia have different opinions about how phasing out coal and gas as energy sources should be managed, and the economic and social implications are probably too complex for Year 8. However, these issues may well be aired in a class discussion. [Or not, TT]. Phasing out coal and gas will impact on employment and job security for some families, and jobs have to be created elsewhere [by whom?-TT], so the change will not be easy. However, in the long term, for the sake of the planet, the change is inevitable, and has to be managed. Otherwise our planet will become increasingly difficult to live on.

While primary teachers might be unanimous on this, the electorate is not, as demonstrated by Scott Morrison's 2016 win, thanks to Queensland coal seats.

Broadcaster Alan Jones has pointed out that schools have successfully lobbied for air conditioning, which should be the first to go if the book's authors are serious about reducing schools' electricity. Kids can also walk, bike or use public transport for school. Hooray.#

Bruce Pascoe, Melbourne University's former aborigine

27 October 2021

Well, well, well. The University of Melbourne seems to have had taken a marvellous lunge towards reality. It no longer describes would-be Aboriginal Bruce Pascoe, its Enterprise Professor in Indigenous Agriculture, as a member of our First Nations. (Fact check: his First Nation is England, there is no Aboriginal line of descent in any of Pascoe's forebears). Professor Pascoe now seems to be just another colonial settler who ought to be feeling guilty towards Aborigines because of his white privilege. Here's the Professor Pascoe story, for what it's worth.

Pascoe, the *Dark Emu* fabricator, is responsible for the faux history bought by 250,000 credulous adults, and *Young Dark Emu – a Truer (sic) History* (60,000 sales), the latter used in schools to brainwash kids to back a two-class setup for Australian citizens. Pascoe's dodgy "history" converts pre-settlement nomadic Aboriginals to dwellers in stone-built towns of one to two thousand. He writes of Indigenous farmers sowing, harvesting and storing their crops. We are to believe they kept their livestock (wallabies? wombats?) secured in pens. Colourful, it is. History, it ain't.

The *Dark Emu* nonsense was demolished first by *Quadrant* writer Peter O'Brien's *Bitter Harvest* in 2019 and belatedly last June by credentialled leftist academics Professor Peter Sutton and Dr Keryn Walshe: *Farmers or Hunter-Gatherers, the Dark Emu Debate*, MUP.

Professor Geoffrey Blainey's take on Pascoe, 19 August 2020:

[T]he famous explorer Thomas Mitchell … never once used the word thousand. The word thousand seems to have been

made up. It's a terrible mistake and it ruins an important part of his [Pascoe's] argument. There's no evidence that there are Aboriginal townships with permanent houses, dependent for most of their food on agriculture. There's just no evidence for it.

Melbourne University has a "Find an Expert" service, where you check out the university's brainiacs. Tap to find that Melbourne University now describes Professor Pascoe merely as "a writer and farmer".

Yet on his appointment as Enterprise Professor, the very first words of the announcement stressed his Aboriginality:

> **Indigenous** *author and advocate Bruce Pascoe has joined the University of Melbourne as Melbourne Enterprise Professor in Indigenous Agriculture in the Faculty of Veterinary and Agricultural Sciences (FVAS).*
>
> *The role, which will sit within the School of Agriculture and Food, has been designed to build knowledge and understanding of Indigenous agriculture within the Faculty and to grow engagement and research activities in this area.*

The university's link on "Bruce Pascoe" takes you to his publisher, Magabala Books, which says, "Bruce is a Yuin, Bunurong and Tasmanian man, and currently lives on his farm in Gippsland, Victoria." Actually Yuin, Bunurong and Tasmanian men – and women – reject his claim.

The Find an Expert body text reads, semi-literately

> *He has published 36 book (sic) including* Dark Emu *which won the NSW Premier's Award for Literatur (sic) in 206 (sic) … He has published numerous essays and journalism (sic) both*

in Australia and overseas. he (sic) is also a farmer and grows
Australian Aboriginal Grains (sic) and tubers.

Find an Expert paints Professor Pascoe as the most unusual professor ever to haunt the cloisters and dreaming spires of the university-by-the-Zoo. The institution credits Bruce with 16 "scholarly works". Its definition of "scholarly" has become elastic, sadly for its alumni and authentic scholars. Pascoe's Scholarly Works list includes (with my elaborations)

 # Fog a Dox ($19.95). "Albert Cutts is a tree feller. A fella who cuts down trees. Fog is a fox cub raised by a dingo. He's called a dox because people are suspicious of foxes and Albert Cutts owns the dingo and now the dox. Albert is a bushman and lives a remote life surrounded by animals and birds. All goes well until Albert has an accident."

 # Seahorse ($16.95). "Jack and his family escape to Seahorse Bay whenever they can. They spend idyllic days exploring the waters of the bay, diving, fishing and cooking up feasts on the beach. Jack cannot believe his luck when he discovers a sunken boat not far off the coast. He shows his father and they decide to salvage it. But what is the story behind this mysterious boat?

 # Found ($24.95). "This gentle story set in the rugged Australian bush is about a small calf who becomes separated from his family." Keep in mind that Pascoe is a Professor in the VETERINARY and Agricultural Sciences Faculty. His agriculture-and-food colleagues will find much erudition to respect in Pascoe's scholarly calf studies.

 # Salt. Selected essays and stories ($26.95) –"… showcasing his shimmering genius across a lifetime of work." A further blurb says, "The title speaks to memories and ghosts triggered by the smell of salt; its ability to clean, to render flesh and skin from bone, to

preserve evidence, to signal cumulative impacts on Country". For Melbourne University scholarly scientific purposes I think this book should be retitled "NaCl: Selected essays and stories."

Dark Emu and its derivatives. More fiction, enough said.

Pascoe's Find an Expert web page also has a category "Projects" with a zero total. In my scrupulous way I sent the following inquiries to Melbourne University:

> *On your "Find an Expert" website, you describe Professor Bruce Pascoe as a "writer and farmer". There is no statement that he is Indigenous. When appointed, you described him as "Indigenous".*
>
> *1. Does Melbourne University no longer assert that Professor Pascoe is Indigenous?*
>
> *2. On the Find an Expert site, there is listed 16 "Scholarly Works" by Professor Pascoe.*
>
> *Of the ten works cited, five are fiction books for adults and children. Is it appropriate for Melbourne University to refer to them as "scholarly works?*
>
> *3. Is Professor Pascoe's appointment to Melbourne University full or part time? Is he tenured? Or is it in the nature of an "adjunct" professorship? To be specific, what Academic Level is Professor Pascoe's appointment, as per Enterprise Agreement 2.14.3. "An Academic is appointed or promoted by the University, at its discretion, to a particular classification level. Appointment and promotion are based on: 2.14.3.1. merit as determined by the University; and 2.14.3.2. the Academic or candidate demonstrating, to the satisfaction of the University, potential capability and competency to advance through the academic levels."*

With commendable efficiency but faint relevance, a reply came a day later from a uni PR Amelia Swinburne:

Here is our statement, which is attributable to a University of Melbourne spokesperson.

The Faculty of Veterinary and Agricultural Sciences appointed Bruce Pascoe as an Enterprise Professor in Indigenous Agriculture to further our work in this area. His extensive knowledge and experience is extending our teaching, research and engagement in Indigenous agriculture. Bruce is a respected member of our Faculty and makes a valuable contribution to our academic community, and we will not be reviewing his appointment.

This reply manages to sidestep every one of my questions. I suspect ambitious uni staff as well as *Quadrant* readers would be interested in pink-cheeked Pascoe's precise particulars. *Crikey!* claims that Pascoe's weird Melbourne University professorship is at Level E, which according to the university's enterprise bargaining agreement, yields $200,000 a year if full-time.

The "newsy" element of the university reply is that the university "will not be reviewing his appointment" an obvious question I hadn't asked. Freudian slip there, perhaps?

Melbourne Uni introduced its "Enterprise Professors" category in 2015.

Criteria for appointment:

2.1. "In order to be appointed to the position of 'Melbourne Enterprise Professor' or 'Honorary Melbourne Enterprise Professor', individuals must:

 # Have an eminent and sustained record of peak level leadership, entrepreneurship and influence;

 # Be widely recognised for their outstanding achievements in industry, business, professions and/or government; and

 # Demonstrate specialist expertise and a highly developed industry/business knowledge base that matches in breadth and depth what is expected of all professors of the University".

As a retired Associate Professor of History Les Louis puts it, "However loosely interpreted, Bruce Pascoe does not meet these criteria."

Roger Karge runs the *Dark Emu Exposed* website with its wealth of debunking research on Pascoe. Karge graduated from Melbourne University with an honours degree in organic chemistry and has built a highly-successful industrial chemistry business. Karge took up Pascoe-debunking for no other reasons than respect for science and indignation at Pascoe's blather.

Karge says Melbourne University was formerly populated with "old school" agricultural scientists appointed and promoted by their success in unlocking beneficial secrets of nature, not on the basis of identity and woke politics. These olden-day academics studied and respected Indigenous plant and insect knowledge, and from their findings global industries developed. He instances his 1970s mentor Professor of Organic Chemistry Don Cameron (tenure 1968-2000) MA ScD (Camb) MSc (Qld) PhD (Manc) FRACI. Karge's own Honours work with Cameron was studying the pigment chemistry of the Australia's indigenous Lac insects.

The university's Media Statement says (author's emphasis),

*Mr Pascoe also sees an opportunity to open the door to greater collaboration with Yorta Yorta people at the Faculty's Dookie agricultural campus in the Goulburn Valley region. "Let's put our food science there ... **we're going to need land***

and we're going to need a research facility that is Aboriginal-owned or has Aboriginal management."

A lot hangs on who Pascoe means by "we". Is "we" Pascoe's private business enterprise or the university or the Australian community? Roger Karge asks why Melbourne University is comfortable with a new professor's apparent agenda to organise an Aboriginal takeover of Dookie's public campus on 2440ha, with its venerable history since 1886.

Karge next dissects Pascoe's record as an entrepreneur, which hypothetically might justify his appointment despite his zero scientific credentials.

In *Dark Emu*, Pascoe says his yam daisy growing venture started about 2012, and predicts widespread commercial dissemination "soon". Nine years later, Karge notes that there is little yam daisy seed to purchase, and those seeds can cost 20c to $1 apiece. Even Pascoe's own business, *Black Duck Foods*, has nothing under "Shop" except for a sign, "Coming soon."

Karge also notes Professor Pascoe's previous business 'enterprise' was called Gurundgi Munjie Pty Ltd, which, in Pascoe's *Dark Emu* is described as "*... a Yuin company on the New South Wales south coast [which] is planning harvests of a number of grains, and early trials of flour production have had spectacular results*".

Karge: "The results could not have been that 'spectacular' given that the company, which was started in 2015 was by 2019 in the process of being 'struck-off' the ASIC companies register, for what 'business' reason we can only guess." (The ASIC page is unchanged at October 2021).

Professor Pascoe's most recent business 'enterprise', *Black*

Duck Foods Ltd is an 'Unlisted Public Company – Non-Profit Company'. Karge writes:

> *If Melbourne University wish to appoint an 'Enterprise Professor', one would expect that they would choose a candidate with a commercially proven background in running an 'enterprise' profitably to generate the funds needed to invest in its business, research and development program.*
>
> *It would be nice to know if Professor Pascoe submitted a business plan to justify the substantial university funds that will be needed to achieve his goals.*
>
> *With all due respect to Professor Pascoe, he is 74 years old, an age at which most people have retired and yet the University believes he is in a position to head up a multi-decade, difficult project such as this.*
>
> *The whole indigenous grass-seed-to-bread theory is just a New-Age fantasy of the Ivory Tower academics of sustainability at the University of Melbourne. A large scale grain-to-flour industry cannot be developed in Australia using indigenous grasses with their poor protein output. Yields are about 50kg per hectare compared with 2000kg per acre for best wheat, which has much lower unit cost. Another indigenous seed producer, after 25 years' work, sold seed at hundreds of dollars per kilogram, which makes for a pretty expensive loaf of bread. Melbourne University's hopes for Pascoe to foster sustainable and low-emission food crops seem chimerical. Apart from the economics, kangaroo-grass cropping requires copious sprays of Roundup and other chemical herbicides.*

Pascoe in *Dark Emu* sets himself up as a pioneer user of Aboriginal plant knowledge, leaving his hugely more successful predecessors unmentioned. Karge says Melbourne University must be "unbelievably naïve" to swallow such Pascoe's claims. Leonard J. Webb (CSIRO) half a century ago repeatedly surveyed Aborigines all over Australia on medicinal plants and identified 124 useful ones. The most famous was a fish poison from the bush *Duboisia myoporoides*. This created the anti-seasickness drug hyoscine (scopolamine), which was given to all D-Day troops to help them fight on the Normandy beaches. Australia today is the world's largest supplier of hyoscine, an ingredient of Travacalm tablets.

Karge tracks Pascoe's media presence and finds it has fallen off markedly since the leftist academics Sutton and Walshe, following Peter O'Brien, demolished *Dark Emu*. However, state education authorities continue to support schools indoctrinating kids with Dark Emu nonsense, and this year Pascoe even became joint winner of the Australian Humanist Award of 2021. CEO of Humanists Australia, Dr Heidi Nicholl explained, "Humanism is a framework for living an ethical, meaningful and compassionate life without relying on supernatural forces." She cites Pascoe for his outstanding achievements 'through a First Nations lens' – as if Aborigines were uninterested in the supernatural.

Amazon last month released a movie *Burning* blaming 2019-20 bushfires on 1degC of warming since 1910, as distinct from substandard forest management, and starring Pascoe and iconic climate hysteric Tim Flannery.

It's good to see that Bruce at Melbourne University is not letting the (kangaroo) grass grow under his feet. I'll check with the PR people in a few months to see if they're still "not reviewing his appointment". #

Proud as punch to be hawking hokum

4 August 2022

It's not true that the University of Tasmania (UTAS) has been treating Tasmanian primary-school kids like lab-rats. Lab work is tightly regulated and I'm sure vice-chancellor Rufus Black would crack down hard on any staffers vivisecting local kids.

The only truth in the lab-rat claim is that UTAS has been feeding the Apple Isle's primary schoolers with apocalyptic scaremongering about global warming, and then checking the kids' trauma level. If it's off the scale, UTAS gives kids helpful hints on how to cope, and directs their panic-stricken families to the loopy counsellors at *Psychology for a Safe Climate*. This is all documented in UTAS's *Curious Climate Schools* exercise. It's a follow-on to a similar experiment on Tasmanian adults called *Curious Climate*. That one was run in conjunction with Their ABC.

The kids' social experiment has been run by a seven-woman UTAS collective with about 30 primary and mid-level schools, 1000 kids and 57 UTAS "experts" involved. It's co-funded by the Tasmanian government no less, through its Climate Change Office. (Hobart's CO2 emissions are about 20,000 tonnes a year versus China's 11,000,000,000 tonnes and rising).

Kids ask climate questions and UTAS' self-styled climate "experts" provide answers. If little Daphne wonders about the "Significance of emotion when encountering climate change", she can ask UTAS emotion specialist Charlotte Jones from the School of Geography, who writes.

Why I do what I do
Learning more about how we feel about climate change has

the potential to lead to social transformation – and that inspires me.

Something interesting about me

I have a secret choc-chip cookie recipe (shhh!)

She's a social scientist, PhD candidate and a Westpac Future Leaders scholarship holder.

UTAS quotes her: "Climate change is an environmental, economic and social crisis and young Australians are at the precipice of that." From her Westpac profile: "I seek to understand how knowledge, emotion and action are co-produced in the context of growing awareness in the 21st century of the extent of human transformation of the Earth." A volunteer with social justice organisations in what she calls Lutrutiwa (I think that's "Tasmania"), she's keen to remedy "intersectional inequalities" via "the dialectic between nature and society".

So she gets a question from a Kentish primary school,

When it comes to future generations, how will they feel about what we have done?

She replies,

The court judgement Sharma vs Minister for the Environment said, "The devastation caused by climate change will largely be inflicted by the inaction of this generation of adults in what might fairly be described as the greatest intergenerational injustice ever inflicted by one generation of humans upon the next … Many young people talk about feeling betrayed and angry and frustrated by actions or inactions of older generations that mean we are now facing significant global challenges. Look at our Curious Climate page on feelings if you want to think a bit more about this.

In another answer to tots, she likens climate activism to the Suffragettes and the US Civil Rights Movement, and congratulates schoolkids for skiving off on School Strikes 4 Climate. She also sees community cooperation during COVID as a model for fast action. (As a Victorian, I actually recall it as Dan Andrews' VicPol coercion – just ask Zoe Buhler in Ballarat, arrested and handcuffed at home in her pyjamas over a social media post advising of an upcoming protest against lockdowns).

Before I get back to the QandA's, I'd better fill in about Curious Climate Schools' mental health concerns. Here's some of the guidance there:

A note for educators: It is important not to tell them [kids] there is no reason to be upset, or to rush to try to fix negative emotions. They are legitimate responses. Children need a safe emotional place to express their vulnerability. If your school has access to a counsellor or social worker, it would be helpful to liaise with them to offer students a person to talk to if they feel overwhelmed.

Validate students' feelings: Support them. This could be by doing an activity as a class, going for a walk together, or having some time to journal or draw in response to listening to the climate change experts.

It is important to remember that emotions about climate change may come up for your students some time after you watch these answers as a class.

Climate change is a challenging topic for all of us. Hearing these questions and answers will likely bring into focus your own complex feelings about climate change. If you need immediate support, you can contact Lifeline.

The UTAS advice for kids:

As you learn more about climate change and listen to answers by climate experts, you will probably experience lots of different kinds of feelings, some of which can be difficult. This is OK and very normal. These feelings can be helpful ... Sometimes our feelings can be uncomfortable, and they can become overwhelming. At these times, we need to find ways to bring our feelings back to a healthy balance ...

Asking for help: If you are feeling really overwhelmed, find an adult you trust to talk to. This could be a parent or guardian, a teacher, social worker, a relative or your doctor. If you need someone to talk to straight away you can go to Kids Helpline.

Taking care of yourself: As you learn more, and listen to experts on climate change, we encourage you to find space to recognise and explore your feelings. This could be through things like journaling, drawing, singing, writing, climbing a tree, going for a walk or talking through your feelings with trusted adults or peers.

The advice continues:

Acknowledge and respect whatever feelings you might have about climate change – does climate change make you angry, scared, worried? Whatever you feel, that's OK! You can talk to your friends and family and teachers about how you feel, and hear how they feel too. If climate change does get you feeling down, remember to look around and see the many GOOD things happening to tackle climate change.

Collective action: Find your tribe and use your voices! Collective events such as the school strikes for climate raise aware-

ness – and they also give climate scientists all around the world hope that the next generation will make changes and vote for the climate policies we urgently need!

Awareness projects in schools – could you and your school-mates become Climate Warriors together? Could you encourage your school to install solar panels, introduce meat-free Monday, ask for more vego options in the canteen, or go single-use plastic free?

Systemic action: Work with your teachers to develop a climate action plan in your school – a guide for how to take climate action from an entire school level to individual classroom and student levels. Contact State and Federal politicians to ask them to make more ambitious changes to climate policy for Tasmania and Australia. [Whether politicians are impressed by the views of 9-year-olds is another matter].

Contact product brands you like, and companies or businesses you use services from, to ask what their carbon emissions are and how they plan to make their products carbon neutral.

It's important to remember too that people don't have to be 'perfect' to be serious about tackling climate change (that would be soooo exhausting and people might give up then!). The big thing to remember is to just do what you can... Importantly, it really doesn't help to make people feel guilt or shame for doing what you might think is not enough ... Remind yourself and other people to feel GOOD about whatever changes and actions you are taking – GO YOU!

The page links to "goodgriefnetwork.org" about how to Process Heavy Emotions like "fear, anger and eco-grief." It urges "creating spaces where people can lean into their painful feelings about the state of the world." It continues,

We, who have been socialized by the dominant culture, do the work of looking at our varying levels of privilege, while undoing our cultural conditioning. When we acknowledge how we have perpetuated systems of oppression, we can stop participating in those systems and refuse to let them live within us.

Curious Climate also refers users to Climate Distress Workshops for people "working on the front line of the climate emergency including climate activists, scientists and policy makers," who need "a safe, containing space for the expression and working through of people's emotional response to climate change."

Enough about feelings, let's get back to the Tassie kids' questions.

Dr Phillipa McCormack, a climate law researcher at the University of Adelaide, was asked: "How much investment is required to make a drastic change?" She tells her pint-sized interlocutor that it will cost $300 billion to $50 trillion [yikes!] to saturate the landscape with subsidised windmills and batteries. This would cost less than unrestrained global warming, she claims, ignoring that CO2 increases have boosted global crop yields to record levels worth countless billions. She continues:

Climate change is making disasters like extreme bushfires and droughts more common, and these kinds of disasters already cost Australians a lot (approx. $3 trillion from 2010-2019!). These costs, which relate to damage and lost income, are going to increase a lot if we do not take urgent action on climate change.

I can imagine the conversation:

Kylie (aged 9), nursing her Cabbage Patch doll: Wow Dr Phillipa, $3 trillion's a lot! Is that the same as $3,000,000,000,000?"

Dr Phillipa: Yes Kylie, your maths are fantastic.

Kylie: My doll's name is Topsy. So the ten-year average cost of our natural disasters has been $300 billion a year?

Dr Phillipa: "Good maths again, Kylie, you clever kid!"

Kylie: "But doesn't Deloitte says the cost only averages $37 billion a year, not $300 billion?"

Dr Phillipa: "Trust me, I'm a senior Adelaide academic. Never mind that Deloitte crowd."

Kylie: "OK Dr Phillipa. That's the bell for playtime. Topsy and me are off to the tuckshop."

Tassie's poor little kids have already been got at by their know-nothing activist teachers, judging by the questions kids served up to UTAS indoctrinators. Here's a sample:

> # I'm thirteen. What do you think climate change will alter about the world in my lifetime, and what can I do about it?
>
> # How will our generation live a full life as it is supposed to get unbearably hot by something like 2033?
>
> # When, or if, we hit past 1.5 celsius degree temperature rise, what will happen exactly and will it lead to Earth's doom?
>
> # Will climate change make us live elsewhere? eg: underwater or in space?
>
> # Will all the reefs die? [The Barrier Reef corals are currently at record extent].
>
> # How do we stop pollution of factories?
>
> # What would happen if all the polar icecaps were melted?

What will the future look like for the animals living in areas affected by climate change e.g., Polar bears [Polar bear populations are increasing, actually].

What will be the first effects of climate change that we will notice in Tasmania? [Tasmania could do with some warming, if you ask me].

How long will it take if we all decide to stop climate change together? [Does "we" include Vlad Putin, Xi Jin-ping and India?].

If everyone in the world was vegan, how would that help Climate Change?

Did Covid stop people from travelling and have a positive impact on climate change? [Kids' hand-me-down priorities are odd].

I particularly liked this reply by Dr Vanessa Adams, a conservation and planning specialist:

Q: What are the main things we need to know about climate change?

A: The science of climate change is settled. [That's great, all those climate scientists can now get off the taxpayer teat and find real jobs].

Over 99% of scientists agree it is anthropogenic – caused by humans.

[She seems to be citing the ridiculous 2015 paper by Dr John Cook, from her own alma mater James Cook University, and even that paper only claimed 97 per cent consensus about climate cliches].

Climate change causes extreme weather – heatwaves, floods, fires, more intense storms and sea level rise.

[No it doesn't, apart from a bit of sea rise which has been progressing since the Little Ice Age ended. For example, global area burnt annually has been declining for decades, and the global cyclone energy index shows a downward trend].

Another ripper answer is from Karen Palmer and Dr Gabi Mocatta. They even peddle the old chestnut about Tuvalu and the Maldives drowning from rising seas. Tuvalu is expanding, as even the ABC/RMIT Fact Check has conceded, and the Maldives is pell-mell building airports and hotels. Maybe the academics are recalling the Maldives cabinet staging a meeting underwater in 2009 as a publicity stunt run by a British PR flak.

As if those howlers aren't enough the academics go on to peddle the nonsense about "millions of people displaced by climate change by 2050", the same scary meme that UNEP was caught out fabricating in 2011.

Ever the professional reporter, I emailed UTAS asking whether its *Curious Climate Schools* program is on-going. Here's the reply from Georgina Sutton, UTAS manager, Education Outreach:

I am very happy to say that it will be going ahead in schools again this year.

General information can be found here (https://curiousclimate.org.au/schools/) and further information will be sent to schools directly in the coming weeks.

We will ensure you are on the distribution list for that information.

Thanks for your interest in this outstanding program. #

Melbourne University circles the green drain

25 January 2022

About 6200 final-year secondary students from 700 schools have been invited to start at Melbourne University (UoM) this year, UoM being a world 30-40th top-ranked university. Good luck to the kids. They've suffered eleven school-years of climate doomism; the university will dish out more of it. Two professors in UoM publication *Pursuit*, for example, see the prospect of another 0.5degC warming by 2030 as a "shrieking emergency siren".

UoM's 2020 annual report says (emphasis added)

> *Planning for a suite of online modules **for all commencing undergraduate students** commenced in 2020 ... The Sustainable campuses and communities module, developed in 2020, explores the impact of humans on climate and the environment.*

UoM is awash in "sustainability", code for anti-conservative politics and zero-emission fantasies. A few months after the toothless 2015 Paris accord, the university adopted its "Sustainability Charter", and then came the 2017-20 plan "Integrating action on sustainability **across all areas of institutional activity** for the first time". UoM's goal is to force Sustainability dogma across every campus, every faculty, every subject and every cafeteria (vegan synthetic steaks, anyone?). Faculty who resist this politicising of their subjects – and the university admits such hold-outs exist – are being counselled on right-think.

"Sustainability" is literally Melbourne University's embedded cross-curricula priority, just as in national and state school curricula. The word means whatever anyone chooses. As one Melbourne University senior fellow has written, "Everyone has a different definition of sustainability." Borrowing from the national school curriculum sounds better but involves crystal-balling:

> *Sustainable patterns of living meet the needs of the present without compromising the ability of future generations to meet their needs.*

As if anyone knows what Australians of 2080 will be prioritising. We might all be speaking Chinese. UoM's 2020 Sustainability Report bemoans "the absence of a practical definition of 'sustainability' research". Canadian *Financial Post* writer Peter Foster put it well a few weeks ago:

> *Like the word 'social,' 'sustainable' tends to vitiate or reverse the meaning of words to which it is attached. Thus 'sustainable' development is development retarded by top-down control. Commitment to sustainability is now mouthed by every politician, bureaucrat, marketing executive and media hack on Earth.*

UoM courses in engineering, architecture and law are already saturated in sustainability hype. But the university says in its 2017-20 Sustainability Plan:

> *By 2020, **all undergraduate degree programs** can demonstrate (at the course and/or major level) that core and compulsory curriculum enable students to understand and apply sustainability knowledge and values to practice in their field … Achieving this depends on significant, **whole-of-University** action.*

Enforcement orders went out to Associate Deans of Academic Divisions. The Academic Board stands over the lecturers to

ensure all formal course proposal and review processes require Academic Divisions to identify how graduate attributes relevant to sustainability are developed through teaching and learning

encourage graduate attributes, including leadership for sustainability, to be documented in students' Australian Higher Education Graduation Statements

Special software was to be developed to "enable documentation of curricular and extracurricular activities demonstrating graduate attributes such as sustainability leadership." Does the converse apply to the records of unwary kids who let slip sceptic sentiments in the uni pub?

Zealous staff and students, surveyed in 2020, wanted to go further to embed and integrate sustainability *"across **all University campuses and all courses**. Introduce sustainability targets/KPIs for faculties/departments. Introduce sustainability training modules and induction sessions for students and staff."*

These true believers want to bring out the truncheon. One proposal cited favorably by the survey report was to embed sustainability

*Through **mandatory subjects** that teach sustainability principles, how the sustainable development discourse has evolved and **how the global power mechanism that maintains neoliberalism was created in the aftermath of colonialism.***

From the 400 self-selected responders came calls (Key Themes) for *"a **mandatory** sustainability orientation module for all students and **staff**".*

I can picture invigilators escorting new professors into the campus's Melbourne School of Design Theatre to be harangued by

25-year-old Extinction Rebels. The professors' names are noted to prove their attendance, and they are set free after passing a multiple-choice exam.

UoM's "sustainability" sidesteps to the UN's 17 Sustainable Development Goals for 2030. The 17 unprioritised SDGs (whittled down from 1400 in bureaucratic bunfights among 120 NGOs) will "end poverty, protect the planet and ensure prosperity for all". (Most members of the 193 UN states which created the SDGs in 2015 are basket-cases run for the personal benefit of their autocrats. Denmark's Bjorn Lomborg has eviscerated the SDG follies.)

I favour Emeritus Professor of Geology Ian Plimer's take on green "Sustainability":

I charge the greens with murder. They murder humans who are kept in eternal poverty without coal-fired electricity. They support slavery and early deaths of black child miners. They murder forests and their wildlife by clear felling for mining and wind turbines. They murder forests and wildlife with their bushfire policies. They murder economies producing unemployment, hopelessness, collapse of communities, disrupted social cohesion and suicide. They murder free speech and freedoms and their takeover of the education system has ended up in the murdering of the intellectual and economic future of young people. They terrify children into mental illness with their apocalyptic death cult lies and exaggerations.

UoM Professor of Education Sophie Arkoudis, whose CV lists no output on climate science but a lot on student issues, led a team looking at how to force the environment into all the university's offerings, saying, *"The challenge lies in embedding sustainability knowledge and values in undergraduate degrees and majors, as some academics may struggle to see the relevance of sustainability to their particular degree program."*

The university in 2017 ran a cross-faculty forum to work out the nitty-gritty. The Professor comments,

*Unsurprisingly, some broader debates about the nature of education have become (and remain) an important part of the conversation: for example ... whether hope **and fear** play a role in an academic education, and the role of advocacy in learning.*

Oh great! Kids' courses larded with hope, fear and advocacy. She foresees in UoM courses:

Management – business students draw from "sociology and critical studies" to identify how some business practices harm people and environments. And kids are to "utilise corporate social responsibility frameworks to guide more ethical business practices." I hope the kids' future employers appreciate that.

Medicine – Students draw on learnings about "Ecohealth". (I'd mention that global warming has saved 500,000 lives in England and Wales alone in the past 20 years, according to the Office of National Statistics newly released figures.)

Creative Arts – Students study "individual and societal responses to environmental challenges in various artistic media." Professor Arkoudis reminds the students to "consider the sustainability implications of an international career" – if she's referring to jet contrails, well said Sophie!

Science – Students use their maths/stats to "anticipate future impacts of environmental change." How nice to be so certain about the future.

Woke staff and students, especially the student-led Fossil Free Melbourne University, demanded UoM divest from fossil fuel companies by 2021, namely the world's "CU200" top coal and petroleum producers, more than 20 of whom – unfortunately – happen to be major supporters of the university. So after thousands of words sucking up to woke activists, UoM discovered that divestment is actually a crappy solution compared with positive investments in low-emission fuels. Sense from UoM, but for the wrong reasons.

UoM is thick as thieves with Premier Dan Andrews' hard-left minions and "stands together with the Victorian Government as a [Take2 climate pledge] founding partner." Covid 19 ('20/'21/'22) created no let-up in UoM zealotry, with the 2020 annual report bragging how UoM "continued to work to tackle the impacts of global warming and to demonstrate exceptional green credentials", and "continued to raise the bar on the University's sustainability goals." One example involved 18 deluded staff and 30 students doing a virtual "Climate Reality" coaching course sponsored by extreme emissions hypocrite Al Gore (net worth $US300m and touting his honorary UoM Doctorate of Laws. Gore's Nashville mansion – one of three – uses as much electricity to heat its pool, as six normal houses in total).

Lifting up more UoM rocks, one discovers in the 2022 course handbook "Sustainability: Hope for the Earth?" worth 12.50 points, and more fit for Religious Studies.

In its Sustainability Charter, the University of Melbourne recognizes its responsibility to help shape sustainability on Earth through "knowledge, imagination and action".

Achieving sustainability on Earth requires global values and

*actions that are ecologically sound, socially just and econom-
ically viable ... We will consider sustainability of systems at
multiple scales and through diverse ways of knowing including scientific, historical and Indigenous perspectives.* [Note
the equating of these perspectives].

The course welcomes all students interested in 'climate change,
land management, extractive industries and more.' (I doubt the
teaching on "extractive industries" is positive). Arts and Music students are invited to "explore the intersection between power, hope
and the arts (huh?) to influence societies (sic) ideas" while Commerce students get "an insight into the history of capitalism" and
the environment (again, don't expect positivity). Youngsters will
emerge "Identify[ing] relationships between all beings and their
physical environments ... There is no exam in this subject."

This planet-saving course bulks up degree courses including Bachelor of Fine Arts (Dance)for "expanded dance thinking
and performance". Extinction Rebellion galoots prancing for the
evening TV news perhaps? UoM claims, *"Expertise in dance as
a way of knowing opens doorways for careers as performers, makers, leaders, activists, collaborators and cultural partners in a global
world."*

For loopiness, try UoM's Environmental Arts & Humanities
Network: *"A post-disciplinary space for stories and conversations
about art-activist-academic thinking-making-being to support living
systems and multispecies justice."* These pampered idiots aim to

*critically and self reflexively investigate intersectional eco-
logical practices and pedagogies, environmental phenomena,
climate in/justices, temporalities, narratives, grief, trauma,
laws, science and activisms in the Global South ... Criti-*

cally and generously question and re-frame what scholarly-artistic-activist knowledge looks, sounds, and feels like in a climate-changing world ... Attend to undervalued perspectives and oppressed knowledges [and] Nourish co-existence on the planet.

Other UoM insights:

Although Pro-Vice Chancellor Mark Hargreaves axed the university's Marx-loving Sustainable Society Institute last December, it's retained several like-minded institutes such as the net-zero "Melbourne Climate Futures".

Among cutting-edge UoM research is a project led by a Dr Julia Hurst, Lecturer, Aboriginal & Torres Strait Islander Historical and Philosophical Studies – "Maternal futures: Motherhood and the climate crisis. Focusing on how the climate crisis is shaping women's experiences around reproductive decision-making and childrearing practices."

#A UoM researcher Amelia Leavesley has written in the university's official magazine, *Pursuit*, a piece headed "Liveable Melbourne a Blessing Amid Weary Lockdowns"

Despite all the hardship, Melburnians have benefited from going through lockdown in one of the world's most liveable cities ... Increased demand for mental health services over the course of this pandemic has seen the Victorian Government invest a record $A3.8 billion funding for mental health and wellbeing in the 2021-2022 State Budget.

When compared to the COVID-19 impacts experienced by other cities – we're in a very fortunate situation. This is not to undermine the sacrifices and hardship of Melburnians' pandemic experience – characterised by an endless loop of new restrictions, general uncertainty, and home-job haircuts ... While the journey isn't over yet, we can be fortified with the knowledge that we have much to be grateful for. Not least, that we're still in this together.

What of individual students? The UoM survey of 2020 found support for lionising and weaponizing climate extremists on campus, i.e. "enable passionate sustainability advocates to develop, lead and/or implement initiatives." These students – perhaps Extinction Rebellion glue-babies – would be "leveraged" to increase their "communications reach." I'll instance two young stalwarts but change a student's name – I wouldn't want her UoM excitements to dog her career.

BA student "Pearl Fearless" won an Australasian 2021 Green Gown award for campus sustainability work. She's an advocate for turning urine from office and apartment blocks into fertiliser for sustainable food production, after getting rid of the faeces and other unsavouries. (Making fertilisers, as normally done, from methane seems simpler and less messy). "Pearl follows her passion for climate and inter-generational justice," said the citation. It cited her leadership in Al Gore's Climate Reality propaganda coaching; representing UoM at the 2020 Global University Climate Forum; and an internship enjoying Tim Flannery's Climate Council hysteria about routine weather events.

But Pearl caught the UoM intolerance virus. Here's how: UoM late last year set up on campus, with $7m federal funding, the Robert Menzies Institute. Apart from being Australia's longest-serving prime minister (18 years), Menzies was a Melbourne University law graduate and Chancellor from 1967-72.

Of course Carlton's ferals mobilised to strangle it at birth, notwithstanding that Western Sydney University has a Whitlam Institute with identical $7m federal funding, and SA University and Curtin University host Hawke and Curtin institutes respectively. Compared with Menzies' 18 years in office, Whitlam served three years, Curtin four and Hawke eight. And every US president is honored with a presidential library.

The ferals' petition claimed Menzies was a "staunch supporter of countless acts of war and genocide", and the proposal "ignores the many who suffered or perished because of him and his political project."

It boasted of Leftists' previous success in stifling a Ramsay (conservative) Centre at Sydney and Queensland Universities (it should also have mentioned stifling the orthodox climate academic Bjorn Lomborg proposed thinktank at UWA). Among signatories was our Pearl Fearless, then an incoming student union official.

Signatories at the university's thought-leading Associate and Professor level totalled close to 25, from departments including law, pure maths, "Culture and Communications" (sic, and heavily represented), German, philosophy, linguistics, anthropology, development studies, literature, art history, management, environment, obstetrics, workplace leadership (sic), biochemistry, and political science. (Another signer: Roz Ward, LaTrobe's Marxist cofounder of the Victorian State's gender-fluidity project aka "Safe Schools". Ms Ward, among other things, considers the Australian flag to be racist).

At the Institute's November opening, students and staff with megaphones rioted at the Old Quad, chanting "F**k the NLP", banging on doors and windows and encircling the event while being held back by security guards. The event was cut short to protect attendees. Two elderly ladies, one with a walking stick, required escorts from the function. The above description is not from the wicked Murdoch press but from the Melbourne University students' Farrago.

I don't know if Pearl was there, but a student union Facebook post said at the time,

Thanks to everyone who came along to the protest against the Menzies Institute yesterday!! ... Incoming 2022 UMSU Education Officers Ben Jarick and "Pearl Fearless" are committed to continue the fight against the Menzies Institute next year, so stay tuned.

A Green Gown UoM "excellence award" finalist was lead kindergarten teacher Harriet Deans, of the Early Learning Centre, and a doctorate researcher. She's gung-ho for educating toddlers about her vision of sustainability:

Her work is directed towards empowering the children she teaches to develop the skills and values to care for others and the environment. Harriet has formally researched (Ethics ID 1646280.1) a unique 'Learning in Nature Program' (LNP) which led to the development of an 'Ecocentric Curriculum' specifically for preschool children ... EfS [education for sustainability] as a priority in the early years provides children with opportunities to develop eco-centric values, attitudes, skills, and behaviours, necessary to contribute to a sustainable life, now and into the future ... Early childhood education can develop children's deeper understandings of and responsibility for current matters of social and environmental concern.

Both Ms Deans and UoM take pride in their role as UN camp-followers. Ms Deans works with the panoply of UN bureaucracies, particularly the Monitoring and Evaluating Climate Communications and Education Project (MECCE). This group, well plugged into UoM, pushes for mandatory climate alarmism in primary schools and upwards, along with "climate justice" and "socio-emotional or action competences" about the "ecological crises". (Actually, global temperatures have fallen in the past six years, according to the satellite data). MECCE says, "Effective education and communication are fundamental to overcoming climate change denial, increasing climate literacy, and supporting climate action."

MECCE is also pushing panic through schools about climate's biodiversity impacts, allegedly involving "mass extinction of species". The UN agencies seek to turn kids' "potentially overwhelming feelings of loss" into "the need to take action." (Fact check: Mass extinction fears 'have little support from science' –and claimed losses 'are absurdly large').

I have to wonder about UoM Vice-chancellor Duncan Maskell claiming UoM teaches kids "how to think".

Duncan, please make that **what** to think. #

PART THREE

A GONZO JOURNO'S LURID BUT TRUE TALES

Born not yesterday but the day before

12 April 2022

They say that bad stuff comes in threes. I can vouch for that.

First, our beloved nine-year-old Cavalier Spaniel, Natasha, got the heart/lung problem common to the breed and began gasping for air. Our vet put her down. Second, on the eve of our three-week holiday to Tasmania my wife, Primrose (pseudonym), and I hid our car keys somewhere unobvious but where they would re-surface automatically. When we got back we couldn't remember who hid them, let alone where. Weeks passed and we steadily lost hope. While using the spare set, I checked the price of new keys: $800!

And third, I advertised my Macbook Air laptop on Facebook for $1250. Our daughters told us Facebook was the best bet with no fee on sale, unlike eBay which charges 13 per cent. But they warned me of Facebook scammers: unlike eBay, Facebook offers no seller protection. "Listen up, Pop! Accept nothing but cash!" said Winsome, my eldest.

I'll now tell you how I got brilliantly scammed by a master (actually mistress) criminal who walked off with my laptop and never paid me a cent.

The Macbook was slow to sell, so I cut the price to $1080 and still got few nibbles, let alone customers at our front door. Then my mobile rang with a woman, Sammy, on the line, quite keen. I gave her our address but she was a no-show.

Next morning, a Friday, a different woman, Hermia, rang, ostensibly a friend of yesterday's caller. She'd be round in 15 minutes. That was great news but just then Primrose announced she off to Woolies for the groceries. I said, "No, you mustn't go yet. This lady might be nervous about entering a house alone with a large virile male. Women have been attacked. You stay here to make her feel safer."

After some marital back-and-forth she reluctantly laid down her shopping list and we spruced up the dining table. The laptop looked pristine in its original box. Alongside we laid its 2019 purchase receipt for $2135 and Primrose brought out the good teacups and some Florentines on the off-chance of socialising with our lady visitor.

"Get cash," Primrose warned me, unnecessarily, as I wasn't born yesterday.

The doorbell rang and there was Hermia. She was 5 feet of heftiness, about 40 and well-spoken. Straw-colored hair was cropped half an inch all round for spikiness. She sported a nose ring and had thrown on a none-too-spotless T-shirt. While she did small talk with Primrose, I had time to study her. At the top of her left arm was a tattoo of an attractive female face with red and yellows flowers in lieu of eyes. Next down was a full-frontal lioness face and on her forearm was a mess of symbols surrounding a naked but modest woman in profile clasping her knees. Her shorts were so baggy and loose that, when she turned to sit down, an inch of plumber's crack came into view. There were leg tattoos which I don't remember. Old thongs completed the ensemble.

Primrose and I exchanged glances. Far from being put off by this lady's appearance, we felt an obligation to re-double our friendliness in the inclusive and accepting way expected of enlightened citizens in the 2020s.

She inspected the laptop. I'd reformatted it and it was asking for a new owner's name, password etc before it did any demo. Embarrassed, I explained that I was a long-retired journalist and she in turn explained her finance and insurance-broking job and its COVID problems. I did wonder about clients' first impressions, but reasoned she could be running her business online, or maybe dealing direct with like-minded ladies.

She admired the laptop and I began mentally slavering. I steered the conversation lightly towards payment, and mentioned how a friend had been scammed selling a large garden fixture.

Hermia (animated): "Facebook is full of scammers! They've tried things on me. People advertise stuff and just want money first and won't let go of their stuff. Be careful, let me tell you."

We all nodded knowingly about this naughty world.

"Well," she said, "I'll take it. It's for my partner. She does graphic design. It's just right."

I felt a surge of relief after weeks of no-sale frustration. What's more, she wasn't haggling me down to sub-$1000.

"Great," I said. "I'll give you a receipt for the cash."

"Oh, I don't have cash on me. I'll do a direct bank transfer on my phone. You needn't worry. Here's my driver's licence to photograph, and I'll screenshot the bank transfer. The funds will be in your account Monday."

She pulled out her driver's licence and photographed it for me. This became a distraction as she made sure the text was well-lit. Primrose was uncomfortable but I was familiar with bank transfers and screenshots. Moreover, I was still in mode, "Be inclusive and tolerant of minorities."

I looked on carefully as Hermia inputted the $1080 transfer and hit the 'send' button. Acknowledgement and receipt followed on-screen. OK, I wasn't getting cash, but the money was in e-transit. I did recall daughter Winsome warning that to be fully safe, accept only transfers between accounts at the same bank, in my case ANZ. Hermia was CBA. But I had her driver's licence, seen the transfer, so what could go wrong?

Hermia and I now bonded. I went to write a receipt but she waved the idea away.

Jumping ahead, I'd forgotten that Winsome, a veteran travel consultant, had also warned me to document any transfer of goods.

Hermia departed with the laptop and a wave of her tattooed arm.

Primrose fretted with her female intuition: "Something isn't right."

I assured her Monday would produce my $1080. But Monday came and went.

Oh well, clearance often take two working days.

Tuesday and Wednesday, still no money.

At this point I was convinced the sale had been on Saturday. Primrose said it was on Friday.

"Give me a good look at that transfer," she said. We pored over it.

"It says the funds are to be transferred on Saturday. Your sale was on Friday. This was a scheduled transfer not a live transfer," Primrose said.

She was on the ball and I was an idiot.

Hermia had gone straight home, logged onto her bank and cancelled the future transaction, which I now know is a piece of cake. Unlike trying to reverse a live real-time funds transfer.

I began phoning and texting: no response. I finally threatened to report her to her local police at Sunshine, an industrial suburb 12km west of Melbourne. Still no response.

My daughters, both financial experts, were incensed I'd ignored their advice on Facebook salesmanship. Winsome took over proceedings.

"It's not a police matter," I told her. "It's now just an unpaid debt."

Winsome: "It's Sunday, we're going to the cop shop right now. We'll play on their sympathies. You are to be a doddering old coot, which in fact you are, who's been robbed of $1000 by a vicious young thief. Get your walking stick out of the cupboard. Shut up there and let me do the talking."

She armed us with our documents and soon we were at the police station, sited behind flagpoles and a high cream-brick façade. It's in a big complex including a children's court. Cop cars were ranked alongside. It was my first time in a cop shop since a motorbike speeding incident in 1963. There were no other customers. The place had a hermetically sealed look and security warnings against photographs. Behind one counter slot was a door covered by a disquieting poster of a big police dog, a German shepherd, held in check by a copper's muscular and hairy arm. On another door was: "Justice of the Peace service here." Other signage:

"Bail reporting here" (with arrows pointing to the south end).

"Firearm licence applications."

"If you are reporting a lost phone you must block the IMEI number first." (Knowledgeable Winsome muttered that this stops anyone using it).

"If you have been affected by crime, support is available at this station." That fits us, Winsome said.

A business-like young cop beckoned. "I'm Constable Matijevic," he said.

Winsome told our tale while I looked on piteously, leaning on my stick and twiddling my hearing aid.

"I'll check if Hermia is known to us," he said, re-emerging doubly business-like. We knew better than to ask if Hermia was a known local rogue.

"I left her a message to contact us. I suggest you make a report."

He took us into a small bare room and inputted our story, not encouraging any emotional embellishments.

"What do you want?" he finished pointedly.

Winsome: "Our thousand dollars."

Matijevic: "Or your Macbook?"

Winsome: "Sure. She lives just a few klicks away. When your patrol's got nothing better to do, why don't they drop in and get it back?"

Matijevic (giving the police version of an eye-roll): "Thanks, we might be in touch. Shame for this to happen to this gentleman."

Winsome: "We're very fond of him. You can see he's quite alert for 81."

Back in our car, Winsome and I de-briefed excitedly. It all went well, the cops are going to prioritise our case.

But weeks passed. Primrose and I came back from our Tassie holiday, and another week went by.

I got a call with "No Caller ID" and was about to give him a mouthful but just in time heard, "Constable Matijevic again. What's your Macbook's serial number?"

Luckily it was on a screenshot on my Facebook ad.

A week later, just before lunch today I got another call.

"Constable Stankic here from Sunshine." (The station could be renamed 'Little Serbia', I mused). "Come and pick up your Macbook. Mention reference 4596B50Y66."

"Wow! Thanks mate."

In an hour I was back at Sunshine Copshop, now crowded with five swarthy young men, a sixth wearing a sweater in vivid red yellow and black, two ladies of Chinese appearance and one other Skip. The men seemed all in tan workboots or black leisure boots. Two were talking quietly about a recent fight. I wished I had better hearing. One bloke was directed to the bail reporting section.

Every few minutes pairs of coppers came in and out, bulked with equipment like Ukrainian commandos headed for Russian lines. I wondered how female coppers could ever lug such burdens and if they were good shots.

A bespectacled blond non-Serbian copper emerged and I gave him my code and my ID. He came back with a huge brown security bag, which I signed for.

I had brought along a box of Guylian Sea-Shell Belgian chocolates and a gift card reading, "Thanks everyone at Sunshine Copshop!" I became uneasy about regulations on such gifts, so will draw a veil over what happened therewith.

Back in the car I fished out the Macbook from the bag. Its outer box and the Macbook itself had stickers, "Cash Converters, $899".

Obviously Hermia had gone there with my Macbook, and Cash Converters had reported the serial number. I wondered whether Hermia had made off with, say, $500 cash from Cash Converters, or whether they avoided paying her pending the police check.[44] Also, Cash Converters pricing was reasonable – $899 vs my imagined $1000.

I was within minutes of Hermia's home and decided to take a squiz. Not a good idea on unfamiliar roads clogged with trucks, and I had two near-misses. My car-navigator took me to a tired 1960s bungalow with white couch, two red chairs and dirty cushions on the verge. But I found Hermia's unit was actually down a long driveway amid middle-class villas backing onto green sward and a creek. Most had mid-tier cars. Hermia's unit was tidy too. I wasn't sure about our line of conversation if she materialised but she didn't.

To wrap up this drama, I now had to make good on the 20 per cent commission I'd rashly promised daughter Winsome for Macbook recovery and also reimburse Primrose for $500 she'd transferred to cheer me up after Hermia's malfeasance.

Primrose had earlier bought me a cute Tibetan Spaniel pup from a breeder in Cairns, and the car keys did turn up this week – Primrose had wrapped them inside a winter nightie. It was unseasonably warm and she'd continued wearing her summer satin ones, labelled Victoria's Secret which she told me was a K-Mart house brand. So good things also come in threes.

Meanwhile, anyone want a 2019 Macbook Air, strictly for cash? #

---

[4] "Cash Converters stores in most states regularly upload a file to their State police service notifying them of all items bought or borrowed against. The police check these reports against their own databases for any matches. If there is a possible match, the police will contact the appropriate store to determine if it is the same item that has been reported to them as being stolen. All outlets are required to hold second hand goods for a period of time prior to them being offered for sale to enable these checks to be made." But Cash Converters also advertises: "Get instant cash for quality items. We buy everything from smartphones, tablets and digital cameras, to musical instruments, jewellery and everything in between."

Memories of the troubles in Timor

2 February 2022

As a 25-year-old reporter in Perth in 1966 I had more zeal than worldly wisdom. I'd never been north of Geraldton and it was a brave decision of my editor at The West Australian, Griff Richards, to send me on a three-week reporting trip to Portuguese Timor with photographer Richie Hann in tow.

I made a complete ass of myself. Before the first week was up the Portuguese governor, José Alberty Correia, summoned the Australian Consul John Dalrymple Colquhoun-Denvers, an ex-artillery officer, and told him my safety could no longer be guaranteed. I would do well to get on the Fokker Friendship to Darwin next morning.

I'd spent the day with the consul in his Land Rover touring the hills to Maubisse amid much bonhomie. He dropped me at the hotel at dusk. As I was changing for dinner (not exactly black tie) a scream at the back of the hotel split the air. A woman murdered? No, just a goat for dinner having its throat cut. Strolling later, I was swooped on by a consular car and rushed to the furious Consul, smarting from a two-hour diatribe about me from the Governor. Barely suppressing his rage, he said I'd been behaving like a second rate juvenile spy. "I won't hear the last of this for months. If you'd just played things quietly, people would have come to you!"

During the Fokker's Darwin stopover to Perth I filed the story of my own expulsion, describing myself judiciously in the third person. In those weird days reporters didn't try to become the news. From my bland report:

Mr Denvers told them [Thomas and Hann] of complaints that Mr Thomas had entered a military barracks in Dili without having obtained permission from military authorities and that he had asked three junior officers for information about Portuguese military strength on the island. He said that the Portuguese also considered that Mr Thomas had been objectionable in questioning troops about Portuguese politics. The junior officers had sent written reports on their conversations with Mr Thomas to their commanding officer.

Mr Denvers said the Portuguese considered the two men's safety would be endangered if they remained on the island because the sentry at the barracks had been sentenced to five days solitary confinement for having permitted Mr Thomas to enter, and other Portuguese soldiers might take individual action against them.

He said the two men had not been expelled but it was in their interest to fly to Darwin on the aircraft leaving this morning...

Tourists Minister Barbosa and the Governor had [earlier] told Thomas he was free to go where he pleased on the island.

The strength of the military garrison was common knowledge on the island and Mr Barbosa, who was president of the Portuguese Union National political party, had given him freely the information about the troops.

The European population of the island consisted largely of soldiers, Mr Thomas said. He had talked to them openly about Portuguese affairs...

I must also have typed in Darwin a long feature about Timor, because in my old scrapbook I've scribbled on it: "Error due to Darwin telex operator".

The reason my trip lasted even five days was that External Affairs Minister Paul Hasluck had given me a letter of recommendation. Paul had been a sub-editor and mentor to my father, Pete, on *The West Australian* in the 1930s and was happy to do Pete's son an apparently harmless favour.

I guess Governor Correia was worried that expelling me might create a diplomatic breach with Australia, as distinct from "advising" me to sod off. Australia was Portugal's sole ally in the region and the Indonesians were itching to push in, although this didn't actually happen until a decade later. I now know that in 1964 High Command ordered the Indonesian Frogman Unit in Surabaya to send an infiltration team to East Timor. The team spent five months as – literally – horse traders (*pedagang kuda*) stirring up trouble.[5]

I must say that, after my impromptu inspection of the barracks, I bumped into a group of soldiers in the street. One who spoke English ranted about how Portuguese soldiers were the world's fiercest. His mates crowded me menacingly but allowed me on my way.

I think the Governor was also perturbed about me getting pally with the Indonesian Consul, Dr Sorosa, who had photos of Indonesian military might on his walls, such as Tupolev "Badger" bombers. Whether the Badgers were airworthy is a separate issue.

One evening Dr Sorosa stopped by me in his Mercedes in a dark street. I hopped in, the car being pretty full already with three administrators from Kupang. He was driving them home after a good dinner. I interviewed till midnight, taking shorthand in the dark.

---

[5] *Faltering Steps: Independence Movements in East Timor – 1940s to the early 1970s –* by Ernie Chamberlain (Edition 3, 2010).

Mr Ataupa, a senior education administrator told me he was one of the island's first high school graduates and first teachers. He taught three schools in one building – the first from 7.30am to 1pm; another from 1pm to 5pm and a third till 10pm. This was how they had done the impossible, he said.

I finished my story, "The mosquitos finally broke up the party." I assume someone reported this odd encounter to the Portuguese.

My chats were admittedly political. Back in Perth I wrote,

[The Indonesian Consul] criticised the heavy Portuguese spending on their army in Timor – I calculated soldiers' salaries alone to equal about two-thirds of the civil [$A3m] budget. He said that because the Indonesia army – if it wanted to – could sweep over Portuguese Timor like an avalanche, the Portuguese were wasting money keeping even a nominal army there. The money should be developing the country, he said.

When I first hit Dili, the Governor plied me with cake and read with respect my letter of recommendation. He extolled his island's peace and progress. He invited me to go anywhere, talk to anyone, and send news to Australian tourists of his happy isle, this precious stone set in the silver sea. Lacking much adult perspective, I took him at his word.

Actually, eight of his less happy breed were arrested only a year earlier for plotting to blow up him and his advisers with hand grenades, as revenge for Portugal's brutal put-down of a revolt six years earlier. I'll get round to that later.

One incident still baffles me. Walking dusty Dili's boulevards, I spotted $A5-10 worth of local banknotes in the weeds. Who lost them in that poverty-stricken town and what odds that it would be me who found them?

One evening disaffected soldiers dropped in, but when I tried to visit one next day, his frightened wife slammed the door. I figure they'd re-assessed me as a loose cannon under watch by the "PIDE" secret police.

I was B-grade chess champ of Fremantle (no big deal, let me tell you). In Dili I'd ask, "Do you play chess?" Obviously a code, the authorities imagined.

On the hill tour, the consul's Land Rover flew the Australian flag. I wrote,

Men and boys on their indefatigable treks to market, would hastily upend the hundredweight of firewood on their heads to give us the slow Portuguese salute, a mixture of respect, servility and sometimes fear in their eyes.

Consul Colquhoun-Denvers played this down as an odd colonial relic. But fact-checking my 1966 juvenilia last month, I chanced upon a meticulously-documented 100-page monograph from 2009 about the failed 1959 revolt. I located author and ex-Brigadier Ernie Chamberlain by phone near Geelong and interrupted his research on Australian and North Vietnamese wartime units. Reading his Timor books and studies jolted me into the realities of Timor around my 1966 visit.

Even in the late 1950s – and maybe beyond – the exploited villagers were disciplined with torture instruments, jocularly called "education devices". In the Viqueque district, central to the 1959 revolt, chiefs and landowners enforced village labour with internal passports, whips called *chouriços* – or 'sausages' and the *palmató-ria*, a ferrule 2cm thick and 40cm long with a special head for beating a peasant's palms. One Timorese explained, "It's really painful. Sometimes they would beat someone's hand until the hand became swollen and was bleeding. If they hit you a lot, you couldn't use your hand for weeks. Sometimes people got it simply because they could not afford to pay the *imposto* (head tax)."[6]

Australia's Timor Oil Company signed on laborers for $A90-300 a year. Administrators doled out a paltry $A21 and pocketed the rest, locking up anyone refusing to work. Farmers were forced to sell their livestock at low prices, while the regime spent little on education and infrastructure. A Lisbon high official visiting in 1956 was appalled and issued a 17-page demand for reforms, which was ignored as soon as he left. My own reports bore little relation to the reality:

> *Eduardo Barbosa, chief of public works in Portuguese Timor, switched off the ABC News on his shortwave transistor. "They have executed four ex-ministers in the Congo," he told me. "This is what happens when you give people independence before they are ready for it."*
>
> *He screwed a monocle under his left eyebrow and ran a finger round the open neck of his shirt. "One time our natives would not work," he said. "All they wanted was to feast. We made them plant rice. They would have starved without a crop.*
>
> *"The United Nations said, 'They are slave labour. You must not do that.' Now if they want to work they can, if they do not our government will not let them starve. They are better off than the peons of Portugal. The peons who do not work, they die."*

---

[6] *Rebellion, Defeat and Exile – The 1959 Uprising in East Timor*, Ernie Chamberlain, 2009, p. 26.

Australia was interested only in security angles. The Consulate reported in the mid-1950s:

The indigenous native is very primitive, and it is usually considered that his intelligence is far below that which would be required to absorb communist doctrines or any other form of political thought ... he is generally regarded as a very loyal person and obedient to the Native Chiefs who in turn are responsible to the Administration. The loyalty of these Native Chiefs is unquestioned.

Just as Waterloo was preceded by Duchess Charlotte's ball at Brussels, the Timor revolt involved an anniversary ball at the sporting men's Club Benfica in Dili.

Informers – including a jilted girlfriend and the Bishop of Dili – had divulged rebel plans to the authorities months earlier. The Indonesian consul deferred the plot to the December New Year celebrations when fireworks would mask the opening attack. This was for a mixed band of Indonesian refugees and Timorese to seize arms depots in Dili, release prisoners and give them machetes to kill revellers and blockade the town. Outside Dili, local officials would be invited to a New Year party and beheaded.

The army suspected freelance rebels might still attack the ball on May 27. The plotting was Dili's worst-kept secret with people arguing in restaurants and the Australian Consul, Francis Whittaker, speculating about bombs being thrown among the revellers. The army upgraded security, and officers (attending out of uniform) waltzed with pistols in their pockets. Whittaker went to the ball anyway, dancing till 3am "without any bangs", as he put it with admirable sang froid.

Within days authorities rounded up 15 suspects in Dili, precipitating an uprising by provincial rebels to forestall their own arrest. They hoped at least for international attention, but nothing public reached the outside world, even Portugal.

The rebels acquired rifles at Uatolori town and at midnight broke into offices at nearby Viqueque. After bashing the guards and throwing them out of upper windows, they seized 70 old rifles but with mismatched bullets. Administrator Ramos escaped by jeep, evading roadblocks and ambushes.

The main battle was at the small fort at Baguia, pitting rebels against prepared defences of machine guns and grenade launchers. Rebels' bullets were exploding in their rifles and they had to turn their heads away, so their aim was poor. The Portuguese, further armed with mortars and bazookas, soon retook the districts. One captured leader was whipped till his back was in shreds and an Indonesian captive died under torture. Others were shot on the spot and Portuguese soldiers crushed one man's head with a rock.

To the east, rebels lost to a 450-strong force of loyal arraiais (warriors). With army protection, they laid waste to tribal enemies' villages, killing dozens and stealing property and cattle. Poor and ignorant villagers beheaded even children to get bounties per head offered by the Portuguese. The army took seven rebels to the Bebui River and Administrator Ramos had them cut them down with automatic weapons fire. Helpers mutilated the bodies with spears and machetes and threw them in the river. (There's now a simple memorial of river stones at the site).

Some 300 Timorese were killed (Portuguese casualties – zero). They tortured prisoners for confessions and dumped them in a derelict freighter in Dili harbour in unbearable heat before exiling them to Lisbon, Angola and Mozambique. The Portuguese burnt down the Dili "Timorese-only" club, considered a centre of anti-colonial subversion. Viqueque Administrator Artur Ramos concluded his report:

I still wish to say that, in my modest opinion, the repression of this movement was much too benevolent and can encourage the repetition of such an event.

And Prime Minister Salazar informed the UN in December 1960:

Any person of good faith can see for himself that peace and complete calm reign in our overseas territories, without the use of force and merely by the habit of peaceful living in common.

After the revolt Australia installed W.A. Luscombe as consul in Dili, apparently a full-time Australian Secret Intelligence Service (ASIS) officer.

Whether the Indonesian government itself had endorsed the revolt remains a mystery. Consul Jakub certainly stirred things up on a freelance basis. He was upset if not deranged over his wife's death in the Dili hospital in 1957, which he blamed on Portuguese neglect. Ernie Chamberlain finishes his account:

Perhaps future reviews and studies by Timorese scholars may yet more adequately recognise the sacrifices of the rebels and the suffering inflicted on the villagers of Viqueque and Bau-cau. The Rebellion might still find broader recognition and acceptance as a "legitimate" contribution to the independence struggle of the Timorese people.

I was lucky I didn't meet a worse fate on my Timor trip. I'd begged the Indonesian Consul for a border-crossing visa but left before I got one. At that time the Indonesian army and death squads had been murdering 500,000-plus Communist sympathisers and other minorities (with CIA and, allegedly, Australian help). My bull-in-china-shop interviewing might have got me killed in some nameless village. I did write third-hand regarding Indonesian Timor,

> *A small girl described to one traveller how she had seen ten Communists led to a hillside and shot.*
>
> *"Communists are outside the law," the [Indonesian] Consul told me. Dr Sorosa said they had moved outside the umbrella of Indonesia's Pantjasila – the five principles of belief in God, nationalism, social justice, humanitarianism and sovereignty of the people. So they cannot live in Indonesia.*

From embarrassment I've put off writing this piece for half a century. I knew that I would one day, and preserved my four 1966 Timor notebooks of shorthand, which have followed me through multiple jobs, cities and marriages. Within another half century I'll get round to transcribing them.#

My tête-à-tête with Mr Gorilla Monsoon

12 January 1968

Brute Bernard, a primitive wrestler from Quebec, gave a roar of rage, climbed up on the ring ropes and made punching motions at the crowd at Perth's Perry Lakes stadium.

Someone had thrown a green plum at him. His reaction provoked another missile. Brute charged into the grandstand, shoulders pumping like pistons. The shrieking crowd parted like the Red Sea and Brute returned in triumph to meet his principal opponent for the night.

The combatants always felt free to leave the ring, either head first in pursuit of fruit throwers, or on the heels of a panic-stricken opponent disappearing into the darkness.

Brute, getting the worst of his slugging match with a 7ft Texan, tumbled through the ropes and crawled furtively up and down in the hope of climbing back in unseen. Tex evicted him twice more with elbow and toe.

That made Brute mad. He jumped onto the ring steps until they collapsed. Then he seized the stoutest piece of timber remaining, and tried to hit Tex's head. Tex grabbed it, whacked Brute, and sent him overboard again. This time Brute found a piece of white cord, and in no time had wrapped it around Tex's neck and was pulling on each end.

Brute does not speak while on duty in the ring, but utters cries like "Aw aw AW AWAW!" He was hardly recognisable later in his dressing room, in a tweed sports coat and dandling a felt money purse.

I tried to think of a winning line of conversation. "How do you feel, Brute? I may call you Brute?" "Tah-yed [tired]," he croaked. "How is Skull?"

(His wrestling partner, Mr Skull Murphy, has hurt his back on active service).

"Not too good."

Pause.

"Is your head naturally bald?"

"When I was a kid, rheumatic fever, I lost hair."

Snarling (from the wrestlers) and roaring noises (from the crowd) floated to our ears across the night air.

Emboldened by my recent tête-à-tête, I headed for Gorilla Monsoon, 32 stone, who was sitting moodily on a wooden bench. Shortly before, he had been pitted against 16-stone Len Holt. Mr Monsoon simply planted his elephantine legs, let Mr Holt climb over and under him for a while, and then fell on him, ending the bout. Having been declared the winner, Mr Monsoon trod on the throat of his supine opponent.

"Where do you come from, er ar?" I asked, tactfully sidestepping the first-name problem.

He favoured me with a bitter glance through black spectacles and sat.

"Gorilla's a mystery man," volunteered the manager. "I don't get buddy-buddy with the wrestlers."

Gorilla's former opponent, combing his hair in the dressing room mirror, seemed little the worse now for the squashing and trampling.

Killer Karl Kox, a notorious bad guy in wrestling, was lounging outside the dressing shed. He specialises in a hold called a 'brain-buster', in which he lifts his opponent shoulder-high and drops him on his head.

"I'm not a bad guy all the time," he explained. "But when I climb through the ropes, I'm in business. I invest my winnings in a feed and grain company in Texas. I got tired of fighting for nothing."

His bout with Mario Milano, a huge Italian, was the piece de resistance for the night. Killer won the first round by twisting Mario's fingers, and Mario won the second with an abdominal stretch.

In the third round, both parties abandoned finesse to hit each other mighty blows on the head. Mario got Killer tied up in the ropes, and every time the referee went to untie him, Mario leaned on the ropes on the opposite side of the ring, to Killer's discomfort.

In time, they wound up brawling in the grass some distance from the ring. Killer was able to run Mario's head into a steel light pole. Mario kept punching, so Killer did it again. Mario began stumbling around in circles, while Killer returned in triumph to the ring.

Mario put his hand to his forehead, and discovered it was bleeding profusely. With a wild cry he hurtled back into the ring and after knocking the surprised Killer almost senseless, lifted him into the air and began to choke him.

The referee, who was on the smallish side, ran in to separate them. Mario threw an uppercut that sent the referee his own height into the air. Picking himself up off his back, the referee returned to the affray and collected another punch from Mario that threw him 10ft. The 15 policemen on duty began to consider taking action but several wrestlers who happened to be nearby rescued Killer and the referee.

The announcer announced a win to Killer Karl Kox, on a disqualification. "That is it for tonight in World Championship Wrestling," he concluded blandly.

Actually, it's since emerged that all such bouts were rehearsed and choreographed. When Mario, as I wrote, "put his hand to his forehead", he was possibly concealing a capsule of blood which he broke on his own skull. #

PART FOUR

FEARLESS BOOK AND ARTS REVIEWS

The Durack clan's tempests and tragedies

23 November 2021

Patsy Millett, daughter of famed Perth writer-historian Mary Durack (1913-94), hasn't spared the vitriol throughout *Inseparable Elements*, her astounding memoir of her mother's tribulations. Least of all does she spare her father, aviation pioneer Horatio 'Horrie' Miller, and Aunt Elizabeth Durack, the celebrated artist of tribal Aborigines.

Dame Mary Durack AC DBE, soft of heart, was beset by rascals, human leeches and time-wasters throughout her long creative life of novels, plays, poems, biographies and kids' books. She was also suckered into hopeless roles in hopeless arts bureaucracies. It's a miracle she ever completed her immaculately researched bio-epics of her cattle-pioneering forebears, *Kings in Grass Castles* (1959) and *Sons in the Saddle* (1983).

The Greeks' Furies would be more tolerant than Patsy in outing Mary's torments and tormenters. Patsy tosses enough grenades for a 100-year war among Perth's society. For starters: Mary's absurd 42-year-long and thankless marriage to brutish Horrie Miller (1893-1980). Horrie helped get Qantas started and criss-crossed WA's North-West in the vintage planes of MacRobertson Miller Airways. As Mary ruminated, "There may have been more selfish men than Horrie, but I never met one." Today Perth Airport's main artery is called Horrie Miller Drive. So why did Mary marry him? Patsy writes

When pressed by the curious as to what – frankly – she had
been thinking, she would resort to speaking in nebulous terms

153

of her children and the felicitous link with an airline that allowed her travel north free of charge…

Clinging to his solitary and abandoned self-image, Horrie bypassed his extraordinary good fortune in having such a wife, such a family, such freedom and means of movement and adventure … Always insisting that he was working his fingers to the bone in the interests of his family, who were insufficiently grateful, he meanwhile steadily drained family company assets.

Horrie's operating style wouldn't cut it these days – he was finally ordered to keep better radio protocol in his Wackett on take-off than, 'Going for a bit of a spin, shouldn't be too long.' As for Patsy, she felt serious urges to patricide when Horrie during his wife's palliative care continued to harass the deteriorating Mary beyond endurance.

Was there not some way to hasten the process of Horrie's departure? To this end, I conferred with the venerable who-dunnit aficionado Ida Mann [a retired outback ophthalmologist], who, all too eager to assist, scrabbled round for the least out-of-date barbiturates from her medical sample drawer. There was no doubt in her mind that such a move constituted a mercy killing. Whether I could have steeled myself to the grim task or whether the intervention of fate saved Horrie from patricide remains undetermined … To the end of my days, I will wake from a nightmare where he is still alive and kicking.

Patsy's tone throughout is wittily sardonic, bordering on incredulous that Mary could absorb so many arrows and impositions mixed with friendly fire from family and in-law elements. Patsy gives Mary's artist sister Elizabeth – a lifetime cadger from Mary – a particularly bad press:

> *Bet could, over the decades, be found supporting some fairly obnoxious political figures, although Joh Bjelke-Petersen was not in the same ballpark as Hitler, for whom during the war years she had formed an ardent admiration. Perforce always chasing the money and power, had her stars been otherwise aligned she might easily have slipped into a role such as that occupied by Leni Riefenstahl [Hitler's movie producer].*

Elizabeth herself could be merciless, prone to

> *… demolish anyone who crossed her path, including, without compunction, those held dear by her sister. Absorbed by her artist's eye, she disposed of [novelist] Ernestine Hill as ' a little scorched-up leaf ', and [historian] Henrietta Drake-Brockman as 'Nicely dressed, clear, fair skin, well done hair, hands that have done no hard work – a numbskull, not even likable like the average nitwit '.*

The family dubbed the elderly Henrietta Drake-Brockman as "Henrietta Great-Frogman" for her penchant for diving on wrecked Dutch galleons.

While all families have their feuds, Elizabeth was capable of furthering them even to the Supreme Court, in her irrational fight over control of Mary's Durack archive. Mary during this unsought fracas was on her deathbed with stomach cancer.

> *Bet was the driver of this runaway bus and her destination more far-flung than the others were able to grasp. Duplicity her stock in trade, she was a virtuoso when it came to pitting one family member against another and switching sides at will.*

After loosing this intra-family wrecking ball and with Mary dead, Elizabeth was surprised not to be forgiven, according to Patsy, who signs her off:

Fatally freed from Mary's restraining hand, she was soon heading for the next – and ultimate – reckless stunt. Eddie Burrup was just over the horizon.

By this Patsy refers to Elizabeth's selling her work in the persona of an imaginary Aborigine, 'Eddie Burrup'. However, Patsy is never small-minded and sums up:

Changing faces and motivations according to requirements, even her pictures subject to caveat emptor, she was a genuine miracle of contrivance – one who would nonetheless produce images powerful enough to eclipse anything that might be revealed by her puny detractors, including this niece.

Among Mary Durack's exploiters was boot-salesman R.M. Williams, who inveigled her onto the board of the Stockman's Hall of Fame at Longreach with blah-blah about her including the north-west cattle industry. He only wanted her name as a PR drawcard. At the 1988 official opening, they seated her with Queen Elizabeth:

Next to the costly ensembles and silly hats, she looked singularly unpretentious, if a little surprised, since prior warning of the prestigious seating had somehow escaped her. The loose perm given way to a neat French roll, she presented a respectable but homespun figure.

As a nod to the madness of the Whitlam times, someone nominated Mary as a potential State governor and there was even press talk of her as our first female Governor-General, in a hypothetical contest with the louche Germaine Greer.

Mary had four daughters and one son by Horrie, and I was startled to learn from *Inseparable Elements* that in 1955, Mary, at the age of 42, had a last child, Johnson, by her live-in odd-job man Bob Hill during Horrie's north-west flying absences.

> *Entering her room one morning, I had seen the house guest going out the window, and my mind shied away from what seemed my mother's descent into some kind of French farce. And so, knowing as I did, I simply dismissed the possibility. In retrospect, what happened is plain enough … She had always regarded Bob as a permanent adolescent who, for all his fooling about with paint and poetry, was no more than a likable ratbag. Predicaments of this sort not unfamiliar to her, it would have been utterly confounding that dear, sensible 'Mare' had fallen to such a folly, the worse for it not being in her sister's nature to avail herself of the practical means of extrication.*

Further particulars are baroque. Horrie, cuckolded, put up with the cuckoo.

Bob Hill himself was the son of Ernestine Hemmings, later "Hill", celebrated author of the Matthew Flinders novel *My Love Must Wait*. Patsy confirms Bob Hill was sired by Kerry Packer's grandfather Robert Clyde Packer, in what was poor Ernestine's probable "one and only dalliance." Ernestine made what Patsy calls "an expedient retreat" to Tasmania and there invented a husband called Mr Hill. R.C. Packer provided some cash support and Bob's school fees to age 11, when Packer died.

Myself a Perth contemporary of Patsy, I'd imagined the Duracks' family home "Mildew" in Nedlands as an oasis of creativity. More the opposite, with Horrie adding his chainsaw to one episode of backyard bedlam.

... enhanced by a multilayered sound track combining John-
son's guitar, Sesame Street at top volume from the TV, a bark-
ing puppy running dangerously underfoot, and [secretary]
Connie's sharp tones directed at the resident mother for her
lack of control over her child.

Anything but a businesswoman, Mary entered gross commitments of time and creativity "with as little concern as she signs
a grocery bill". Case in point: script-writing for a Swan River
Saga theatrical, grossing $10,381 and for which she was paid $259.
She labored gratis over months to edit the legends of an Aborigine called Butcher Joe, and was taken aback, Patsy says, to learn
that writer Hugh Edwards (Island of Angry Ghosts and a score
more) required a $5000 grant to complete the job.

Mary suffered her cruellest blows from the deaths of two daughters, Julie, at just 27, and outback nurse-pilot Robin at 35. Julie
was felled during pregnancy from complications stemming from a
botched operation by an incompetent medico when a child. Robin
in the midst of her daily work flying trauma cases to hospital, was
struck down by melanoma.

Julie in Broome in 1949 got a bad stomach ache. The available
locum, somewhat the worse for wear and, according to Patsy, biased by an extra-marital affair he was having with Elizabeth, assumed an appendix problem. Julie's pain was actually just from
eating unripe mangoes. Describing the "shocker" of an operation,
Patsy says,

Unable to find the appendix but convinced of his diagnosis,
the doctor kept cutting until, located at last, a normal and
uninflamed appendix was removed. A long time recovering,
Julie was left with a livid scar from the right side of her abdo-

men to the navel. But by 1952, the event was no more than a bad memory and Julie restored to good health and cheer. Not even Horrie, acquainted as he was with the concept of connective elements, foresaw the forging of the first awful link in a tragic chain.

Twenty years later, in an under-equipped small hospital, she died of complications from another faulty operation to fix the original damage.

Sister Robin authored two best-sellers about her flying nurse role. Perth Airport's Sugarbird Lady Road is named after Robin. In Patsy's words,

Through her hands passed a gruesome parade of burns, bashings, botched suicides and incomplete abortions; victims massively haemorrhaging within the confines of a small aircraft all over her and other patients aboard. And always for her the most heart-rending sight : the limp little hands of dead or dying children. Unmasked and vulnerable, she sat cheek by jowl with infectious diseases: tuberculosis, hepatitis, glandular fever ... It was the pilot's responsibility to restore the cabin to a sanitary state, and that for Robin included taking linen and seat covers home for washing and mending.

By 1975 Robin herself was gravely ill. Her rigors were worsened by an incorrect pathology report leading to an overdose of radium therapy. Her torments included her despicable and parasitic husband, Dr Harold Dicks (according to Patsy), a Royal Flying Doctor Service stalwart and president. In her last days, Robin woke to see Harold forcing a "vulgar embrace" on her sister Anne-Marie. "Stop it, Harold," Robin said. "I know what you are doing." Within days of Robin's death, Harold was also coming on to an outraged

Patsy as well; within three weeks he found a new girlfriend and in six weeks installed a woman among Robin's belongings at suburbia's inaptly named Mt Pleasant. Patsy later discovered Harold surreptitiously visiting Mildew.

> *Suddenly overcome with revulsion and rage, and having the hose in hand, I flushed him off the property – down the garden path, past the 'bear-pit' where with Robin he had so often enjoyed the hospitality of the house, and out the gate. Unfortunately, the weak water pressure made it a symbolic gesture that dampened rather than cannoned him away on the end of a jet. 'How do you live with yourself, Harold Dicks!' I shouted rhetorically, to the wonderment of my watching children.*

Robin's headstone had the quotation from aviator Antoine de Saint-Exupery: "Can these be the same stars? Is this the same sky? How bright, how clear, what safety I have reached."

Patsy also has much to recount of Mary's involvement in Aboriginal theatre and politics, including city-based climbers fostering race-hatred and pushing aside tribal members and their "fossilised culture". We get vignettes such as Mary trying to organise an Aboriginal Theatre Foundation performance in Broome, with women from La Grange Mission "who modestly insisted on dancing in white bras and pink slips".

A Whitlam grant despatched a 140-strong troupe to a festival of black artists in Lagos, Nigeria, where amid chaos our urban "black power" members trumped their tribal rivals. (The roll-call was 30 tribals vs 110 urban hangers-on).

> *In the prevailing melee, the one performance of a genuine corroboree failed, along with the sound and lighting. Eighteen members, disassociating themselves from the messages of dis-*

cord from their city brothers, pulled out. Unique Australian Aboriginal culture had, in a final mockery, been represented by a sassy urban group dancing Filipino jazz ballet to American soul music. Kath Walker, there to promote black literature, had blamed the whites and the tribal groups for 'being out of their element' and producing a 'flop'. Amid widespread criticism at home, the $203,000 grant that had gone into the project was put down to the folly of the previous government.

Mary's years of work for the Aboriginal Theatre Foundation, and the ATF itself, has now gone down the memory hole.

That there is today virtually no record of this enterprise to be found in any public institution raises conjecture that it has been 'disappeared' as inconvenient to more popular (or less contentious) constructions of Aboriginal contemporary history.

Mary's attempted sponsorship of the scattered remnant of the original Carrolup Aboriginal artists of the south-west provides another vignette. She located Aboriginal artist Revel Cooper in Fremantle Prison, his life a disquieting "tale of confusion and alienation that could be applied to so many of his countrymen".

And all too poignantly predictable was the end of the story. On his release, having blown his cheque from the publisher, Cooper began to turn up at [Nedlands family home] Mildew to demand further payment from his patron. With a waiting taxi full of his extended family, if he found no-one home he would bail up neighbours. Sadly knowing that it was just a matter of time, Mary could only see him away with the contents of her purse. Periodically re-incarcerated, he would eventually be killed in a drunken brawl.

Utterly poignant was the official treatment of Aborigines and their culture when, in 1971, the Ord Dam drowned the Duracks' Argyle holdings.

Bulla, keeper of the ancient stones and *tjuringa* boards, forfeited his entire cache to the waves. Why, he continued to ask, had 'the old boss' left his properties to strangers rather than to the Aboriginal workers he had trained and who belonged there? He was genuinely bewildered by this. 'We feel we lose everything that we belong,' he said, and his sorrowful summary of the situation for himself and his people became the title of the coming ABC Big Country episode.

Patsy has little to nothing to report on the alleged "stolen generation" crimes of Mary's parents' era, other than forced removals to quarantine hospital of those afflicted with leprosy, and pastoralists' casual 'picking up' of Aboriginal children to raise for station labour.

"I suppose we can't sit in judgment," Mary wrote, "no-one in the old days would have suggested blacks had human rights."

The Durack-Miller clan had something in common with the forlorn Trappist missionaries of the 1890s north-west. Mary wrote:

They expected to find 'crosses' and to embrace them – even martyrdom, but the greatest crosses they had to bear were not from external discomforts or persecutions but from their own inner conflicts and each other.

Inseparable Elements is a moving and fascinating insight into the heartland of a great Australian family. As Patsy sums up,

Through the pages of my mother's diaries, I relive our close and sometimes embattled relationship – the furious love and jealous guardianship of her creative flame that yet demands my vigilance. #

Book and Bench: Nick Hasluck's judicious musings

24 October 2021

A bit of judicial biffo goes on all the time as appeal courts rule on whether a trial judge got it right or wrong. A case in point is the High Court's 7- 0 critique of two Victorian appeal judges who sent the innocent Cardinal Pell to prison. Such court language has a polite veneer. But do you ever wonder what judges really think? To find out go buy Nicholas Hasluck's *Book and Bench*, (Arcadia, $44). It's his two-year diary from 2000 when he became a WA Supreme Court judge. He retired in 2010.

Barrister Nick, also novelist, memoirist and poet, took crimson while continuing as chair of the Literature Board of the Australia Council and finishing a Jacobean-era novel, Arbella's Baby, writing as "Margaret Martin" in a post-modern identity twist.

Book and Bench publishes for the first time his private biffo with ex-High Court Judge Sir Ronald Wilson over the latter's *Bringing Them Home Report* of 1997, source of the "stolen generations" story and alleging government-administered "genocide".

Hasluck's father, Paul, was Commonwealth Minister for Territories running Aboriginal policy and administration in the Northern Territory from 1951-63, and Governor-General 1969-74. Paul Hasluck, with his devotion to Aboriginal welfare, didn't actually spend his time stealing part-Aboriginal kids from their wailing mother's arms. (The same could be said of WA Labor Premier (1953-59) Bert Hawke , uncle of advocate for Indigenes Bob Hawke).

Equally absurd is that Paul's bureaucrats did the stealing behind Paul's back; Paul was fanatical about portfolio detail.

163

Yet if *Bringing Them Home* were true, Paul had to be a genocidal monster. Paul's son, Nick, was not having any of that.

The intra-judicial explosion detonated when Sir Ronald wrote effusively to Nick congratulating him on becoming a judge (their Perth homes were only 7km apart as the crow flies). Sir Ronald doubtless expected a grateful reply. But Nick was stewing over Sir Ronald's telling the National Press Club in 1999 about NT 'genocide' in the Hasluck era. Nick blasted Ron; Ron lashed back. They banged heads to mutual exhaustion. And later, Ron admitted to Patrick Carlyon of *The Bulletin* (June 2001) that his 'genocide' claim was a crock – which hasn't stopped the Australian wokerati spraying the term around regardless.

Drafting his *Book and Bench*, Nick overcame qualms about publishing the letters.

Sir Ronald wrote *"to express the congratulations, pleasure and approval I feel in your appointment to the Bench ... As you will understand, I have felt a real affinity with your fine leadership of the Equal Opportunity Tribunal over the past ten years and congratulate you on your work in that regard..."*

Nick fumed for several weeks. Then, on a quiet Saturday afternoon, between writing up two court judgements, "I realise that the time has come to send a candid response. I can't prevaricate or postpone the unpleasant task any longer. I work away at it for a while and eventually settle upon a somewhat lengthy reply in these terms:

> *... I cannot pretend to agree with much of what you have had to say in recent years about the so-called 'stolen generations' issue, especially in regard to the Northern Territory in the post-war era. Accordingly, I feel that I would be lacking*

in moral courage if I simply responded to your letter with a bland, and thus insincere reply.

It is apparent from your Bringing Them Home *report and your subsequent utterances that you will allow no merit or humanity to anyone involved in the administration of Aboriginal affairs prior to 1972. This, inevitably, brings with it a condemnation of my father, the late Sir Paul Hasluck. Indeed I saw you on television at the National Press Club saying, unequivocally, to a vast viewing audience, that 'genocide' was being perpetrated in the Northern Territory throughout the 1950s as a deliberate policy; that is to say, during the period my father was in office as Minister for Territories. And yet, it is also apparent from your report that no serious attempt was made by you or your colleagues to explain the policies of the day or to allow any of those involved to be heard in their own defence.*

I regard this lack of due process as reprehensible and the meagre exposition in your report as a travesty. This makes the characterisation of my father as a genocidal murderer doubly offensive, especially when one remembers that Paul Hasluck's call in his maiden speech in Parliament on March 14, 1950, for the rights of Aborigines to be respected was, to use Gough Whitlam's words, 'the most thorough speech ever to have been delivered in the national Parliament.' Now, under your leadership, an insidious attempt is being made to demonise Paul Hasluck and many others like him.

Perhaps you will be inclined to respond to this with semantics, and seek to convince me that 'genocide' is being used in some special sense that doesn't encompass a murderous intention to exterminate an entire race.

But that is not the way your followers see it. At Writers' Week in Adelaide recently, Bob Ellis and many other speakers had no compunction in comparing the so-called 'genocide' in Australia to the use of gas chambers in Nazi Germany, and those responsible for the former as being in the same ring of hell as Hitler, Goering and Goebbels. Inflammatory comments of this kind are now de rigueur in Australian intellectual life, as I discovered again at a recent conference at the National Library in Canberra. This is the level to which debate in this country has now sunk as a direct consequence of your report ...

Hasluck next criticised Wilson for

tarnishing the names and reputations of many people of an earlier generation – the patrol officers, the nurses, the teachers, the missionaries, the administrators – who laboured in good faith with limited resources to confer benefits on those who might otherwise, at that time, have been left without a future. I cannot see that defamations of this kind are a necessary or desirable part of 'reconciliation' ... it is a tragedy that as a consequence of your report so many Australians of goodwill now feel that this is a subject that is 'out of bounds' and can no longer be discussed.

Hasluck attached a letter he wrote to the *Sydney Morning Herald* on 11 March 1999, quoting Paul Hasluck himself on the NT that

an earnest effort was made to change Australian neglect and indifference towards Aborigines, to improve their conditions and raise their hopes for the future. We strove for full recognition of their entitlements – legally as citizens, socially as fellow Australians.

Wilson responded within three days that his inquiry had solicited evidence from all quarters and by 'genocide' he referred to cultural not physical destruction. He denied trying to demonise Paul Hasluck, and said the report's finding of genocide was based on the states' Protectors conference of 1937 aiming "to persuade all governments to adopt the policy of biological absorption of Aboriginal children of mixed descent into Western society" and eliminating the children's cultural identity and traditions.

Wilson: *The Report voices the changing motivation underlying the assimilation policies from biological absorption to what was thought to be best for the children. Unfortunately the stripping away of all traces of aboriginality was still thought to be in the best interest of the children, such was the insidious impact of the racist White Australia policy on this aspect of Australian life.*

Sir Ronald ended by saying the Report's *"credibility is beyond question. I am truly sorry that it has occasioned you such distress and anger. Yours sincerely, Ron. PS Please do not feel obliged to respond to this letter."*

Within three days, Hasluck did indeed reply:

... To my mind, your Report's failure to take account of contemporary sources of this kind [namely Paul Hasluck's book Shades of Darkness*] is inexplicable and justifies my earlier reference to the Report's "meagre exposition".*

Hasluck complained that Wilson's Report also ignored the PhD of Colin Tatz on NT administration in the 1950s, which has "not a single word about forcible removals, genocide or human rights abuses of any kind."

Wilson replies, ending the exchange:

I sadly agree that we shall have to agree to disagree. I believe the gulf between us centres on our respective understandings of the breadth of the term 'genocidal'. The Report acknowledges that removal may have been motivated by the belief that it was in the best interests of the children.

In a later glorious aside, Nick Hasluck remarks:

The credibility of the report is not assisted by the fact that its principal author, Sir Ronald Wilson, was a Senior Crown Prosecutor in WA for many years during the assimilation era, but failed to prosecute anyone for the crimes of the kind he now contends were taking place his home state during the period he was in office. Paradoxically, it seems that as a former Moderator of the Uniting Church and as a member of the governing board of Sister Kate's hostel for part-Aboriginal children, Wilson was an active collaborator in the policies and practices he now condemns.

In his lawyerly way, Hasluck quotes the High Court case, *Kruger* (1997), and Full Federal Court, *Cubillo-Gunner* (2001), affirming that NT child policy was oriented to their welfare, not genocidal in any sense. Likewise the Wilson report itself says the final report of the Royal Commission on Aboriginal deaths in custody "contains the specific finding that child removal policies were adopted not for the purpose of exterminating people, but saving them."

Hasluck also had little time for "the sanctimonious Sir William Deane", another one-time High Court judge (1982-95), who was Governor-General from 1996-01. At the 2001 Centenary celebrations, Deane was "managing to suggest, as usual, and very piously, that any members of the audience who are not ashamed of their nation's past are clearly in need of Orwellian re-education."

Keep in mind that *Bringing Them Home* of 1997 suggested 100,000 or so "stolen" children, and Kevin Rudd in his 2008 Apology said "up to 50,000". The alleged total is an elastic figure.

But try this: When Paul Hasluck became Territories Minister in 1952 he asked for a report on numbers of NT Indigenous children removed from camps and sent to hostels and schools in Darwin and Alice Springs. This pre-dated any "stolen" controversies. His officials told him that, from 1927 to the World War II, the incomplete records indicated 77 boys and 32 girls had left their families, all with the consent of the mothers. That's under ten per year, from an NT Aboriginal population of around 17,000.

Nick Hasluck: *The number since the War, where records were complete [to 1951], was 45 boys and 65 girls, much less than 1% of the Aboriginal [NT] population and less than 3 percent of the [NT] Aboriginal children of the period. Not exactly the picture of widespread removals now presented to the Australian public in the 21st century by activists with an axe to grind!*

Neither Paul nor Nick refer to whatever happened to part-Aboriginal children in other states, since Paul's ministerial remit was solely the NT. The South Australian archives, for example, have now revealed that numbers of removed children in SA were even fewer than in the NT – averaging two to three per year from 1840-1940, including a SA government count of five per year from 1900-13, and that's for all reasons.

Keith Windschuttle from his archival research for *The Fabrication of Aboriginal History* (Vol. III, p. 617) puts the national total of child removals from 1880 to 1970 at 8,250 or 92 per year for all reasons, including orphaning, neglect, jeopardy and consensual transfers for fostering and education (those dominate the NSW data). Only one compensation court case has ever succeeded, involving a well-meaning but misguided Adelaide welfare officer who separated infant Bruce Trevorrow from his family in defiance of state policy against such removals. Trevorrow was awarded $775,000.

The late Professor Colin Tatz AO mentioned by Nick Hasluck spent the early 1960s in the NT doing his PhD thesis (1964) on Fifties era administration of NT Aboriginal policy. This is a crucial contemporary record. Tatz, previously a crusading South African lawyer, was well placed to note any malpractices (let alone genocidal tendencies). Nick read Tatz's thesis in the ANU libary. He found a mere 11 people had accessed the thesis, none from the Bringing Them Home inquiry.

He writes,

Tatz was given entry to every corner of the NT in the early 1960s. Whilst there ... he interviewed some 300 people, officials and others active in Aboriginal welfare. His thesis mentions administrative shortcomings and even suggests that not enough was being done to implement the assimilation policy of the time – that is, a policy to ensure that Aboriginal people had the same entitlements as other Australians. Curiously, as I now confirm by a careful study of his text, there is no mention whatsoever of any problems concerning the 'removal' of part-Aboriginal children from their parents. How is it that Colin Tatz, a human rights campaigner, failed to protest, or even notice, the 'genocide' that was allegedly taking place at the time he was writing his thesis? Probably because, contrary to current [2000-01] propaganda, it wasn't there to be noticed. Perhaps it simply wasn't happening!

Tatz authored *Australia's Unthinkable Genocide* and the question-begging, *Genocide in Australia: By Accident or Design?* (2011).

Hasluck cites a 1959 book, *Medicine Man*, by an NT medico, Dr F. McCann, many years before the "stolen" controversy:

It establishes, contrary to [academic] Robert Manne's contentions, that many 'half-caste' children (a term used in that era) were abandoned by their communities and were 'rescued' by removal to places such as the refuge in Alice Springs, the Bungalow , and the Retta Dixon Home in Darwin.

If Nick Hasluck was concerned in 2000 that the genocide myth was taking root in a "constant note of recrimination and hysteria", he must be in despair today. Every schoolchild is now coached that Australian governments sponsored genocidal "stolen generation" policies. Only last week NSW's $605,000 bureaucrat, Jim "I got fired" Betts, farewelled his Department of Planning, Industry and Environment (DPIE) in these terms:

I hope DPIE continues its journey towards genuine reconciliation with our First Nations people, acknowledging the reality of the genocide inflicted upon them ... DPIE can make a difference by taking its own bold steps on the journey to Truth, Voice and Treaty. Maintain the rage.

Cue applause for Mr Betts. In today's Australia, impeccable historical accounts, judicial findings to High Court level and plain common sense count for zilch in rebutting the genocidal child-stealing myth. #

Risdon Cove: the truth massacred

22 June 2022

There's nothing like a gruesome massacre story to get our woke folk writhing in white guilt, even if the "massacre" is sheer malarkey. The 1804 "massacre" at Risdon Point near Hobart is a case in point.

On Australia Day 26 January 2011, called "Invasion Day" by its detractors, Michael Mansell of the Tasmanian Aboriginal Land Council stood outside Hobart's Parliament House and made a fiery speech.

He said many Australians sorrowed for the 35 killed by Martin Bryant at Port Arthur in 1996. "But not one of those Australians can even remember that a whole tribe of people, men women and children at Risdon Cove, were slaughtered by the cannons of the people, the pioneers, who came to Tasmania." (Audience members cry "Shame! Shame!" at any whites present).

Risdon Cove is 7km north of Hobart. In 1803 Lt John Bowen led a group of 49 there from Sydney to become the first white settlement in Van Diemen's Land. In February 1804 Lt-Col David Collins arrived at Hobart, leaving some troops, settlers and a dozen convicts at Risdon Cove.

Three months later, on 3 May, 200 or so Aboriginals arrived on a kangaroo round-up drive. They seized two dead kangaroos, and harassed a settler who'd built a hut on their tribal ground. The commander Lt Moore sent troops to rescue the settler, with orders to fire only as a last resort, but one trooper shot dead one of the Aborigines. Things worsened and Moore ordered a shot to be fired from one of two 12-pounder ship's cannons to "intimidate".

The presumption is that a blank was fired producing only sparks, flame and smoke, since the cannon was sited 1km from the action and the white community was mid-way in the line of fire. There were no reports of dismembering from canister shot, but the earth-shaking explosion was heard even in Hobart.

The official accounts by Moore and Collins, compiled just after the affray, reported three Aborigines killed, some wounded, and the rescue of an orphaned black two-year-old. Governor King in NSW replied with alarm about the "unfortunate event" with concern for the welfare of the Aboriginal population.

This does not add up to what Mr Mansell calls the slaughtering of an entire tribe by cannon fire. Nor does it add up to what's on the Massacre Map of Newcastle University historian Lyndall Ryan, an expert on Van Diemen's Land. Her map puts the "massacre" at a definite 20 and possibly 30-50.

Why and how the "massacre" accounts? Because on 16 March 1830, 26 years after the event, there was an inquiry in Hobart into deteriorating relations with blacks. An old convict lag Edward White, who claimed to be an eye-witness to the Risdon Cove affray, gave compelling and detailed evidence of a "great many" unarmed natives killed and wounded during a three-hour all-out battle.

Because of his credible recorded testimony, historians thereafter treated the official stories as self-excusing lies. (Actually the inquiry did not even access the official accounts, only a diary of a church minister which included a transcription of a surgeon's brief first-hand account). The inquiry, remarkably, produced its findings within two days of hearing the last witness. With each re-telling of the story based on convict Edward White's account, new colourful and horrific details appeared, turning the "massacre". into the opening shots in Tasmania's shameful "Black War" that climaxed with the late-1830 "Black Line" campaign.

In 2004 Professor Lyndall Ryan re-told "one of the best-known massacres in Australian history." Drawing on Edward White's evidence plus hearsay, she added that at least one barrel of Aboriginal remains, perhaps already dissected by the Risdon surgeon, was sent to Sydney on the ship *Ocean* after the massacre. Her upper death toll of 50 came from a boy James Kelly who was 12 years old at the time and living in Hobart, not Risdon, and not an eye-witness.

Ryan's account has delighted woke museum curators. Those at the Tasmanian Museum & Art Gallery came up with a fanciful "bones in the barrel" exhibit with explanations about the 1804 surgeon "stripping of the flesh off the bones of these two Aboriginal bodies", for study by Sydney and possibly London medicos. The curators have cooked up a realistic-looking sealed barrel addressed to "Colonial Surgeon, Sydney, May 1804", a macabre exhibit currently sending shivers up the spines of schoolkid groups.

A decade earlier, in 1995, Tasmania's Liberal Premier Ray Groom sought to atone for all the white guilt. He handed the 79-hectare Crown site to Aboriginal descendants of the "massacre" represented by Michael Mansell and the Tasmanian Aboriginal Land Council. It's all heritage-listed and I'll detail later what happened to it.

Now for the reality check on the "massacre" attested by convict Edward White. A trio of amateur historians, Scott Seymour, George Brown and Roger Karge, after a decade's research, have proved that the convict White was a con-man who arrived in Van Diemen's Land between 1808 and 1811, considerable years AFTER the 1804 Risdon affray and not an eye-witness by a long shot. Probably seeking government rations and slops (clothing) in his old age, he concocted his massacre gossip.

Scrub out White's account, and our knowledge of the Risdon Cover "massacre" comes back to the two official accounts of three killed, regrettable of course but unplanned in a sadly-typical cultural confusion.

The research by the amateur trio is laid out in a beautifully-presented book *Witness? Truth-Telling at Risdon Cove* ($44.95, Risdon Cove Publishing, April 2022). It describes each step in the complex job of "outing" con-man White via the archives. In addition it provides on its pages facsimiles of the hand-written documents for the reader to cross-check. This professional treatment is a huge embarrassment to the black-armband historians whose work has substituted myths for history.

The amateur trio were inspired simply by a craving to get at the truth. (Their opening illustration is a statue of the female Roman god Veritas, with a caption, "Truth is Mighty"). Their expertise includes state-of-the-art data-base software capable of sifting and analysing vast historical archives in London, Ireland and Australia, nailing the lying convict.

The trio's professional rivals are also no slouches and their own "history" appears well-rooted in documentary evidence for White being on-the-spot.

Apart from Lyndall Ryan, the major player is Tasmanian historian Phillip Tardif. Tardif managed apparently to document how Edward White got to Sydney and then Risdon Cove prior to the "massacre". The only problem was that Tardif focused on the wrong "Edward White" – a common mistake with common names. Tardif won funding from the Tasmanian Historical Research Association for his settlement history in the bicentennial year 2003.

His book *John Bowen's Hobart: the beginning of European settlement in Tasmania*, claims that Edward White did embark from

Cork, Ireland, for Sydney on the ship *Atlas* in 1801. The amateur trio prove however that he never disembarked, having died during the voyage. (The voyage death toll was 63 out of 151 convicts).

Tardif's (deceased) Edward White somehow got from Sydney to Risdon Cove with a reinforcing party before the 1804 "massacre". Tardif's thesis cries out for a document naming "Edward White" among the dozen convicts left at Risdon Cove by Lt-Col Collins. White would thereupon become a potential eyewitness to the May 3 conflict.

In his history, for the first time, Tardif was able to cite despatches from Lt-Col Collins to NSW Governor Philip King naming the convicts at Risdon Cove as "mostly useful Mechanics, Sawyers and Carpenters". On the list, Tardif writes, is "Edward White". Eureka! That's verification of White's eye-witness claims 26 years later.

As historians do, Tardif footnoted his important discovery (p163) for verification:

Port Jackson, Despatches, Original Correspondence, Colonial Office (CO 201/33 pp 240-42) Collins to King, 31 July 1803[sic – read 1804], in HRA Series 111 Vol. 1, p. 254.

Only the first reference ("pp. 240-42") is relevant for Tardif's case. All three pages are in facsimile in *Witness*. The listing of what historian Tardif says are "13" convict names reads "George Clark, John Jackson, Wm Wright, Wm Garratt, Edwd Barnes, Dennis McCarty, John Jones, Joseph Parnell, Richd Wright, Wm Cole, John Harris, Mary Lawler." The amateurs count 12 names, not 13, and there is no "Edward White" listed. They write,

We have tried to contact Phillip Tardif for clarification on this discrepancy but he has not responded. The Australian newspaper has also reportedly sought comment from Tardif, but "Mr Tardif could not be contacted". Failing a forthcoming explanation for this discrepancy, we believe Tardif's book misleads its readers into believing that Edward White's name was on Collins' list, when clearly it was not. Readers are led to believe that documentary evidence exists that places an Edward White at Risdon Cove in 1804, when the sources cited in the book do not support this at all.

Co-author Scott Seymour says he was initially delighted that Tardif had confirmed White was at Risdon Cove in 1804. He went to Tardif's reference to see Lt-Col Collins' own handwriting and had to do a double-check and triple-check: why wasn't White's name there? He became perplexed but not surprised, since there is no record of an Edward White being shipped from Sydney to Risdon Cove in 1803 or 1804.

The three authors then set out to solve the enigma, "Who was the convict Edward White who gave his bogus testimony to the inquiry in 1830, 26 years after the affray?"

For history buffs, their research is better than a detective novel. They are able first to track some of his post-inquiry adventures. He petitioned the authorities, with support from respectable citizens, four times from 1831-35 to get government sustenance. His case was that he was too ill to support himself. His four preambles are shown to be less than truthful, while he harps on how he came forward with important evidence to the inquiry.

Lt-Gov George Arthur, unconvinced, never granted the free rations. The *Witness* authors say an Edward White died of a fever in Hobart on 13 February 1840 and was probably the same man.

They then embark on tracing his origins prior to the 1830 inquiry, while ruling out confusion with various other "Edward

Whites". The records were often themselves faulty, with convicts lying to shorten their terms. These errors are then repeated in standard data bases used by families and scholars to research convict lives. The trio's vital need is to establish on what vessel this Edward White (among another half-dozen similar names), came to Sydney and thence to Hobart.

To sift the evidence they applied their SAT software, crunching data about Spatial (where), Associates (which friends and contacts were involved) and Temporal (timing).

They picked up that he won a 30-acre farmland grant in 1823 which he sold or quit in 1828. This enabled them to track him in court cases back to 1818, and his probable freedom from 1815. This rearward-facing trail then ran cold.

The authors decided to change tack and start their search for White back in 1800, scanning court records and convict ships from Ireland and England for traces. With luck, this search would join up with their 1815 discovery, like tunnellers meeting in the middle of a mountain.

They found 11 potential convict "Whites" and to cut an intricate story short, finally established that their Edward White, also called "Edmund White", was transported at 27 from Tipperary via the ship *Tellicherry* in 1805. His arrival in Botany Bay was recorded in 1806.

To their surprise, they found he'd been sentenced to death in Tipperary, later commuted, for "running away with" a Judith Prendergast. He might have abducted or kidnapped her, or was framed by relatives over an elopement.

In Sydney, court records show him getting 200 lashes for an escape attempt, and absconding again in 1808. This second offence likely had him sentenced down to Hobart, but they couldn't find records of it. They conjecture that those records were in the nine and a half tons of documents deliberately burnt or pulped by the authorities from 1863-70 to save money on storage, a horrendous loss to all historians.

The best the authors can do is to place their Edward White at a Hobart muster in 1811. He was claiming falsely to have been transported from England on the Hercules in 1802 with a seven-year sentence, not on the *Tellicherry* in 1806 as a 'lifer'. The lie would have got him his liberty on or after 1811.

The researchers were amused to find that in their final sifting of three Edward or Edmund Whites, all arriving on different vessels, they turned out to be the one Edward White pulling identity scams.

The authors conclude, "It means that his [1830] testimony should be expunged from the historical record of Tasmania. Whenever the topic of the Risdon Cove affray arises, the words 'convict eye-witness' or the name 'Edward White' should never be seen or heard. His name and testimony should only appear as a footnote in the History Wars, and even then, only when teaching students critical thinking, archival research or the perils of 'presentism'..."

Professor Lyndall Ryan of the "massacre map" and Michael Mansell of the Land Council were indignant when contacted by *The Australian* in February. Ryan was quoted,

> *To claim that Edward White was not a witness to the massacre is ridiculous. None of the 19th century historians query White's testimony. If White was a fake, he would have been exposed long ago. This is the latest in a long line of massacre deniers.*

Mansell insisted the official accounts were a cover-up and White's evidence was credible. Neither provided evidence to rebut the book, "because they couldn't", the authors say. "Why have they devoted decades of scholarship and activism to shoring up White's story and this particular massacre? Is it a case of intellectuals 'liking' genocide?" they ask.

They note that the Risdon "massacre" story has helped trash our global reputation, Ryan writing that it is "part of the national and international literature on the colonial encounter." Her version is also taught to students and is leant on by journalists as remote as *The Wall Street Journal*. Among today's Tasmanians (black and white) some are labelled as assassins and others as victims. The authors claim an increasing number "are wondering whether this whole sorry tale is just one big shakedown."

They conclude, *"Hopefully this book will provide the basis for a reckoning and an end to this divisive madness that has pervaded Tasmania for a generation. It is in every Tasmanian's interest that we wake up and begin the slow but steady path to true reconciliation."*

End-note: I mentioned above the 1995 Liberal government handover of Risdon Cove's 79 hectares to the Aboriginal Land Council. The Tasmanian Government, which acquired the site in the 1950s for a reserve, has always found the Risdon settlement embarrassing because of the 'massacre'. They were only too happy to declare the grounds no longer a historic and tourist site. It had been a popular historical interpretative centre with signage, replica huts, a monument to founder Lt John Bowen and pamphlets for visitors on soldiers and convicts. The interpretative building has now been converted to a small school for Indigenous children.

Soon after the 1995 handover the signage disappeared, one hut burnt down, others were vandalised and levelled, the Bowen monument destroyed, plaques wrenched off with crowbars, relics sent to the tip and archaeological trenches filled and covered. The grounds are now overgrown with grass.

"This is another outcome of con-man White's false evidence in 1830 about a massacre," says co-author Seymour. "We've lost the oldest colonial-history site in Tasmania. It's unique because it's remained in the original state as a farm with no urban-sprawl encroachment. The only road through it is the one marked on the 1804 maps. What a tragedy, based on a convict's lie." #

Comrade pupils, here is today's history lesson

9 June 2022

School education is bathed in a green-Left miasma, and so a new Victorian Year 12 history text is unlikely to create much of a fuss. It's Volume 1 of a four-part lavish and expensive series from Cambridge University Press, *Analysing Australian History – From Custodianship to the Anthropocene* ($49.95). In production and multimedia values it's state of the art. It's also keyed specifically to the Victorian Certificate of Education syllabus.

The five woke authors begin with a racist apology for being "all non-Indigenous Australians, mostly of Anglo-Celtic descent … Each volume has been reviewed by First Nations educators … and checked by many people, including the Victorian Aboriginal Education Association Inc and teacher forums."

Despite being "checked by many people", the textbook is replete with howlers such as how we've been "exporting" brown coal. We don't.

The politically-naive authors refer to *Tribune*, the official newspaper of the Communist Party of Australia, as "the union newspaper The (sic) Tribune". They unwittingly provide a 100-word slab of 1958 Tribune agitprop for kids to study the "struggle around issues of benefit to the people generally". On the same page is an hero pic of Whitlam's far-left minister Tom Uren on the march, "a respected federal Labor politician" – the others presumably being less-respected. (Uren successfully sued the Fairfax and Packer news organisations in 1963 over allegations that he had links to communists which amounted to his being a traitor).

In the Introduction we view a lone forlorn sheep, backside facing us, suffering from the so-called Anthropocene at "Pejar Dam in southern NSW, 2005" near Goulburn. On page 261 a pic of the very same ewe becomes "An exhausted sheep searches for food on a farm near Ivanhoe, New South Wales, 2002." Googling suggests that Mrs Ewe took the three years to trot 730km south-east from Ivanhoe to Goulburn. No wonder she's done in.

The authors are Richard Broome, president of the Royal Historical Society of Victoria and an emeritus professor at La Trobe; Ashley Keith Pratt, vice-president of the History Teachers Association of Victoria; James Grout, a junior and senior history teacher at Geelong; David Harris, teacher and environmental historian; and Geoff Peel, teacher, school department head and examiner.

The book's title itself is a howler. There is no "Anthropocene", as the authors claim. It is only a so-far-unaccepted recommendation by the Anthropocene Working Group (AWG) to the International Union of Geological Sciences (IUGS) to bolster the global warming narrative. This wished-for "Anthropocene" has lasted a mere 70 years. Officially we are in the Holocene era (12,000 years) of the Cenozoic (66 million years). The IUGS has declined to declare any "Anthropocene", preferring to wait maybe 50,000 years until some evidence of it shows up in rock strata.

In the book, kids must elaborate on this misleading brief: *"Evaluate the significance of the scientific community's adoption of Crutzen's idea of the Anthropocene."*

Like those 'brown coal exports', this is just plain wrong.

Now flip to the full page opening picture of Chapter 8: "Environmental movements contest the Anthropocene [sic], 1986-2010." We see a triumphant crowd of Labor Party members in 2007 raging against coal and led by rock star Peter Garrett and flanked on his left – wait for it! – by a beaming Anthony Albanese, aged 44. Our Prime Minister had then the gravitas of Manager of Opposition Business in the House and Shadow Minister for Water and Infrastructure.

As well as three "Australian Labor Party" banners, the pic shows the Labor Party heroes surrounded by placards like "Quit Coal" and "Clean Coal a Dirty Lie". The caption reads, "Marchers led by Federal MP and Labor's environment and climate change spokesman Peter Garrett start the Walk Against Warming in Sydney, 11 November 2007."

Flip past a second heroic pic of Bob Hawke, and conservatives will be affronted by a quarter-page image of the official Greens Party logo. The authors claim the party got up in 1992 because state and federal governments "were overwhelmingly reluctant to enact changes that might jeopardise economic growth for the purposes of conservation". The book makes no reference to the international Green movement's actual origins with Nazi philosophy morphing into the admitted paedophile-tainted German Greens movement, which involved up to 1000 child victims.[7] Kids should get extra marks for independently researching that.

In apparent role as Greens recruiter, the book intones (emphasis added)

> *Over time, the Greens developed socially-conscious policies beyond environmental issues, but maintained its initial strong focus on conservation matters. Its platforms have continually advocated matters such as recycling, water manage-*

---

[7] For the Nazi's environmental credentials, see R. Darvall, *The Age of Global Warming – A History*, Quarter Books, London, 2013. p. 40: "Were it not for its crimes, the Nazi record on the environment would have been praised for being far in advance of its time..."

ment, habitat loss, specie extinction, deforestation and pollu-
tion, but above all, democracy.

Kids will assume conservatives oppose democracy. The book then serves up retiring Greens leader Bob Brown's absurd manifesto to his "earthians":

So far it seems like we are the lone thinkers in this vast expanding universe. (If not, why are they not communicating with us?). They have extincted themselves. They have come and gone. And now it's our turn. Just as we are causing that destruction, we could be fostering its reversal. Indeed nothing will save us from ourselves but ourselves. So democracy – ensuring that everyone is involved in deciding Earth's future – is the key to success.

As a clincher, kids are treated to an adoring pic of five Greens demonstrators in yellow shirts with Greens logos and matching placards, "Clean energy clean air: The Greens". They hold high a globe of the purportedly endangered planet. The caption reads:

Greens activists dressed as surf lifesavers march through the city to condemn Prime Minister John Howard's inaction on climate change ... 7 September 2007.

The book's standard question-boxes require kids to spout knowledge about the Greens formation (but ignore Hitler and Green paedophilia) and its local electoral strength, followed by

What is Bob Brown's basic solution for the world's environmental problems?

Another topic goes:

In Australia profit will always be valued more highly than the health of the population and environment. Discuss.

Fans of even-handed history will be delighted at how kids are now taught about the Cold War. The book gives the West and the Communist states precisely-equivalent treatment, e.g.,

Historians have identified several causes that led to the out-break of the Cold War, including the desire of both the United States and Soviet Union for geopolitical dominance at the end of World War II, the ideological conflict between these superpowers, the emergence and existential threat of nuclear weapons, the fear of communism in the United States and the concomitant fear of capitalism in the Soviet Union.

Quoting historian Timothy White, it continues:

While scholars may have been blinded by loyalty and guilt in examining the evidence regarding the origins of the Cold War in the past, increasingly, scholars with greater access to archival evidence on all sides have come to the conclusion that the con-flicting and unyielding ideological ambitions were the source of the complicated and historic tale that was the Cold War.

In other words, the Communist dictatorships which murdered 100 million of their own people and defenceless "class enemies" are really just the mirror image of the Western law and market-based democracies.

Apparently reluctant to offend Russia's top dog Vlad Putin, the authors say that un-named "leading nations and world rivals" got some atomic bomb secrets by spying. The authors put in favourable references to "peace movements" actually inspired or controlled by Moscow, as documented by KGB defector Vasili Mitrokhin. Talking of peace, the book refers identically not once but three times to what it regards as the historic founding of Greenpeace in 1971. In reality co-founder Patrick Moore quit after 15 years, unable to stomach Greenpeace's irrational and destructive policies.

The book even directs kids to the ridiculous Doomsday Clock cooked up by leftist scientists. To elaborate, those idiots in 2018 set their clock to "two minutes to midnight" or comparable with the H-bomb stand-off of 1953, because of President Trump and climate change. Nothing more relieves hormonal teens' angst these days than a Doomsday Clock. The book demands of them, "At what time has the Doomsday Clock been set at most recently? Why has it been set at this time?" I can answer that: it is set (pre-Ukraine war) at 100 seconds to midnight, "the closest it has ever been to civilization-ending apocalypse", but with sponsors' hope that President Biden will be our planetary saviour. Our kids, by the way, are also offered a diet of "the 14 most frightening films about nuclear destruction" such as the corny Melbourne-based *On The Beach* of 1959.

The book devotes multiple references to avowed Communist Jack Mundey of Green Bans fame. He gets almost as much messiah treatment as the Green's Bob Brown. Kids are told to debate the topic, "Jack Mundey was an environmental hero."

Needless to say, the uranium and nuclear industry get a bad rap, starting with kids being fed a Moscow-friendly conspiracy theory:

In August 1945, the United States used nuclear weapons on two civilian targets in Japan – the cities of Hiroshima and Nagasaki. The action was ordered by President Truman, ostensibly to hasten the end of the war in the Pacific. However intense controversy remains about the underlying motives of the United States, with many people arguing, both then and now, that it was unnecessary at that point to defeat Japan and, in fact, the bombing was primarily carried out in order to intimidate the Soviet Union.

There was nothing "ostensible" about the 82-day casualty toll on Okinawa shortly before (ignored by the authors) which let the Americans know what to expect on the home islands: 100,000 civilians or a quarter of the Okinawa population killed or dead by suicide, 45,000 American troops killed or wounded and 100,000 Japanese troops killed. It was this high toll that persuaded President Truman to use atomic weapons, rather than send an invasion force into Japan.

On the home front, the history authors are respectful of would-be Aborigine and Melbourne University Professor Bruce Pascoe's *Dark Emu* nonsense about the thriving agriculture of town-dwelling pre-contact Aborigines. He gets half a dozen references. For the susceptible kids, the authors rank *Dark Emu* (2014) with Geoffrey Blainey's 1975 *Triumph of the Nomads*, although, in what looks like a desperate last-minute addition, the Cambridge authors say,

> ... *anthropologist Peter Sutton and archaeologist Keryn Walshe in their book* Farmers or Hunter-Gatherers? The Dark Emu Debate *(2021), argue that Pascoe has exaggerated his case for Aboriginal farming and used evidence loosely. But clearly in some areas, Aboriginal food production was intensified.*

Pascoe's map of a purported original Aboriginal "grain belt", covering half of the continent and dwarfing modern wheat cropping, is reproduced across almost the full page. The original map-drawer Norman Tindale was talking about grain collecting/harvesting, but the Cambridge authors twice refer to it as "production". I find it odd, especially in a class textbook, to conflate Aboriginal gathering of sparse native seeds with modern wheat productivity.

A litmus test in textbooks is whether such authors hit kids with Murdoch Derangement Syndrome. This history doesn't disappoint. It quotes activist journalist Maria Taylor, author of *Global Warming and Climate Change: what Australia knew and buried*, which she helpfully assures visitors to her website is "suitable for secondary, tertiary studies and research and as a case study in environment environmental education, environmental policy, science and society studies, political science, policy and political economy, contemporary Australian and western history, climate change studies, media and communication ..." On the climate wars, the Cambridge authors quote her thus:

> *Great influence was also exerted by News Limited, with a virtual monopoly in Australian print media circulation. The Murdoch media shared the notion that accepting climate science is unwarranted and a threat to business and has spent the last 20 years conducting a 'culture war' on this issue. Through politics and media these reasserted beliefs and values had **taken over the whole society** [what!!!] by the early 2000s and have returned in force in 2014.* (My emphasis. I assume she refers to Tony Abbott's election).

I googled Dr Maria Taylor, wondering how any Canberra-zone journalist could think *The Age, Sydney Morning Herald, Financial Review, Canberra Times* and *The West Australian* are part of a Murdoch hegemony. Dr Taylor publishes a monthly semi-rural community newspaper focused on sustainable lifestyles, does some part-time lecturing on journalism to ANU undergraduates and in 2007 wrote a score of articles for the *Bungendore Bulletin*.[8]

---

[8] Dr Taylor's ANU profile cites an ANU Press book she wrote on global warming which includes this quote: "... *one of the most unnerving scientific pronouncements ever made: Humanity is conducting an enormous, unintended, globally pervasive experiment whose ultimate consequences could be second only to a global nuclear war*".

Australia's mining and petroleum producers ought to riot about use of this text in class. The authors dismiss the global impact of the 1960s mineral boom in the style of the ex-ABC's Emma Alberici:

The Fitzgerald Report [1974, for the Whitlam government] revealed who benefited from this boom. The Report showed the mining industry paid $263 million in royalties to the government from 1966–67 to 1972–73, but five times that amount went overseas in profits to parent companies. The same thing occurred during Australia's most recent mining boom in the early twenty-first century. Government fuel subsidies, equipment tax deductions and other benefits led to high profits from mining, amidst record high metal commodity prices ...

Through gritted teeth the authors acknowledge that "Mining is important to human development and livelihood" but laud every anti-mining success that activists can cook up:

Mining is also destructive of the environment and the Aboriginal peoples' custodianship of the land. Iron ore, bauxite and some coal mining is done by open-cut mining. The existing vegetation and topsoil are bulldozed aside, the fauna is destroyed or retreats, and large excavations are made to expose the minerals, often resulting in water and dust pollution. The holes and trenches expand as mineral extraction increases ...

Flip a few pages and kids get a section in praise of extreme Left-dopey arts and culture, like "George Turner's 1987 dystopian work *The Sea and Summer* depicting a Melbourne of the future drowning under rising seas of climate change." No wonder kids suffer education-inflicted pessimism and mental health issues extending even to suicides. The book offers this alleged "poem" of Ms Oodgeroo Noonuccal, aka Kath Walker:

The miner rapes
The heart of the Earth
With his violent spade
Stealing, bottling her black blood
For the sake of greedy trade.

There follows John Williamson's 1989 *Rip Rip Woodchip* song and its chorus,

Nightmare Dreaming, can't you hear the screaming?
Chainsore, eyesore – more decay.

The book's question box includes

Identify specific ways in which the [woodchip] lyrics suggest that the environment is being destroyed

Why do you think the song resonated with society?

In a gesture to impartiality, the authors do give brief air-time to conservatives Hugh Morgan (ex-WMC) and Keith Windschuttle (*Quadrant* editor-in-chief), and more so to Geoffrey Blainey. I couldn't avoid the entirely subjective suspicion the authors selected weak quotes to enable kids to knock the conservatives down. For example, Morgan is cited arguing that "2000 years of Christian tradition supported the rights of companies to mine". His cited views in the book include the correct point that Aboriginal culture "demanded vengeance killings and in the past had involved cannibalism" which I assume is inserted to set him up for kids as a nasty hateful rich person. Question: "What might have contributed to Morgan's views on Aboriginal peoples and Christianity?"

The authors in their onslaught against the invading colonialists don't mention the prevalent "coming in" of Aboriginal families to missions and stations for easily-accessible rations. They do provide kids with a positive quote that

> *The rate of economic progress in Australia between 1820 and 1850 far exceeded that of any other British Colony, and approached that of Britain herself.*

But they match it with an opposite:

> *The squatters and their flocks drove away the game, and the sheep ate the plants and killed the roots upon which the Aborigines lived. But the transformation did not stop there. The grazing of sheep first opens then kills forests, first converts grassland to wealth then reduces them to indigence [poverty] … biological impoverishment now began in Australia.*

Emotionally exhausted, I have yet to tackle Volumes 2-4 of this curious history series. But at least it puts its cards on the table. #

Blacks, gays, feminists, a-sexuals – all classroom history fodder

8 July 2022

The lugubrious tone of history teaching in Victoria is shown in a second volume of the new four-part Cambridge University Press series *Analysing Australian History – Power and Resistance, 1788-1998* ($49.95).

The book for the Victorian Certificate of Education course is by Ashley Keith Pratt, series editor and "passionate history educator"; Bill Lewis (history and geography teacher); James Jacobs (history); and Angie Pollock (history and English). Richard Broome, president of the Royal Historical Society (Vic), is also a series editor. They apologise that they are "mostly of Anglo-Celtic descents".

The cover shows a naïve 2015 painting of the Port Phillip colonists in 1842 hanging two Aboriginals who speared two white whalers. It's by Indigenous artist Aunty Marlene Gilson, a descendant of a "King Billy" and a "Queen Mary" around Ballarat. It's repeated in soft format inside, and then with a miniature of it overleaf. There's a close-up of the hanged men on page xiv, and we get the full version again on page 24 with kids to answer a battery of questions. There's pics of whites massacring Aboriginals on pages 11, 21, 22, 27 and 30 and a memorial on page 35.

By the opening page of Chapter 1 ("Timeline") we get "1842: Kilroy poisonings", repeated a few pages later. The place in Queensland was Kilcoy, not Kilroy, which doesn't inspire confidence in the authors' thoroughness. A further minute's checking and one finds the poisonings are factually contentious, e.g. from an historian's UQ honours thesis on it (1980): "The Kilcoy Massacre has been widely accepted as a fact; it is often overlooked that no convincing proof of its occurrence has ever been produced." Maybe evidence has turned up post-1980 (or maybe not). By 1847 the "Timeline" notes "Whiteside poisonings", also in Queensland, which also involves factually contentious material.

Kids are stuffed with dire versions of slaughters (30,000) claimed by historian Henry Reynolds. They're directed to the University of Newcastle's contentious and half-baked "massacre map" and told to use it to check out the nearest massacre site to where they live. The number of massacre victims blows out from estimates like 20,000 Australia-wide two decades ago, to recent "careful estimates by historians" of 60,000 – and that's just for Queensland!

The other main groups assigned to noble victimhood and resistance in what the book editors call *"these magnificent textbooks"* are women and gays. For want of anything more exciting, authors Bill Lewis and Angie Pollock go to town about the two "barroom suffragettes" of 1965:

> *Areas of the public sphere closed to women included the public bar of pubs and hotels, which sparked one of the **most iconic protests for women's equality** – the 'barroom suffragettes' Merle Thornton and Rosalie Bogner who chained themselves to the public bar of Brisbane's Regatta Hotel in 1965.* (My emphasis)

Ms Thornton in 2020 recalled,

> *After another half an hour or so we left for home, glassy-eyed with exhilaration, to see it replayed on the evening news. It's a wonder that any of us got any sleep at all that night … It was audacious of course, but our protest triggered a tsunami of responses that no one could have predicted … [i.e. press ar-*

ticles in UK, Russia and 'around the world']. The Regatta Bar *demonstration was recognised as a* **leading activist moment in second-wave feminism.** *I couldn't have been happier or more energised by what might now be possible.*

Questions from the text:

Explain what Rosalie Bogner and Merle Thornton were protesting against

Describe the atmosphere in the Regatta Hotel. [Photo includes indifferent male drinkers].

Explain how Australians reacted to the protest.

Why do you think people around the world would be interested in this protest? [From Alaska to Togo, I assume].

Four years later a union activist, smartly-tailored Zelda d'Aprano, chained herself to the doors of the Arbitration Commission in Melbourne, "over the injustice done to women in terms of equal pay, 1969", we learn. In the opening Timeline we get the 1968 assassination of Martin Luther King on "World events" matched locally with Zelda's clanky protest a year later. (Another amusing Timeline "World events" extract goes, *1991: Soviet Union dissolves, ending the Cold War. 1991: Susan Faludi publishes Backlash; Anita Hill's testimony and Riot Grrrl punk movement spark Third Wave Feminism).*

Feminist politics takes centre stage, albeit "split by different goals and thinking". Political scientist Verity Burgman tells kids about *"liberal feminism, radical feminism and socialist feminism ... liberal feminism strove for reform, working within the system ... Radical feminists held that the source of all oppression was the structures of patriarchal society. Socialist feminists held that the capitalist system was the root of female oppression."*

The identity grievances never let up, e.g. "The Constitution was made by white men and mostly voted in by white men." We even discover that in the early 1990s, "racism was ascendant" in Australia.

The source selections leave me uneasy, e.g. "As Australia was a man's country according to popular wisdom, so the 1950s seemed to be a man's decade. The long tradition of male solidarity in Australia was reinforced by **men's experience as soldiers and prisoners of war** and the postwar introduction of national service for eighteen-year-olds. Women's difference – their distinctive claims and interests as women – **had been eclipsed** by their positioning in the family." (My emphases. Quote from Lake et al).

Does the throwaway phrase about "prisoners of war" refer to Changi and the Burma-Thai railway? Is that experience of our captured men of the 8th Division somehow the counterpoint to eclipsing of feminist egos? And am I reading too much into this?

In similar vein, I noticed in the Endnotes that the above-cited feminist historian Marilyn Lake co-edited in 1995: *Female desires: The meaning of World War Two.*

Capitalism of course gets a bad rap, despite having taken humanity out of nasty, brutish and short lives. Port Phillip pioneer John Batman and his crew are introduced as "capitalists" , with a helpful annotation, "Someone engaged in business activities with the primary purpose of making money". I guess the pizza shop around my corner is also run by capitalists, who are depicted in the book's old cartoons as menacing fatties in top hats, and even worse, as a horned and fanged devil grinding down a hungry working-class wage slave.

At this point I'll interrupt my narrative to describe how kids are reacting to this merciless conditioning. VCE Australian History enrolments are plummeting, down from 1245 students in 2014 to just 632 in 2019, or a tiny 1.27% of VCE students. Barely 50 schools offer it. There was a slight rise to 710 in 2020. This new set of four VCE history texts, believe it or not, is supposed to woo kids back into the history corral. As *The Age* puts it:

> *The new version of Australian history will replace the current study design … with four deep dives into distinct themes, including Aboriginal land management, race and immigration, landmark environmental fights such as the Franklin Dam campaign and struggles for women's equality. Topics including the fight for LGBTQ+ rights and the frontier wars between First Australians and colonialists will also be given more exposure.*

Now let's get back to our text. Discussing post-war anti-colonialism, authors are cited such as "the Palestinian Edward Said" who "critiqued the underlying ideologies and racial inequalities of colonialism".

Research-minded kids can look him up, to find him endorsing "that Israel's mistreatment of the Palestinians is rooted in a Judaic requirement for Jews to commit crimes, including murder, against Gentiles". He also "praised the historian Shahak for describing contemporary Israel as a nation subsumed in a 'Judeo–Nazi' cultural ambiance that allowed the dehumanization of the Palestinian Other."

As for gays, the book's authors relentlessly group them as "LGBTIQA+", as in "What struggles were faced by the LGBTIQA+ community in this period?" Fair enough, I thought, let's be inclusive of Intersex and whoever those "Q" folk are. The book educates,

The nineties also saw a move towards more diverse un-derstanding of sexuality identity, with the use of the term 'queer' encapsulating a desire to not be placed in a binary gay/straight dichotomy. Dennis Altman observed that 'queer' quickly took on a variety of uses, united by the desire to es-cape specific identities while retaining a sense of opposition to the dominant sexual and gender order.

But then I wondered, "What the heck does the 'A' in LGBTQIA+ stand for?" Dr Google advises, "A is for a-sexual, a-gender, a-ro-mantic." The history fails to cover the liberation struggle of a-sex-ual, a-gender and a-romantic folk against the colonial patriarchy. I trust the omission will be rectified in a second edition.

Meanwhile the kids' history authors are open to yet more ini-tials being added to LGBTIQA+:

*Indeed, while [the] current term for those who have identities different to heterosexual individuals is LGBTIQA+, **and may continue to evolve over time**, in the period we are discussing the words homosexuals, gays or lesbians were used.*

A story on the Michael Smith blog – possibly apocryphal – has a Grade 6 boy who posed this question in our class meeting today: "Why do the Anzacs only get one minute a year but the LGBT get a whole month?"

The book refers mysteriously to some connection of homosexu-al men with the Cold War, namely that gay-ness was "seen as both a perversion of 'godless' communist influence and a potential threat to national security." Kim Philby's Cambridge spy ring did im-mense damage (not "potential" damage) to Western interests and was strongly homosexual. Western officials who were homosexual in the "illegal" era were subject to KGB blackmailers.

After failing to impart this key information, and calling the 1950s "the darkest decade of the twentieth-century for Australian lesbians and homosexual men," the text authors harangue kids, "Why do you think ASIO attempted to stop employment of homosexuals in public service positions?" (Incidentally, lesbian practices were never illegal here so I don't know why lesbians suffered that 'darkest decade' – lesbian partners could keep their public service careers while married heterosexual women were terminated).

The textbook sums up:

> *However, the resistance against power and authority is never complete. Women, First Nations peoples and people of diverse gender continue to struggle to gain full equality in Australian society, as do all people of colour, refugees [do they mean 'asylum seekers'] and those with diverse abilities.*

The authors mention without comment the dominance of female university students, 58% females vs 42% for males in 2016, and my updating shows no change by 2020.

On a page headed "Continuities", we discover, "Power continues to be predominantly in the hands of heterosexual people." A bad thing, obviously.

Re this following loaded question, kids seeking high marks should avoid answering 'Yes': *"Could Australia claim to have ever been an egalitarian society between 1788 and 1998?"*

Returning to the book's teaching about so-called "First Nations", the authors cite the curious research of would-be First Nation stalwart and Melbourne University Professor Bruce Pascoe, whose shtick includes explaining the kumbaya peace-loving ways of pre-contact tribes:

> *Indigenous traditional ideas of conflict were based on the no-*

tion of feud, not war, by which only those who had wronged you specifically were attacked, not the whole group. This approach to fighting led to a controlled conflict, which kept the numbers killed at a lower level than in an all-out war. The writer Bruce Pascoe explains:

Aboriginal populations were relatively low ... probably 1.5 million for the whole country [what a high figure! TT]. Traditional warfare developed in accordance with this limitation and the death of one warrior was treated symbolically as defeat or the point from which the conflict was resolved through diplomacy. Strategies of war which countenanced large numbers of war dead could not be sustained.

First, the essence of Aboriginal pay-back systems and witchcraft was that any third party – man, woman or child – could serve for retribution. Second, from William Buckley's account in the south to others of northern regions, black-on-black massacres could be as horrific as whites'. In "Journey to Horseshoe Bend", anthropologist T.G.H. Strehlow described a black-on-black massacre in 1875 in the Finke River area of Central Australia, triggered by a perceived sacrilege:

The warriors turned their murderous attention to the women and older children and either clubbed or speared them to death. Finally, according to the grim custom of warriors and avengers they broke the limbs of the infants, leaving them to die 'natural deaths'. The final number of the dead could well have reached the high figure of 80 to 100 men, women and children.

The Murngin (now Yolngu) in NE Arnhem Land during 1920s practiced a deadly warfare that placed it among the world's most lethal societies.

Incidentally, the book says of the 1816 Appin massacre in NSW, "some Europeans were killed in [lead-up] conflicts", followed by the massacre of 14 or so Aborigines. The vague words "some Europeans" actually refers to about 17 killed in the previous two years, including mothers and children, along with an unknown number of Aborigines. I wonder whether the phrase "some Europeans" instead of "17 Europeans" was demanded by the Aboriginal reviewers with veto powers over the text?

Kids are even cross-examined to make sure they absorb Pascoe's peculiar views:

1. How does Pascoe describe the nature of war before European arrival?

2. How does Pascoe describe the British view of First Australian's attitude to war?

In a rare glimmer of common sense, the authors don't describe Pascoe as a paid-up First Nations member. But they fawn over activist/poet Bobbi Sykes as "Indigenous":

Indigenous commentators such as poets Roberta Sykes and Oodgeroo Noonuccal ... all argued for Indigenous sovereignty, land rights, and greater respect for First Nations cultures by mainstream Australia.

Hey historians! Check wiki as first port of call:

Sykes was raised by her mother and purportedly never knew her father. Sykes says in her autobiography that his identity is unknown, and her mother told her a number of different accounts about her father; variously that he was Fijian, Papuan, African-American, and Native American. However, her mother has revealed that he was an African-American sol-

dier, Master Sergeant Robert Barkley. Although she fought hard for Australian Aboriginal rights, she herself was not of Australian Aboriginal descent. She was sometimes criticised for not correcting the record when others assumed she was Aboriginal.

This Sykes error is small beer compared with the authors' claim that "First Nations peoples have managed to maintain traditions in the face of violence and upheaval across the entire continent." As historian and *Quadrant* editor-in-chief Keith Windschuttle points out, the last traces of "High Culture" were dying out in the centre and north by the 1950s, and elsewhere long before.

Windschuttle also dismisses the new history series' main claim that British "invasion" stamped out traditional Aboriginal society, i.e., that the invasion "created massive traumas, wrongs and human suffering that Australia is still addressing to this day." He says:

We did not take the Aborigines' land and their law. The great majority of them gave up their previous culture and beliefs willingly. They "came in" to the new white society and its economy.

Venerated anthropologist W.E.H. (Bill)] Stanner wrote: "The blacks have grasped eagerly at any possibility of a regular and dependable food supply for a lesser effort than is involved in nomadic hunting and foraging. There is a sound calculus of cost and gain in preferring a belly regularly if only partly filled for an output of work which can be steadily scaled down. Hence the two most common characteristics of aboriginal adaptation to settlement by Europeans; a persistent and positive effort to make themselves dependent, and a squeeze-play to obtain a constant or increasing supply of food for a dwindling physical effort. I appreciated the good sense of the adaptation only after I had gone hungry from fruitless hunt-

ing with a rifle, gun, and spears in one of the best environments in Australia".

The book scores an own goal on the so-called "Stolen Generation". It sets out the five main demands of the Aboriginal "tent embassy" in Canberra in the early 1970s. None of the demands refer to any stealing of Aboriginals' children. If it really involved 50-100,000 stolen kids, the "embassy" members would surely have protested? Similarly, the 1970 ten-point "policy manifesto" of the National Tribal Council and the 10-point demands in 1970 of the Black Panthers of Australia make no reference to any "stolen" children. Smart kids should ask their teacher to explain this anomaly.

As retired WA Supreme Court judge, Nick Hasluck, has written (*Book and Bench*, Arcadia 2021) in criticism of Sir Ronald Wilson's *Bringing Them Home* farrago (1997), Wilson was

> *tarnishing the names and reputations of many people of an earlier generation – the patrol officers, the nurses, the teachers, the missionaries, the administrators – who laboured in good faith with limited resources to confer benefits on those who might otherwise, at that time, have been left without a future. I cannot see that defamations of this kind are a necessary or desirable part of 'reconciliation' ... it is a tragedy that as a consequence of [the Bringing Them Home report] so many Australians of goodwill now feel that this is a subject that is 'out of bounds' and can no longer be discussed.*

Paul Hasluck, former Minister for Territories in the NT from 1951-63, wrote to the *Sydney Morning Herald* on 11 March 1999, that

> *an earnest effort was made to change Australian neglect and indifference towards Aborigines, to improve their conditions and raise their hopes for the future. We strove for full recog-*

nition of their entitlements – legally as citizens, socially as fellow Australians.

This history book under review has no use or time for such rebuttals.

The book deals gingerly with the dismissal of Whitlam. The Rex Connor/Jim Cairns multi-billion "Loans affairs" get not one mention, with gallant Whitlam ostensibly grappling with "the end of the long post-war boom and an economy facing the pressures of higher unemployment, stagnant growth and inflation". Well, if you budget for a 46% growth in government spending in a single year 1974-75, don't expect stability. It was only conservatives, the book believes, who saw the Whitlam era as "chaotic, wasteful and too left-wing".

Whitlam's "legacy reverberated for decades" – in a good way, they mean. He allegedly (according to Communist-friendly historian Stuart Macintyre) was *"the last national leader to follow his convictions regardless of consequence, he rose and fell as the possibilities for a confident and expansive national government ended."* Whatever that means.

An academic, Geoffrey Robinson of Deakin, blames Whitlam's misfortunes on the "shrinking capitalist economy" which actually increased in GDP by 3.9%, 2.6%, 4.1% and 1.35% from 1972-75. The punchline to Robinson's article in *The Conversation* (not quoted in the book) reads, "We could argue that the 1975 version of Whitlamism remains a winning formula."

Kids must then answer: "To what extent did the dismissal of the Whitlam government impact on the liberation movements?" Which liberation movements? They don't say. Maybe Pol Pot's.

Volumes 3 and 4 of this series yet await me. I might crowd-fund for my mental-health counselling.#

The sadly ubiquitous Karl Marx

14 January 2022

The Left fights the culture wars in various ways. They fight hot wars by censoring, cancelling and firing opponents. They fight cold wars by monopolising the information-space, such as newspapers and the ABC excluding questioning of climate alarmism. But the 'progressives' most insidious and successful campaigns put the emphasis on "culture" so that kids and citizens absorb the desired world-view without even noticing.

I have an unlikely case in point. My wife and I enjoy watching Welsh orange-haired Professor Alice Roberts on SBS prancing about compering her TV series *Britain's Most Historic Towns*. We get bits of history and a lot of entertainment – she's still looking yummy at age 48.

Professor Roberts doesn't appear to have a political bone in her body but, actually, she's active on several fronts. She's the atheist president of the charity Humanists UK, which campaigns for state secularism and for "a tolerant world where rational thinking and kindness prevail". She campaigns against state-funded religious schools, although she did enrol her two daughters in a classy Church of England school.

Her *Historic Towns* pieces are made for UK's Channel 4, a hybrid State/commercial TV outfit. Its remit is to be innovative, educational and catering for Britain's diverse community, including the religious. However its initial Easter show called *Jesus: the Evidence* suggested the Gospels were unreliable and Jesus was into witchcraft, if he had existed at all which the program doubted.

As an Alternative Christmas address in 2008, Channel 4

handed its pulpit to Iranian President and Jew-hater Mahmoud Ahmadinejad, who spoke on how Christ would have censured the evil United States. Channel 4 followed up with a "Masturbate-a-thon", called Wank Week, involving a mass masturbation event (cancelled after protests) to raise funds for Marie Stopes International's sexual health work.

So if you're getting my drift, Professor Alice and Channel 4 aren't in the Maggie Thatcher mould. All the same, Alice's Historic Towns seem an unlikely vehicle for Left brainwashing — until you dial up Series Three, Episode 7: *Manchester and the Industrial Revolution*. It was in the Reading Room of the 15th century Chetham Library in Manchester that Karl Marx in 1848 cooked up much of his *Communist Manifesto*. Alice is told by a local Marx-adoring historian, Jonathan Scofield, that the Marx-Engels liaison "seems the closest, most important friendship in world history". Alice gives Jonathan a feminine gasp: "Ohhh!"

She visits the library like a pilgrim: *"I am heading for the desk where Marx and Engels actually sat and collaborated … He (Marx) sits at this desk and chats and gets books out."*

The librarian lets her touch the first edition. Alice rhapsodises, *"Look at this, this is a copy of the original Manifesto! I'll skip to the end, it doesn't take long, 50 pages in total:*

'Let the ruling classes tremble at a Communistic revolution. The proletarians have nothing to lose but their chains. They have a world to win. Working men of all countries unite!' "

She pauses to let this inspirational message sink in, and says, *"Isn't it amazing, such a small book, such HUGE impact on the 20th Century. This call to arms would become arguably the single most influential publication of all time. Its theories underpin the*

Russian Revolution of 1917 and creation of the Soviet Union." (A good thing in Professor Roberts' opinion, apparently). That's it: she has no inkling that Manchester-originating Communism was not a boon to the 20th Century.

She's so impressed with Marx and Engels that her show runs grabs from the *Communist Manifesto* at the front as a highlight and teaser. Her overall thesis is about Manchester being a *"workshop of radical ideas that changed the world".*

TV-wise, she lumps Marx and Engels in the middle of heroes from the Peterloo martyrs of 1819 to the Corn Law and Parliamentary reformers, the activists against working-class squalor, the Manchester anti-slavery movement praised by Abraham Lincoln and freed slave Frederick Douglass, Dickens, Disraeli, Benjamin Franklin, reformist author Elizabeth Gaskell and finally the women's liberator Emmeline Pankhurst.

Alice's woke credentials are cemented by interviewing "Caroline", who is no relation to the original Pankhurst but changed her name to Caroline Pankhurst. This re-named virago, who is every man's nightmare of a feminist, says *"Pankhurst would be horrified to see how social media has added another way of silencing and oppressing women."* Huh? If you say so, dear.

Alice poses against a mural of two black men and one black women, all wearing Adidas gear, with a label, *Hated, Adored, Never Ignored.* "It is great to see that tradition of protest thriving in this century," she says, although I think it's actually an Adidas ad. Alice ends her show by laying a wreath at a statue of Ms Pankhurst, saying, "I can't think of a more fit way to end my time in Manchester than to pay tribute to Emmeline Pankhurst and all the Manchester radicals – those brave men and women who call out inequality and injustice wherever they saw it, who fought for the greater good, for what was right. And their work goes on."

In the case of Marx, his work does go on in China, North Korea, Venezuela, Cuba …

If you find Professor Alice a bit odd, keep in mind that the mainstream leader of the British Labor Party from 2015-20 was Marxist/socialist Jeremy Corbyn. You can currently find Marxists galore teaching kids in our universities.

Presidents Bill Clinton and George W. Bush created a memorial to the "Victims of Communism" in Washington DC. Its pedestal reads, *"To the more than one hundred million victims of communism and to those who love liberty."* You can argue all day about whether Marx's disciples slaughtered 60 million, 80 million or as the memorial claims, 100-plus million. The means include murder, war, politically-engineered famines such as the Ukrainian Holomodor (about four million died of hunger), and being worked to death in gulags.

Brooding about the program, I decided to read (for the first time) Marx's *Communist Manifesto* and its drafts and 1848 sequels. Professor Alice clearly hasn't. She has a husband and two girls: Marx proposed abolition of the family, and kids being handed over to State educators for indoctrination from when they first lisp and toddle:

> *But, you say, we destroy the most hallowed of relations, when we replace home education by social. The bourgeois clap-trap about the family and education, about the hallowed co-relation of parents and child, becomes all the more disgusting, the more, by the action of Modern Industry, all the family ties among the proletarians are torn asunder, and their children*

transformed into simple articles of commerce and instruments of labour ... Our bourgeois, not content with having wives and daughters of their proletarians at their disposal, not to speak of common prostitutes, take the greatest pleasure in seducing each other's wives.

Under Communist State aegis, Professor Alice would be lumped into Marx's "community of women" pool:

Bourgeois marriage is, in reality, a system of wives in common and thus, at the most, what the Communists might possibly be reproached with is that they desire to introduce, in substitution for a hypocritically concealed, an openly legalised community of women.

It's worth the mentioning, I suppose, that Marx's *Manifesto* urges the abolition of private property. Professor Alice, as one of Britain's most adored scientists (so far showered with five honorary doctorates), would have a lot of material goods to lose. Marx:

(T)he theory of the Communists may be summed up in the single sentence: Abolition of private property ... In one word, you reproach us with intending to do away with your property. Precisely so; that is just what we intend.

Much of Marx's *Manifesto* involves snarling against other more moderate reform groups. Professor Alice can thank her idol for terms such as "the idiocy of rural life" and "Lumpenproletariat" viz:

The social scum, that passively rotting mass thrown off by the lowest layers of the old society, may, here and there, be swept into the movement by a proletarian revolution; its conditions of life, however, prepare it far more for the part of a bribed tool of reactionary intrigue.

I hadn't realised that Mao's Great Leap Forward was foreshadowed by Karl Marx. In his paradise to come, *"existing improvements and scientific procedures will be put into practice, with a resulting leap forward which will assure to society all the products it needs"*. Mao's Great Leap Forward (1958 to 1962) killed 45 million, or nearly twice the current population of Australia.

Marx like two other monsters, Stalin and Pol Pot, wanted his nirvana to be fuelled by "an entirely different kind of human material." Meanwhile this crazed scribbler Marx imagined that

> *the difference between city and country is destined to disappear. The management of agriculture and industry by the same people rather than by two different classes of people is, if only for purely material reasons, a necessary condition of communist association.*

Marx dreamed that under his Communism, someone would organise

> *construction, on public lands, of great palaces as communal dwellings for associated groups of citizens engaged in both industry and agriculture and combining in their way of life the advantages of urban and rural conditions while avoiding the one-sidedness and drawbacks of each.*

The palaces would house his "industrial armies, especially for agriculture." Sure, Karl, that makes sense!

As an atheist, Professor Alice would be untroubled by Marx's replacement of all religions with Communist catechisms.

Question 22. Do Communists reject existing religions?

Answer: All religions so far have been the expression of historical stages of development of individual peoples or groups of peoples. But communism is the stage of historical development which makes all existing religions superfluous and brings about their disappearance.

While Marx was penning the *Manifesto* he was also formulating "Demands of the Communist Party in Germany". Law firms, like Labor friendly Maurice Blackburn, will be disturbed to learn Marx's demands included, "Legal services shall be free of charge." Victoria's Marx-friendly bureaucrats will be equally dismayed, as Marx decreed

all civil servants shall receive the same salary, the only exception being that civil servants who have a family to support and who therefore have greater requirements, shall receive a higher salary.

An unintended consequence could have been a spate of babies among Victoria's half-million public servants.

I'll close with a couple of paragraphs from Solzhenitsyn's *Gulag Archipelago*, to suggest where Marx's ideology led. Solzhenitsyn mentions a peasant during one of Stalin's famines:

Because he had six mouths to feed he devoted himself wholeheartedly to collective farm work, and kept hoping he would get some return for his labor. And he did – they awarded him a decoration. They awarded it at a special assembly, made speeches. In his reply, the peasant got carried away. He said, "Now if I could just have a sack of flour instead of this decoration! Couldn't I somehow?" A wolflike laugh rocketed through the hall, and the newly decorated hero went off to exile, together with all six of those dependent mouths.

There are plenty of documented horrors of Communism in the

three volumes' 1000 pages, but here Solzhenitsyn writes of a specu-
lative one:

> *There was a rumour going the rounds between 1918 and
> 1920 that the Petrograd Cheka, headed by Uritsky, and the
> Odessa Cheka, headed by Deich, did not shoot all those con-
> demned to death but fed some of them alive to the animals in
> the city zoos. I do not know whether this is truth or calumny,
> or, if there were any such cases, how many were there. But I
> wouldn't set out to look for proof, either. Following the prac-
> tice of the bluecaps [secret police], I would propose that they
> prove to us that this was impossible. How else could they get
> food for the zoos in those famine years? Take it away from
> the working class? Those enemies were going to die anyway,
> so why couldn't their deaths support the zoo economy of the
> Republic and thereby assist our march into the future? Wasn't
> it expedient?*
>
> *That is the precise line the Shakespearean evildoer could not
> cross. But the evildoer with ideology does cross it, and his eyes
> remain dry and clear.*

I suppose one can cut Professor Alice some slack. She was only
16 when the Berlin Wall came down and like almost everyone else
in the West under the age of 50, has no idea what Communism was
about. Her qualifications are in medicine, biology and anatomy, I
suppose she's doing history travelogues because she's photogenic.
But I'd prefer she sticks to anatomy.

Disclosure: Tony Thomas was a member of the Communist
Party of Australia (Willagee, WA branch) between 1960 and 1962
from the ages 20 to 22. #

The write stuff

9 May 2021

Invited to a War is Air Vice-Marshal Alan Reed's memoirs of a 37-year RAAF career, spanning what he calls "a fortunate life".[9] The war was Vietnam and the "invitation" was from the US government.

Reed retired in 1990 and died in 2021 at 87. In 1967 he was on exchange to train USAF pilots in Phantom fighter-bomber reconnaissance roles. He felt inadequate without Vietnam experience but the Pentagon couldn't order a foreign national to go to war. Hence the "invitation" to which Reed responded, in effect, "Yes, please." On his first night bunking down at Tan Son Nhut airbase with his "Blackbirds" group, the Viet Cong sent in a rocket salvo, burning a C130 transport.

Kitted with his shoulder-patch "Alone Unarmed and Unafraid", he was told that over-flying Cambodia was taboo but by omission, it was OK to over-fly North Vietnam and Laos, where the locals were known to skin captured pilots alive.

He did ten "out-country" sorties, winning two Distinguished Flying Crosses. The first was for photographing a surface-to-air missile site under construction and heavily defended. The citation said, "Despite intense and accurate automatic weapons fire and antiaircraft artillery fire, he made multiple passes over his target to ensure complete photographic coverage." The second DFC was for spotting a Phantom crash site. A total of some 761 Phantoms – US Air Force, Navy and Marines – were lost during the war. In one loss in Reed's group, Major General Bob Worley was consumed by

[9] Altech International, 2020, 314pp. Amazon, $43.73.

fire before he could eject, becoming the only USAF General killed in combat.

In contrast, Reed was always lucky. He was one of 13 pilots graduating from No 13 Course at Archerfield base, Qld, in 1954. Against the odds, none died in action. Curiously, Reed's steed was the only Wirraway ever to shoot down a Japanese Zero – by Pilot John Archer above Gona in 1942.

On Good Friday 1955, Reed was rostered second pilot for a Lincoln bomber making a midnight dash from Townsville to Brisbane with a blue baby and nurse. He did the pre-flight checks and strapped in the bassinet, but then was 'bumped' by a squadron leader keen to visit Brisbane. Reed declined an offer to sit in the back of the plane. The skipper mistook Toowoomba's lights for Brisbane and all died in the crash 100 feet below the top of Mt Superbus.

Later, flying an F111 at Mach 2.4 or 3000km an hour, an intake vent problem caused an engine to stall and surge. It felt like he'd hit a brick wall, but he was able to regain control. (The F-111's top speed was Mach 2.5). His nearest-miss, ironically, was in retirement as co-pilot of a Tiger Moth in peaceful Wooloomanata, near Lara, Victoria. The pilot stalled the left wing at 50 feet and Reed grabbed control a second before the plane was about to cartwheel into the dirt. Strangely he'd learnt the "unload to live" manoeuvre flying a Phantom.

His career ranged from command of Australia's No 6 Phantom squadron to leading our first F-111 squadron at Amberley and high-level staff work. Indeed he signed the RAAF's final recommendation for F-111s rather than more Phantoms, against spirited opposition from Russell Offices. Later an F-111 pilot sent a recalcitrant deputy secretary an F-111 photo with the bureaucrat's office window marked with target cross-hairs. F-111 "Pigs" or "Aardvarks" served Australia well from 1973 to 2010.

With some trepidation, Reed included in his book his flights photographing Indonesian air bases during "Konfrontasi" in 1959-60. It was also 1960 when Russians caught spy pilot Gary Powers after downing his U2 with a missile – the Americans didn't believe such missiles were capable of reaching such a high-flier. The big risk in Indonesia was from contrails alerting MIG15s and 17s. Reed's role as "Little Reed" was to fly half a mile behind the lead bomber piloted by "Big Read" – Group Captain Charles Read – and alert him with VHF "clicks" to switch altitude if contrails formed.

The pair of intruders avoided Java but inspected bases at islands including Ambon, the Celebes, and Lombok. Reed doesn't know if they were detected. At the time he was sanitising his logbook with official cover stories about "contrail research" so he's short on remembered detail. Reed and Read were awarded Queen's Commendations, without specifics mentioned. Today Reed thinks his memoirs are the first public disclosure.

Two years' later Reed's flight of five Butterworth-based Canberras had just finished war games with USAF F-100 Super Sabres when the Cuban missile crisis hit. Reed writes that the same F-100 base-buddies were on the tarmac readying for a one-way flight to China with a nuclear weapon apiece.

His Biggles-like yarns are a constant delight. In a 1980 war game, his F-111s' job was to hit the carriers USS *Constellation* and HMAS *Melbourne* before their planes could attack Hawaii. The "Pigs" dealt with HMAS *Melbourne* but the formidable *Constellation*, with its 80 interceptors and two Hawkeye early-warning aircraft, was coming in undetected from the north, with more strike-power than the whole Australian Defence Force. When it was spotted, the admiral in Hawaii ordered Reed to attack it with four F-111s – suicidal against the carrier's radar coverage and F-14 defenders. Still without opposition 200 miles from target – which was weird – the F-111s split up and at 100 feet, surged over the carrier from the four points of the compass at 600 knots. It turned out that one of the carrier's two Hawkeyes had just landed with a fault, and the second hadn't yet taken off. Next day, with both Hawkeyes vigilant, Reed was once more coming in at 100ft when a defending F-14 streaked underneath him and pulled up ahead in a victory roll.

Reed has no embarrassment recounting his early love life – they called the Townsville nurses' quarters "the bulk store". With superb candour he relates how he teetered on a third-floor balcony to jemmy the shutters of his irate wife's locked bedroom at Butterworth. Instead he fell off and broke two arms, one wrist and his pelvis, and when just recovered and running Point Cook, got his sound left leg broken playing rugby.

His ultimate embarrassment was in the late 1980s at Laverton, between Melbourne and Geelong, when taking a lady on a joy flight in an antique Tiger Moth. He'd misjudged his fuel, the engine cut out and he glided to a landing in the Werribee sewage farm. They were rescued by old lag with a rowboat. Reed and his PR flacks managed to hide from the curious media that an Air Vice-Marshal was the shitty pilot. #

PART FIVE

DON'T TRUST THE MEDIA – HERE'S WHY

The sickest ABC joke in ages

20 August 2022

There's something endearing about tax-fed ABC people's lack of self-awareness. Those in Entertainment are convinced they're on a mission to "entertain, surprise, delight and help us understand the world we live in" and to this end they have mobilised "the best of new and established Australian talent". They want to take risks and push boundaries, deliver public benefit with impact, and nurture new talent "with heart and purpose".

Sure you do, ABC execs. But what's on the very same ABC page as those lofty sentiments? A photo of two luridly-clad grinning blond drag queens, one sporting purple-tinted tresses and resting a beefy arm bedaubed with tattoos. Their merriment concerns a placard they hold (trigger warning): "Where do you hide your DICK?"

This is as subtle as the graphic on Episode 4 of the ABC's 2020 *At Home Along Together*. That one shows a kneeling woman being penetrated by three men anally, vaginally and orally. It's ABC comedy, you see.

The blondes' placard pic is on a webpage soliciting entertainment proposals from external film producers, to show what the ABC really likes, i.e. "What we're looking for … to hold our loyal audience and attract new ones too."

I chanced upon the page when studying the ABC's Diversity and Inclusion Guidelines for contributors. Diversity is something their ABC really is passionate about: just watch the screen's parade of ABC Aborigines, young ladies of a certain religion, Sri Lankan asylum seekers and an eclectic mix of anyone-but-Anglos. ABC execs back-stage busily tick boxes. They enter every glimpse of a "diverse" Australian into spreadsheets for annual ABC reporting.

There is one minority the progressive ABC overlooks, and that's the 49 per cent of conservative voters. Imagine ABC Guidelines demanding that both its content and its crews comprise 49 per cent conservatives, to reflect the national culture and make-up. And imagine executives having to organise career paths to ensure conservatives rise to ABC leadership roles.

With that exception, the Diversity Guidelines are draconian in intent, a term which references the ancient Greek Mr Draco, who decreed death for pinching a turnip. I don't mean that chair Ita Buttrose and MD David Anderson would literally execute anyone for putting to air and video too many Anglo-WASP types. But the ABC guidelines have Draco's implacable tone:

> *Your intentions for representation will be captured in a Diversity and Inclusion Plan and submitted for consideration within our commissioning process.*

The ABC helpfully provides a worked-out Example Plan for three one-hour science pieces – a big deal, obviously. I am not making anything up here. First, the applicants have to answer,

> *Does this program reflect the diverse Australian community? (i.e. in its representation of theme, story lines or subject matter)?*

and

> *Please explain how this program will help the ABC achieve its diversity and inclusion goals in terms of on-screen and off-screen representation.*

For the characters/presenters, this model has mobilised 18

CIS-females and only 15 CIS-Males, reflecting the ABC matriarchy. (The ABC clarifies that "CIS gender" people are those who are born male or female and none-the-less continue to think they are male or female, respectively). The model also has one gender-diverse lass/lad/whatever, and one shy gender-creature who "prefers not to say". Also involved are 11 non-Anglos, five Aborigines, three Torres Strait Islanders, two disabled, and a handsome tally of eleven LGBTQI+'s.

The ABC defines the LGB alphabet soup as "Stands for people who identify as lesbian, gay, bisexual, transgender, queer or questioning, people in intersex variations, plus other diverse sexual orientations and gender identities". Maths-minded readers will twig that the LGBABC's total is 16 per cent of the applicant group – I'll get back to that percentage shortly.

The non-Anglos break down into a Norwegian playing the movie lead (another Norwegian has snuck in as third assistant-director); and two supporting Koreans (I hope they're not the Kim Jong-Un variety). There's a Polish presenter; three Indonesian extras run by the "Indonesian/Australian" producer (looks like jobs for the boys/girls/whatever?), two German extras and three more extras from – you won't believe this – Iceland! The ABC doesn't name them but the trio must be Bjork Asgeirsson, Ingibjorg Einarsdottir and Gudmundur Ragnarsson, who are household-name movie extras in their capital Reykjavik.

For the off-screen crew of this ABC hypothetical, they include 36 CIS males and females and only one gender-cranky person; four Aborigines; no Torres Strait Islanders (there'll be riots in Badu and Dauan over that); five disabled; and only three gays (What? Why? I need a safe space!). An Australian/Korean has found his/her/their niche in standby props and an Australian/Japanese is working on Continuity. Let the credits roll, say I.

More generally,

The Commissioning for Diversity and Inclusion Guidelines for screen content place diversity and inclusion at the heart of our planning, commissioning and content making processes.

Here's some ABC hurdles for those pitching:

1/ Scripted: Content that reflects the identities of the many cultures and communities in Australia, through stories and characters that reflect the experiences of under-represented groups.

2/ Non-scripted: Content that explicitly and predominantly explores issues of identity relating to under- represented groups, including Indigenous matters, gender, cultural diversity, or has a specific focus on LGBTQI+ communities, people with disability or other under- represented groups.

The cast shall include:

At least one main cast member is Indigenous Australian, culturally and linguistically diverse, a person with disability or identifies as LGBTQI+ AND at least 50% of the main cast are women or gender diverse.

In yet another clause, headed "Nothing about us without us", the ABC demands that

*All productions about a specific diverse community or subject must include **at least** one person who is representative of that diversity within the core creative team." (My emphasis).*

In other words, when filming about Eskimos make sure you've got Eskimos on the taxpayer payroll.

You will recall that in the first worked-out table, the ABC has arranged, consciously or not, for 16 per cent of the series' characters to be LGBTQI+. This slightly overdoes the ABC's Guidelines, "What does it mean to look and sound like Australia today?" There it claims, "11% of Australians identify as LGBTQI+". The implication is that ABC programming should reflect at least that ratio.

While I kow-tow to the LGBTQI+ industry as enthusiastically as everyone else, I reckon the ABC's 11 per cent figure is a fantasy. It would imply that in my short street near Essendon, there reside around 30 gender-diverse citizens, enough for a my-street mini-Mardi Gras next February.

The ABC quotes its source: *"In 2012, the Department of Health and Ageing estimated that Australians of diverse sexual orientation, sex or gender identity may account for up to 11 per cent of the Australian population."* ("May" and "up to" seem rubbery). Others citing the department's 11 per cent include the Human Rights Commission (2014) and Latrobe University, suggesting the figure has achieved urban-myth status.

The Health Department has provided me with its 2012 report which itself provides no source for its 11 per cent claim. Contrary to that figure, the 2016 National Drug Strategy Household Survey estimates that 3.2% of adults identify as homosexual or bisexual and 2.4% as "not sure/other" orientation.

Based on the Australian Bureau of Statistics 2014 General Social Survey, 3.0 per cent of adults identified as gay, lesbian or as having an 'other' sexual orientation (ABS 2015). The 2016 Census showed same-sex couples were only 1 per cent of all couple families. The

ABC might be comfortable with its 11% because the ABC's heavy with capital city-dwelling, well-educated and affluent types, where the LGBTQI+ group is over-represented.

It celebrates any of its minorities with double-identity status. For example, it has at least two proud gay Aborigines. One is Jack Evans – ABC Behind The News reporter: "Growing up as a queer Aboriginal man, I struggled to see myself reflected in the media. The ABC has provided me with the platform to be the representation I never had."

The other is the ABC's ACT newsreader Dan Bourchier. He says, "I also regularly speak about my Indigenous heritage, and about being gay and part of the LGBTQIA+ community."

The ABC imagines that its new programs are

brave, bold, ambitious and accessible stories that reflect shape and enrich our lives … distinctive, intelligent, innovative and culturally diverse … ignite national conversations, foster understanding and create meaningful change … sound like contemporary Australia and creatively take risks and push boundaries.

Here's the reality, like fawning over would-be Aborigine Bruce Pascoe's *Dark Emu* nonsense:

Based on his award-winning book, author Bruce Pascoe leads us on a revelatory and inspiring journey across Australia to present a very different history of our nation and the First Australians. This is a story you have never heard, facts you were never told. The true story of Aboriginal achievement. The First Australians as farmers, bakers, designers, traders and astronomers. This 2 x 1 hour series will redefine Aborigi-

nal history and will present lessons from our past that can shape our future.

The ABC did its best to railroad the innocent Cardinal Pell to prison, but the ABC website skites:

Reputation Rehab sees co-hosts Kirsten Drysdale and Zoe Norton Lodge find reputations in distress and provide a unique opportunity for transformation and redemption. We are living in an age of outrage culture and everyone is tired of it. Barely a week goes by without someone getting publicly crucified in a torrent of angry tweets, by opinion pieces, radio and TV punditry, for real or imagined mistakes.

Are you listening, Louise Milligan?

This series is a timely response to the culture everyone wants to change. It tackles shame head-on and breaks the outrage cycle by using comedy and empathy. Steeped in the conventions of reality TV, Reputation Rehab draws inspiration from scandals, personal failure and public humiliation.

I also noticed the ABC take on Australia Day 2021:

The ABC aired January 26 bringing an Indigenous perspective on (sic) the event, with crosses to Survival Day and Invasion Day events across Australia.

In a curious omission, the ABC brags that since its 1932 Charter, it has been "independent and innovative ... widely appealing and specialised" – blah, blah, blah, finishing with, "We are Yours, Australia." But in the listing of seven Charter responsibilities, the website omits the crucial one:

... to ensure that the gathering and presentation by the Corporation of news and information is accurate and

impartial according to the recognized standards of objective journalism.

A Freudian slip perhaps.

I've decided to pitch some stories myself to the ABC commissioning department, with striking ideas inspired by true events. Adhering to the brief, I've tried to be

... bold, provocative, original, and push people's buttons. They should create conversations and make you think, laugh or cry – or all the above. Please think of our previous successes as a challenge to aim high with your ideas – ambitious concepts are welcome! Factual series that dig deep into unique stories and worlds we haven't seen before, or characters that we don't see on TV every day. They can be issue-based, cultural, political, historical, or presenter-led, but must be contemporary in tone and style.

Here I go:

Pitch One: "The Girl Who Fought Against Union Power"

Episode One: Fatima gets a photocopying job at headquarters of the National Blacksmiths Union. Anglo-Saxon red-necks make fun of her hijab. But with her sassy and loveable competence, and support from an Aboriginal accountant from the Wadeye community, she becomes secretary to the boss. Quickly mastering legal lore, she helps stonewall regulators who are persecuting him over the union's accounts. The episode ends positively with boss and assembled staff toasting her with 1964-vintage *Veuve Cliquot*.

Episode Two: Fatima notices sheafs of receipts from union credit cards in the boss's trash. He's been visiting odd places and sending his comely co-directors on shopping trips to Paris, accommodation courtesy *Hotel de Crillon*. She emotes to camera, "Our low-paid

226

blacksmith members are being robbed blind by these union heavies." She confronts the boss, he confesses and intends to board a flight to Peru. They struggle for a phone, she manages to dial the corporate cops at ASIC and ICAC. They arrive in squad cars with sirens blaring seven years later. Meanwhile she visits blacksmith members and signs them over to the Coachdrivers Union where she becomes the first martial-arts-capable President. Ends.

Pitch Two: "The Winds of Change"

Episode One: An admired Greens leader, Dr Robert Sepia, retires with a friend to a pristine island home called Erewhon, off Tasmania. Here they enjoy studying the migratory birds. Cue Beethoven's *Pastoral Symphony* as they splash through wetlands at sunrise. A new neighbour turns up – a jobless Aboriginal 'dozer driver named Uncle Mick. His kids are hungry because Dr Sepia has stifled mining and logging projects. Flashbacks show Uncle Mick driving his 'dozer up to Dr Sepia, who has chained himself to mining equipment. Cue scary music and a suspenseful closure.

Episode Two: Dr Sepia has heartily recommended a windfarm consortium to the Government to reduce planet-killing CO2 emissions, but the company decides that his Erewhon Island is ideal for 163 bird-mincing turbines. Dr Sepia recruits Uncle Mick and his dozer to push down the project's fences and they battle balaclava-wearing windfarm security guards. Sound track: Tchaikowski's *1812 Overture*. With their flower-children supporters, they force the evil wind farmers to relocate to Sandy Bay near Hobart CBD. Dr Sepia and Uncle Mick are reconciled; Mick, speaking *palawa kani*, welcomes Dr Sepia to *lutruwita* (Tasmania). Dr Sepia prepares Mick's kids a vegan feast of lentils and tofu. Ends.

The ABC will love my pitches. I'll just need to fill in those 27 Diversity and Inclusion forms. #

The media is the massage
21 February 2022

Why is the media so mistrusted? That's not a question much raised at journalism schools or debated on the ABC's *The Drum*. The mistrust is because the left-leaning media dispenses such muck that only fools give it any credibility. Read on and I'll document that statement – understatement, really – using as case studies the giant global news wholesalers such as *Agence France Press* (AFP) and *Associated Press* (AP), and the *New York Times*, flagship of America's progressive newspapers.

In Australia reporters are the second-least trusted of 30 occupations, ahead of politicians but behind delivery drivers. That's according to a *Readers Digest* poll last year. Australians who trust the media were 43 per cent, which is less than in Poland, Croatia and South Africa.

Among 46 countries, the US media is the least trusted (29 per cent), according to a Reuters Institute poll last year. Within the US, last October's Gallup Poll assessed trust in media at 36 per cent, the second-lowest on record. Only 11 per cent of Republicans – who comprise half the population – trust the media, and only 10 per cent of Americans trust the media's reporting on COVID.

The normal focus is on mastheads like the *New York Times* and *Washington Post* – and here *The Australian*, *The Age* and *Sydney Morning Herald* (SMH). But such a narrow focus detracts from the less obvious role of news wholesalers i.e. newswires AFP, AP, Reuters and Bloomberg. Without them your morning paper or online bulletin would be half empty.

In days gone by the wire services' watchword was political

and ideological neutrality. Playing such a straight bat made them unremarkable. But now AFP, Reuters and Bloomberg have literally signed the climate pledge and partnered with 460 other media groups at Covering Climate Now (CCN). That "partnership" involves hyping warming and cancelling whatever doesn't fit the narrative. And AP, in a jaw-dropping breach of journalistic ethics, this month began hiring 20 climate-crazed reporters using an $US8 million gift from five green/Left billionaire philanthropies. From now on we'll be reading the best AP climate news that can be bought with activists' money. Here's a snapshot of the agencies' reach:

AFP: This world's oldest news wholesaler (186 years) has 1700 journalists operating in 150 countries. It's independent but gets about 40% of its funding from French government subsidies.

AP: A 175-year-old New York-based non-profit group of US newspapers and broadcasters, with 3300 workers wholesaling and sharing news with 1300 print and broadcast outlets in 99 countries.

Bloomberg: The Manhattan-based, 40-year-old, privately-owned business conglomerate with 20,000 employees globally. It was co-founded by Michael Bloomberg, who is now now worth $US70 billion. Print and broadcast media are just one leg of its operations, with financial software the mainstay.

Thomson Reuters: 170-year-old London/Canada-based news wholesaler running 3,100 reporters and photo-journalists worldwide and reaching 1 billion readers.

Taking AFP specifically, its impartiality statutes include (emphasis added)

 # Agence France-Presse may under no circumstances take account of influences or considerations liable to compromise the

229

exactitude or the objectivity of the information it provides;
it may under no circumstances fall under the control, either
de facto or de jure, of any ideological, political or economic
grouping;

 # Agence France-Presse must ... provide French and foreign
users with exact, impartial and trustworthy information.

By partnering with Covering Climate Now, AFP has trashed those ethics. CCN's founders view fossil fuel executives as criminals against humanity. They also want to "revoke the social licences" of "deniers" in the same way tobacco companies were shafted last century. CCN pushes absurdities like a billion "climate refugees" by 2050.

I'll get back shortly to AFP and its malign influence on our local media, including Murdoch flagship *The Australian*. AFP's lapse is small beer compared with the grotesquerie of rival AP taking that $US8 million handout from the likes of Rupert's green/woke spawn, James Murdoch, and his wife, Kathryn. Young James' political sympathies can be easily discerned from Open Secrets' register of his generous donations to Hillary Clinton and Democrat state committees far and wide.

Julie Pace, AP senior vice-president and executive editor, explains the alliance with CCN: "This far-reaching initiative will transform how we cover the climate story." The converse would involve the Institute of Public Affairs and Pauline Hanson giving $A11 million to *The Australian* to hire 20 conservative journalists to report on The Greens's electoral campaigning. Obviously, AP's bought-and-paid-for climate team won't be writing anything critical about warmist dogma or dodgy people manipulating temperature data at the IPCC or NASA.

AP explained candidly that, among other motives, it needed the money:

The announcement illustrates how philanthropy has swiftly become an important new funding source for journalism – at the AP and elsewhere – at a time when the industry's financial outlook has been otherwise bleak.

Concern about conflict of interest is out the window, as AP admits without blushing:

For many years, journalists and philanthropists were more wary of each other. News organizations were concerned about maintaining independence and, until the past two decades, financially secure enough not to need help.

AP hails other newspapers and mastheads for also accepting foundations' tainted money for their journalism.

Here's some detail about AP's five generous donors

Hewlett Foundation: Assets $US13 billion. Awarded the Climate Works lobby a massive $US460 million in 2008, and an ongoing stream of further grants. Opposes fossil fuels and coal and gas developments.

Rockefeller Foundation: Founded in 1913 by the oil barons (of all people). Assets at least $US4 billion. Many worthwhile medical and education projects, but its track record also includes a wartime study that infected hundreds of Guatemalans with syphilis and, before that, the funding of a German eugenics laboratory frequented by Dr Josef Mengele en route to his human experimenting at Auschwitz.

Quadrivium: About $US20 million in assets. Co-founder and president Kathryn Murdoch, wife of co-founder James Murdoch.

Her net worth is said to be $US2 billion. She also works for Hillary Clinton's Clinton Climate Initiative. Quadrivium's viewpoint:

Climate change threatens the security and stability of our country and our world. We recognize that communications around this threat have been politicized and we are working with organizations that are capable of reaching a majority of the public, regardless of country or political tribe. We are helping to expand the successful Climate Matters program which uses meteorologists as trusted messengers of the links between extreme weather and climate change.

Walton Family Foundation: Assets of about $US7b. Climate activists on agriculture and water resources.

Howard Hughes Medical Institute: Assets $US29b. Supports and mentors medical researchers and scientists. Not much obvious climate preoccupation but its research emphasises the controversial alleged link between warming and the spread of malaria.

New York-based climate communicator Marc Morano juxtaposes AP's acceptance of the $US8 million with the Code of Ethics of the US Society of Professional Journalists, and writes:

SPJ Code of Ethics: *"Be wary of sources offering information for favors or money; do not pay for access to news."*

Reality Check: The AP will NOT 'be wary of sources offering information for favors or money,' but instead, it will be seeking money from additional donors for a job well done promoting climate hysteria.

SPJ: "Deny favored treatment to advertisers, donors or any other special interests, and resist internal and external pressure to influence coverage."

Reality Check: Instead of 'denying favored treatment' to 'donors', the AP will be dishing out 'favored treatment' not only to its current funders of the news but to any other potential donors who could help expand their 'climate' reporting.

SPJ: "Be vigilant and courageous about holding those with power accountable."

Reality Check: The AP will now be subservient and timid 'about holding those with power accountable', especially those who gave them untold millions to promote climate propaganda

The $US8 million to AP would also batter down Australia's MEAA (journalists) Code of Ethics:

5/ Disclose conflicts of interest that affect, or could be seen to affect, the accuracy, fairness or independence of your journalism.

6/ Do not allow advertising or other commercial considerations to undermine accuracy, fairness or independence.

7/ Do your utmost to ensure disclosure of any direct or indirect paymentmade for ... stories.

I trust that all AP climate stories recycled by the Australian media will include a footnote: "This reporting funded or influenced by money from green/Left foundations".

Rupert Murdoch's daily broadsheet, *The Australian*, had been a beacon of sanity against the billion-dollar ABC, the *SMH* and *The Age*, Malcolm Turnbull-created *Guardian Australia*, university-and-tax- funded *The Conversation* and Murdoch's online leftists at news.com.au. Within *The Australian* there have been obvious pushes by woke elements towards a green-Leftism, until now without much success. *The Australian* continues to run commentaries by the unfashionable climate analyst Bjorn Lomborg, by long-term Labor apparatchik Graham Richardson and all politics in between. The good work of its environment reporter Graham Lloyd airs material that both fits and doesn't fit the warmist agenda. But *The Australian* is coming to resemble a cold-store apple – healthy on the outside but starting to rot within. The rot's coming from propaganda and drivel in its AFP feed from "global coordinator for climate change", Marlowe Hood, who has laughably self-titled himself "Senior Editor, Future of the Planet". He tells us he was "born at 314 ppm (when CO_2 was 314 parts per million)" and is now a "herald of the Anthropocene." Ta-da!

The Australian has run more than 20 Hood pieces, nearly all falsely dubbed by its sub-editors as "Breaking News". They have headlines like "Acceleration of global warming 'code red' for humanity" and "Climate cataclysms set stage for key UN science report."

Marlowe Hood has done nicely from his climate shrieking. Last year he applied for and won 100,000 Euros ($A160,000) cash from green/Left Spanish foundation BBVA. Blurbing the prize, BBVA extolled Hood as "one of the foremost environmental journalists and communicators of his generation". Qualified in Chinese (that's it, but), Hood praised to BBVA the "largely unheralded but quietly influential" climate reporting by agencies like AFP. Agencies, he kids himself, are not just news-breakers but "impartial arbiters that set the tone and steer the global narrative."

His submission for the 100,000 Euros says he was at an Oxford conference in 2009 on (supposed) impacts of a (supposed) 4degC warming. "And suddenly the reality of global warming and the human misery it will trail in its wake hit me in the gut and left me gasping for air," he hyperventilated. In preacher mode, he told BBVA how "Humanity is standing at the crossroads [of a "sixth mass extinction", no less] and doesn't have long to decide which path we will be taking."

In a soliloquy of self-delusion, he asked himself if his journalism is "the best way to wield influence, since an agency's job is to deliver news, not opinion." He yearns "to explicitly denounce what I know to be harmful or wrong, and to champion what I think is the right course of action" but manages (he says) to restrain himself. He boasts how his activism earns him under-the-table scoops from the UN-based catastrophe spruikers:

These stories are not only directly accessible to tens of millions of people through AFP's media clients, they are also read by other journalists who take their cue from top level agency reporting.

As for his teaching duties to 100 young journos a year, he asks what he describes as the question for anyone interested in environmental communication:

How do you scare people enough to take it seriously, and at the same time show them that there are solutions and hope, so they don't just throw their hands up in despair? It's all about striking that balance.

I nearly choked over Hood's latest "news" piece in *The Australian*, 14 February. The propaganda, almost beyond satire, is illustrated with a nameless city cocooned in lush green parks and dappled skies lit by the sun's rays. But the artists change it to a hellscape of broiling heat, fires and parched cracked earth thanks to the evil of carbon dioxide emissions. *The Australian*'s sub-editors have grabbed the illustration from the range of Goebbels-standard propaganda pics on offer at Shutterstock including dying polar bears on ice floes, drought-stricken deathscapes and wind turbines glowing in heavenly pastel landscapes.

Hood's story, based on leaks from his alarmist pals, says the IPCC is going to release another "harrowing" Summary for Policymakers on 28 February, more of the doom that UN people have claimed is just around the corner, every few years since 1990. Hood parades a litany of fake facts. Species extinction, ecosystem collapse, mosquito-borne disease, deadly heat, water shortages, and reduced crop yields are already measurably worse due to global heating, he claims:

> *Just in the past year, the world has seen a cascade of unprecedented floods, heatwaves and bushfires across four continents. All these impacts will accelerate in the coming decades even if the carbon pollution driving climate change is rapidly brought to heel, the IPCC report is likely to warn.*

Is "global heating" really making "reduced crop yields measurably worse"? In fact there's been slight global cooling in the past five years, as measured officially by satellites and from the surface. On 2 February, the UN's Food and Agriculture Organisation estimated last year's world cereal production at yet another record of 2793 million tonnes, with a graph showing the rising trend from 2012. Yields for virtually every major crop have been on that rising trend during 60 years' worth of global warming. Closer to home, Australia has just had its coolest year since 2012, according to the Meteorology Bureau, and in 60 years Australian cereal yields have more than doubled.

Hood drives his truck through AFP's guidelines for proper sourcing within its news articles. His piece in *The Australian* includes the bland, "experts and advocates say". But AFP Protocols stress:

Analysts should be clearly identified, along with the orga-
nization for whom they work and their area of expertise ...
Anonymous analysts lack credibility and must not be quoted
... AFP is a global news agency and we should seek out ana-
lysts who offer conflicting points of view and not be content
with analysts who follow a particular narrative.

Hood's "news" piece looks even more stupid considering the
IPCC summary he's blurbing is not finalised and its authors are
continuously changing the draft. Moreover, Hood is just another
mouthpiece for the orchestrated campaign by activist scientists
and lobbyists to hype the impending Summary. Verify this by looking at other tame journalists' output, like AP's science writer Seth
Borenstein's version headed: *"Scientists and governments meet to*
finalise UN report on 'nightmare' impacts of global warming". Borenstein is at least more frank in sourcing his garbage to an activist
group, writing:

The IPCC's horrifying evidence of escalating climate impacts
is set to show a nightmare painted in the dry language of sci-
ence," Teresa Anderson, who heads climate justice issues at
ActionAid International, said in a statement.

If you think the agencies' output is on the nose, you'll gag at
the stench from once-eminent mastheads like the *New York*
Times, Washington Post, Wall Street Journal, LA Times and *Chicago*
Tribune. The *NYT* took $US100,000 a month from the Commu-
nist Party of China, via the CCP's *"China Daily"* mouthpiece, for
the decade to early 2020 to run pages of advertorials like "China
Watch: Diaoyu Islands Belong to China."

The *NYT*, the progressives' "paper of record", takes pride in
its archives stretching back to the 1850s pre-Civil War. But when

caught out getting paid for CCP material, it furtively deleted those 200-plus pseudo-news pieces from its archives. The slimy deals with the CCP were exposed only when Republicans in Congress forced *China Daily* to properly disclose its US influence-peddling since 2016.

The *NYT* was further hostage to the CCP over its heavy investments in China a decade ago. This might (or might not) have influenced its determined efforts in early 2020 to discredit and smear as 'racists' and tinfoil-hatters those suggesting COVID leaked from the Wuhan laboratory part-funded by Dr Fauci's team. In turn, *China Daily* sometimes played back the *NYT* hit-pieces to its own domestic audience.

All up, Xi Jinping's men needed to pay a paltry $US20 million to get their messages to the US public via the cream of America's progressive newspapers. Was Trump wrong to say this media is "the enemy of the people"? And are we wrong to so distrust the media?

Murdoch-owned Fox News demolished left-liberal rivals MSNBC and CNN in early February, out-rating their combined offerings among both total day and primetime viewers for the 25th straight week. The dismal-ratings fate of left-liberal US cable channels demonstrates that media shills can't fool all the people all the time. #

What the ABC decided you didn't Need to know

20 April 2022

Let's do a case study of the ABC's handling of an important political controversy. That is, the contents of the laptop abandoned in a Delaware repair shop in 2019 by Joe Biden's dissolute son Hunter. The *New York Post* exposed it just three weeks before the election. Key thing to remember is that the ABC loves Hunter's pop Joe Biden to distraction, as the comments below demonstrate:

Stan Grant: *"Joe Biden's appeal to decency, to bring Americans together ..."*

Leigh Sales: *"When you talk to people who have spent time around Joe Biden, including Republicans, there is one word that keeps coming up ... 'extraordinarily decent person' ... 'the most decent, honourable politician I've ever known' ... 'a person with decency'."*

Joe actually leads a sleazy family of grifters. For example, on 13 August 2018, after son Hunter drove to Las Vegas from LA in his Porsche at up to 175mph, one prostitute warned him to stop using more than two prostitutes simultaneously because they might steal his stuff.

Hunter has traded on his father's position to enrich himself by multi-millions of dollars As a quid pro quo Joe got his cut from Hunter – who whinges at having to hand over half his earnings to Dad as part of their comingled paypacket. In the past decade Hunter was soliciting riches from corrupt Ukrainian and Russian oligarchs and from princelings in China tied to the Communist Party – indeed cash connections extending all the way to China's then-rising star Xi Jinping:

Hunter Biden had business associations with Ye Jianming, Gongwen Dong, and other Chinese nationals linked to the Communist government and People's Liberation Army. Those associations resulted in millions of dollars in questionable transactions. Republican-chaired Congressional Investigation Report, 23 September 2020.

Joe Biden, as US vice-president and president, falsely denied any knowledge of the drug-addled neophyte Hunter's business deals.

One 2017 email on the laptop referred to Hunter warehousing for Joe 10 per cent of profits from a multi-billion China belt-and-road funder, called CEFC, associated with Chinese intelligence actors. It controlled "more money than God", said Hunter, who cruised to China on Air Force Two in 2013 when Dad met Xi Jinping. The 10 per cent was for "the big guy". As one of his partners put it: *"Don't mention Joe being involved, it's only when u are face to face."*

Hunter referred to another CEFC official as "the f***ing spy chief" and told cronies that CEFC was "coming to be MY partner to be partners with the Bidens." The Bidens' windfall from CEFC cash was $US5 million. CEFC founder Ye Jianming gave Hunter a 3.16 carat diamond after their first meeting. In Hunter's later divorce suit, its value was put at around $US80,000.

Rupert Murdoch's *New York Post* front-paged the material. For six hours it seemed an election-winner for Trump – until Twitter and Facebook blocked the story from circulating online, even suspending the *Post's* own Twitter account. One post-election poll showed 36 per cent of Democrat voters didn't know about the laptop, and 13 per cent would not have voted for Biden if they had known.

The ABC's team was comfortable with Twitter/FB's censorship jihad and themselves trashed the *Post*'s story as Russian-inspired disinformation or worthless. They were impressed by 51 retired senior intelligence executives who claimed the story had all the hallmarks of Russian hackdom – citing no evidence whatsoever.

Last month, the *New York Times* finally conceded Hunter's laptop contents were the real thing. The *Times* had suppressed the truth for well over a year. The *Washington Post* next day sheepishly followed suit.

Contrition? None, of course, and none yet from the ABC. As for those 51 intelligence "experts", the *New York Post* splashed their portraits as a rogue's gallery of lying Deep State operatives. One of them, 28-year CIA veteran John Sipher tweeted: *"I lost the election for Trump? Well, then I (feel) pretty good about my influence."*

Now let's get forensic about the ABC's laptop coverage.

First, the *Post*'s initial bombshell was that Joe Biden was lying that he had no knowledge of Hunter's lucrative business dealings with dubious offshore players. The laptop emails showed Hunter setting up Joe for a meeting in 2015 with the corrupt Burisma operatives paying the unqualified Hunter $US83,333 a month. However, the laptop's email wordings were ambiguous whether the meeting was consummated. The ABC repeatedly seized on the "unconsummated" interpretation to protect Joe Biden. After eight months of denials and stonewalling, the White House admitted last year that Joe did attend the meeting at Café Milano's private Garden Room in Georgetown DC, on 16 April 2015, but claimed it was just a "drop by" because Joe (improbably) wanted to meet a Greek Orthodox priest there and no business was discussed. As Miranda Devine notes, "That's not how it works. Joe just has to show up and shake hands. All that matters is that Hunter demonstrates his pulling power" to justify pocketing $US83,000 a month.

Among other invitees were Moscow billionaire Elena Baturina and husband, the corrupt Moscow mayor Yury Luzhkov. Baturina the previous year had wired $US3.5 million to Hunter's business, a transfer US Treasury flagged as a suspicious transaction.

The ABC might now protest that it knew nothing of those dinner facts at the time. But since the facts have emerged, the ABC has declined to inform its Australian public or correct its previous smears.

Here's the ABC's reporting timeline.

15 October 2020:

Associated Press/ABC runs an unsigned 'Explainer' about why Facebook and Twitter were suppressing the laptop story. The ABC describes as "an unfounded idea" that Hunter Biden "may have enriched himself by selling his access to his father." Well, useless crackhead Hunter certainly collected multi-million payoffs from bagmen from America's antagonists like Russia and China, but for no reason, apparently.

The piece continues, "Disinformation experts have said there are multiple red flags that raise doubts about (the emails') authenticity [they're authentic], including questions about whether the laptop actually belongs to Hunter Biden." [It did]. The ABC quoted one "disinformation expert" that the emails could be either hacked or forged or both. [The emails weren't hacked or forged or both].

The mere involvement of Trumpers Steve Bannon and Rudy Giuliani is viewed as "another potential alarm" – though the ABC never viewed as "potential alarms" any leak from double-dealing Democrat FBI/CIA chiefs, hookers, grifters or nameless "officials".

AP/ABC next spin the story as Twitter and Facebook limiting "hacked" material on their platforms "ahead of the election", rather than desperately censoring material damaging to candidate Biden. (After the election Twitter CEO Dorsey admitted the emails weren't hacked, and Facebook never published its promised Fact-Check).

The ABC inserts a correction to the story three months later, walking back a detail that had been over-favourable to Biden.

16 October 2020:

Planet America with John Barron – also of the US Studies Centre, Sydney University – and "comedian" Chas Licciardello claim that struggling candidate Trump, with Murdoch's backing, is "desperately resurrecting" his attacks on Hunter Biden.

In a vile *ad hominem*, Barron in his smart grey suit spits at the legally-blind albino repairer of Hunter's laptop: "He is a piece of work!" This repairman, Mac Isaac, legally owned the laptop in August 2019 when Hunter failed to pay and collect it. His father, a retired Air Force colonel, reported the contents properly to the FBI, which declined to even receive the laptop. In December 2019, however, the FBI had second thoughts and seized the laptop from Isaac's shop. In the national uproar, Isaac's public-spirited act tore his life apart. He got violent threats, feared for his life and closed his thriving business to move interstate. He has since brought suit against Twitter for its lie that he 'hacked' the laptop.

Barron also calls the *Post* story "a pretty poor piece of journalism" and "a very very credulous piece of reporting". This applies exactly to the ABC's coverage. If anyone is "a piece of work", it's ABC's John Barron.

The pair agree that Twitter/FB's censorship is "extraordinary" but put that down to the "fishy" laptop story being "simply bunkum" from Russian hacks and misinformation.

The pair run the gamut of laptop excuses, e.g., that

Hunter maybe didn't give the laptop to the repair shop (he did).

Hunter was living in Los Angeles and the shop was in Delaware (pundit Chas seems unaware that for generations the Biden family seat is in Delaware).

The laptop would have been password protected (Well, doh!)

Why didn't the repairer contact Hunter? (He tried in vain).

The FBI did nothing about the laptop because "there was nothing to it" (No, because the material was dangerous to Joe Biden).

Why didn't the repairer charge more than $US85? (So what?)

Why would Hunter agree to forfeit the laptop if not collected in 90 days? (Perhaps because he was on crack cocaine and anyway it's standard repair boilerplate).

Wasn't it "convenient" the repairer couldn't recognise Hunter? (Come off it, he was legally blind).

The repairer was a "rabid Trumper" (as were 74m Americans).

The media has to be very careful about foreign election interference and Russian email hacks (except when covering the Democrat-funded "Steele" dossier fakery about prostitutes peeing on Trump's bed in Moscow).

The emails on the laptop aren't significant or smoking-guns – "there was nothing actually there". (So why the unprecedented Twitter/FB crackdown?)

20 October:

The ABC's David Lipson runs a three-minute audio piece headed, "America's top intelligence official dismisses Russian disinformation campaign." This was a reference to John Ratcliffe, Director of National Intelligence. I thought, "Good for you, David, some honest ABC reporting at last." But Lipson's actual audio was the usual disgusting ABC spin. The item was introduced as "Reports of a Russian disinformation campaign" and Lipson, claiming "big questions about the veracity of the story", next cut to Democrat Congress Intelligence Chair Adam Schiff saying, "The whole smear on Joe Biden comes from the Kremlin."

Lipson clings to his conspiracy: "Multiple news outlets have suggested the FBI is investigating whether the report is part of a Russian disinformation campaign." He then commendably inserts intelligence boss Ratcliffe saying it's not Russian spooks and he intends to "stop people using the intelligence community to leverage some political initiative." Lipson scoffs and dismisses Ratcliffe's words with a sneering:

> *Here is the kicker! Before his appointment Ratcliffe was a Republican member of Congress and a staunch Trump loyalist who defended the President in his impeachment trial … Now he is America's most senior intelligence officer and weighing in on an intelligence issue 15 days out from the election!*

The trouble with Lipson's *ad hominem* is that Ratcliffe was right and Lipson is a goose.

22 October:

The ABC's Steven Smiley and Angela Lavoipierre introduce an audio on the laptop: "Donald Trump's favourite news story is the one about Hunter Biden, he won't stop bringing it up. By contrast most of the reputable news media will not touch it, and Twitter and Facebook have both put brakes on related posts. But do they have good reason?"

Lavoipierre: Sometimes you end up with a terrible story that might not stack up.

Smiley: Yeah which is a pretty good description of latest chapter to the Hunter Biden saga.

A certain Adi Robertson, who sees herself an expert on office furniture at an obscure US blog, *Verge*, is quoted damning the laptop story because, or so she claims, the repair-shop man "subscribes to some weird anti-Clinton conspiracy theories" and Trump's Rudy Giuliani at some point unwittingly endorsed a Ukrainian MP later exposed as a Russian agent.

Democrat leader Adam Schiff is also quoted: "The origins of this whole smear is from the Kremlin. The President [Trump] is only too happy to have Kremlin help to try to amplify it."

The on-air trio then bruit (without evidence) that the laptop story is a lookalike to how the Russians allegedly hacked the Democrat National Committee and Hillary Clinton's private servers in 2016. Robertson hedges her bets but says the laptop story is "really troubling" and they agree it's "dubious" and "really strange if not outright disinformation". She concedes the censorship is beyond normal Twitter/FB practice – but no, it's not suppressing a story "that might harm the Biden campaign". It's just that social media allowed too much disinformation in 2016, so Twitter/FB are over-correcting: "Once bitten, twice shy."

They all agree that "many conservatives" claim it's a violation of free speech, but conclude that the problem is merely "platform power" involving "news distribution".

23 October:

The ABC's Matt Bevan admits the laptop scoops have been coming from the Murdoch Australian press, while US rival outlets "wrestle with whether or not to publish". Indeed. Bevan sneers that the laptop "supposedly" belonged to Hunter Biden (it did), and that its murky stories of Joe, Hunter and Ukrainian gas company Burisma are inconclusive or false. What Bevan omits is why Burisma was paying Hunter Biden, a libidinous crackhead, $US83,000 a month and billionaires from Moscow and China were showering him with millions.

Bevan touts Russian conspiracy:

Then, starting at the beginning of 2020, reports emerged [huh?] that Russian government hackers had gained access to the emails of Hunter Biden, and were planning to release them before the 2020 election, timed to do maximum damage to his father's campaign, in a direct re-running of their 2016 US election interference campaign … Journalists [un-named] at the New York Post *have told the* New York Times *and* New York Magazine *that they are concerned about the veracity of the story."* [That's weird because the story was correct.]

There are a few possibilities for what has happened here. One is that Mr Giuliani, despite his recent record of lying about this story repeatedly [no, it's the ABC lying repeatedly], *really did by incredible coincidence come into possession of these materials.* [The repair shop owner, after long FBI indifference, turned to Giuliani to make something happen. That's not an "incredible coincidence"].

The other is that Russian intelligence hacked into Hunter Biden's information and then laundered what they found through a laptop and a drop at a friendly computer shop. [Yeah right, Matt, taxpayers ought to dock your ABC salary for that nonsense].

Either way, the information on the laptop is highly questionable. [No, it's accurate].

Which is why American news outlets have been hesitant to touch it. [No, it's because they are in bed with Democrats and the Bidens].

But Australian media has shown no such qualms. [You mean, the Australian Murdoch media has run rings round the cowardly, truth-suppressing ABC on this affair].

Bevan's piece required two incidental corrections by the ABC itself.

24 October:

ABC's David Lipson surprisingly concedes the laptop is not Russian disinformation. But then he spins it as "more sideshow than showstopper" because Biden probably didn't attend that Hunter dinner [he did].

Lipson even mentions laptop emails describing Joe Biden "as the 'Big Guy' in business deals being sought in China", but forebears the detail that this "Big Guy" was to be cut in for a secret 10 per cent of the money warehoused by Hunter and Co. Lipson spins: "But the emails are dated May 2017, when Biden was no longer serving as vice-president." In other words, the Hunter Biden/China financial sleaze was just during Joe's private capacity, so who cares? Lipson approves Joe's zinger in the third debate that his tax returns show no "untoward" money. Actually, Matt, politicians keep dirty money out of their financial records and the laptop provides how-to examples.

1 November:

The ABC's Echo Hui and Hagar Cohen do a long "investigative" piece about a wealthy Chinese expat blog "New Federal State of China" touting the laptop. The ABC narrative thus associates the scandal with a bunch of what the audience is encouraged to regard as odd/crazy Chinese diaspora activists. This group's anti-CCP stance is a particular black mark:

> *Dr Anne Kruger, the director of Asia Pacific at the fact check organisation FirstDraft, studied the group's operations and said followers flood the internet with questionable material. "Their main tactic is really to try to appeal to people that might have a gripe against the Chinese Communist Party and to push conspiracy theories," Dr Kruger said.*

This blog became, say the ABC duo, "the centre of Hunter Biden's laptop scandal" (what nonsense!). The duo add that "most mainstream US media have not reported the allegations because the source and substance of the material could not be verified." This Chinese blog, according to ex-members cited, is "very, very dangerous to any country, and the misinformation it recklessly spreads will seriously harm democracy."

3 November:

The ABC's "music and pop culture reporter" Paul Donoughue brazenly instances the "discredited" laptop story, and says Twitter "briefly" stopped users from sharing the "misinformation". ("Briefly" meaning two of the crucial three weeks until election eve).

Donoughue quotes UWA academic Michael Douglas likening Twitter/FB's crackdown to legitimate censorship of child exploitation material: "In my view, suppressing **dubious** content designed to influence an election is also justified."

Donoughue also cites another deluded academic: "Professor Bruns and other researchers say there is no evidence that social platforms are biased against conservative voices." Reality: Twitter censored the Trump campaign 625 times from 31 May 2018 to 4 January 2021, while censoring of the Biden campaign totalled zero.

March/April 2022:

Despite their favourite sources, the *New York Times* and *Washington Post*, now admitting the laptop is bona fide, the ABC reports nothing about it. Another angle the ABC ignores is that Leigh Sales' chum Hillary Clinton's 2016 election campaign and the Democratic National Committee (DNC) were fined $US8,000 and $US105,000 respectively on 30 March 2022, for lying about their $US1 million funding of the anti-Trump "pee" dossier.

Maybe the next conservative government here will set up a Truth & Justice Commission into the ABC. It seems needed. #

The other Watergate scandal

3 August 2022

When the Watergate movie *All the President's Men* came to Canberra in 1977, I rushed to the cinema. Half an hour into this engrossing drama, a middle-aged man in the row in front of me turned around and cursed me, "Thanks to you, I can't see any more of this and I'm going home." I was upset by his outburst, but in my high tension, I'd been heedlessly kicking the back of his seat.

I'm sure all the Press Gallery tribe were equally engrossed. Bob Woodward and Carl Bernstein ("Woodstein" for short) and the *Washington Post* broke the mould and won glory with their investigative journalism. They demonstrated the White House's guilt for the Watergate burglary and forced the first-ever resignation of a US President, namely the Republican's "Tricky Dick" Richard Nixon. Forty or so members of his fiefdom were convicted. Journos ever since, including myself, have fantasised about ourselves making history and millions with exposures of high-ranking evildoers.

There were actually two burglaries of the Democrat National Committee (DNC) offices in Watergate within three weeks in mid-1972. The first involved some successful phone-bugging; the bungled second burglary was mainly to photograph a large volume of documents. Security guards caught the five-man team red-handed. A sixth burglar lurking nearby escaped detection, never to be officially identified but now named as CIA contractor Lou Russell.

That was all half a century ago. The Woodstein burglary narrative was full of contradictions and non-sequiturs – especially given that Nixon enjoyed landslide popularity (he carried 49 states out of 50 a few months later) and any Democrat strategies were not worth knowing. But people became too excited to care as the Nixon cover-up drama took priority. The prosecution and conviction of the burglars involved guilty pleas and few revelations emerged.

Over the decades various mystery elements were solved. But only now has most of the real Watergate story been put together, via lawyer John O'Connor's *The Mysteries of Watergate – what really happened*, published last month. (Post Hill Press, $A31.75, 425pp).

O'Connor is no lightweight. He was a federal prosecutor from 1974-80 and in recent decades counsel for Mark Felt (1913-2008), the *Post*'s "Deep Throat" who led the Watergate investigation as FBI deputy director.

O'Connor was the first to publicly identify Felt, in a *Vanity Fair* article in 2005. Felt allowed O'Connor to tell his Watergate story because otherwise Felt's legacy post-death could be trashed and distorted by the *Post*'s ungrateful Woodstein duo. Felt knew too much about Woodstein's agendas and Watergate realities.

O'Connor published Felt's revelations as *A G-Man's Life* in 2006, but O'Connor claims sales were sabotaged by his own publisher in league with the *Post*, and the book's disclosures made no impact on Woodstein's sainthood. Here's O'Connor's conclusions in his new book, after Woodstein again declined to cooperate by providing their own rejoinders:

\# The falsities, distortions and cover-ups by the Democrat-loving *Post* and its reporters were as bad or worse than anything Nixon was accused of.

\# The burglaries were done not by a White House team but by a CIA team for its own purposes, after the perpetrators got some low-level sign-offs by White House dupes about "national security" concerns, and financing from a White House fund for Nixon campaigning. Only one out of six burglars, James McCord, was from the White House and he was probably current CIA claiming to be ex-CIA.

\# The CIA burglars' target was not to get hold of Democrat electoral strategies to benefit Nixon's White House, as they had claimed to Nixon officials. There was no Democrat election campaign at that time, and the burglars ignored the office of the Democrat's director Larry O'Brien. Instead they bugged the phones of a minor Democrat functionary Spencer Oliver Jr, who was seldom in his office and didn't even work for the DNC. His phones were actually being used by a secretary to match up randy Democrat visitors from out of town with high-class hookers mostly run by a "lush blonde" pal of the wife of a White House counsel.

\# *The Washington Post* was (then as now) founded and run for the benefit of the Democrat Party, and its Watergate burglary reporting aimed to hide from the public the Democrats' sordid call-girl centre operations. It's now owned by the world's second-richest person, Amazon's Geoff Bezos.

\# The CIA team wanted the "explicitly intimate" calls and trysts for potential blackmail, also for CIA people's own prurient enjoyment, and possibly to thwart the team leader's rival contender for a cushy job running a public relations firm Mullen & Co. as a disguised CIA front.

\# Since long-standing CIA operations against domestic US citizens were illegal (domestic surveillance was the FBI's role), the CIA hoped the burglary authorisations and cash extracted from White House dupes could retrospectively authorise a raft of past CIA criminal surveillance of US citizens.

\# The CIA was obsessed with sex behaviours, both to compromise and blackmail US citizens and keep tabs on what foreign agencies were doing. The CIA's dossier or what it called its "fag file" on US homosexuals ran to 300,000 names, and it had voluminous tapes of people's activities in brothels.

\# When the burglars (minus one) were caught, the CIA was keen for Woodstein to focus on the White House, not themselves. CIA records show that James Bennett, head of the CIA-front global PR firm Mullen & Co, made a deal with Woodward soon after the burglary that he would feed Woodward stories and "a suitably grateful" Woodward would then "protect" Mullen and its CIA ownership. Keep in mind that the chief burglar, Howard Hunt, was a full-time Mullen executive while holding down a part-time job in Nixon's White House as a supposedly "retired" CIA man to do "sensitive assignments". The author says that Bennett provided Woodward with only a few lame stories and Woodward and the *Post* protected the Mullen firm for reasons of their own.

\# The CIA's problem was that Mark Felt's FBI, resenting the CIA's grab for power and influence and manifold illegalities, was doing its own investigating of the burglaries, by all accounts an honest and professional FBI effort. Felt kept leaking to Woodstein (and some other journos) to prevent Democrat-friendly media and agencies from sweeping the real stories under the carpet.

\# Six years later, *The Washington Post* cheered on the authorities who falsely convicted Felt of federal procedural crimes, causing Felt's wife such shame that she filched his service revolver and shot herself. Felt was later exonerated. Specifically, the 'crimes' were warrantless break-ins for evidence against the Weather Underground group which had done 50 or so bombings of government buildings. Felt's defence was correctly that national security concerns overrode Bill of Rights provisions. The Felt case led to the FISA precautionary system which unhappily was then abused by the FBI to surveil President Trump in the Russia-gate hoax organised by the Democrat Party.

At the height of the Watergate drama, as documented by Woodstein and in the movie, Deep Throat aka Mark Felt, in high anxiety, warned them that "Everyone's life is in danger". Woodstein implied it was themselves at risk, but made no attempt to clarify any detail for readers. This omission made them seem heroic and enabled them once again to avoid pinpointing the CIA's gangster-like roles in Watergate.

The reality, as O'Connor documents, was that the CIA was ready and willing to assassinate **witnesses** (not reporters) capable of testifying to courts about how the CIA ran the burglaries and other domestic illegalities. Don't think that's far-fetched – it's on the record that the CIA had discussed with a White House dupe how to assassinate a muckraking columnist Jack Anderson who had twigged the CIA involvement (the CIA cited the mooted assassination as "Operation Mudhen"). In the event, the CIA terrified Anderson into silence by ostentatiously tailing and surveilling him.

One of two key potential witnesses against the CIA, the sixth burglar Lou Russell, died of poisoning in circumstances parallel to the planned assassination of Anderson, and just one day after Deep Throat warned Woodstein of CIA assassination tactics. Russell had another CIA role taping prostitutes at work and post-burglary he was getting hush money payments from the White House. He'd been subpoenad to testify shortly to a Senate committee, and died claiming someone has switched poison for his heart medicine.

The method the CIA suggested to the White House dupes about Jack Anderson was called "aspirin roulette", or the planting of a poison pill within the victim's normal medication pills. Russell's friend, Detective John Leon, a Washington wire-tapping expert, was scheduled to tell all at a press conference on 9 July 1973 about CIA and Democrat wiretapping. He also never made it, dying suddenly of a heart attack just before his press appearance.

Dorothy Hunt, the wife of the CIA burglary team leader Howard Hunt, and herself an undercover agent, was carrying $US10,000 in a briefcase – a small fortune – in alleged hush money to a source in Chicago. She died on 8 December 1972 when the United airliner crashed en route with 43 fatalities among among 61 passengers. It was a few weeks before her scheduled appearance to testify. O'Connor makes no claim that the CIA aided the crash (it was officially ruled as pilot error), but does note that CIA and FBI sleuths were strikingly quick to the search at the crash scene.

By this time I'm sure you're wanting to know where and how O'Connor got all his evidence. The book reads like a prosecutor's summing up of his case to a jury, with the evidence to follow. In this case, he has already provided documentation and footnoting in a 2019 volume Postgate: *How the Washington Post Betrayed Deep Throat, Covered Up Watergate, and Began Today's Partisan Advocacy Journalism* (Post Hill Press, $A37.90).

The new book is for lay readers, myself included, who would find the encyclopaedic details indigestible. I've taken a quick look at the first, documented, version. Only experts and Watergate aficionados would vouch for sure – the story is as convoluted as the Kennedy assassination – but the tale he weaves from on-the-record material alone is perfectly plausible. For anyone indignant that Woodstein and the *Post* are shown in such poor light, just check their cheerleading of Russia-gate and the *Post's* pre-election coverage of Hunter Biden's laptop, involving public lies and silence about the truths.

As O'Connor notes, in the pre-internet 1970s, documents like new Congressional and official reports on Watergate were not readily accessible by the public and readers relied on the press to honestly summarise them. O'Connor tests the *Post*'s good faith by checking back on how honestly they reported those emerging reports, and he gives them a 'fail' grade. In other words, the *Post*'s failures of omission and commission were not accidents but strategically motivated.

For example, the *Post* declined to report that one of the burglars, Eugenio Martinez, had a desk key on him and fought guards to conceal it. It turned out to be the key to a drawer in the office used as a switchboard for call-girl appointments. Woodstein's claim was that they were *au fait* with the important Watergate details – so how did they miss this "key" detail? And when the Republican minority report on Watergate came out in 1973, exposing top-tier secrets, why did the *Post* ignore them and focus only on its boring, mundane passages? One unreported detail: CIA internal admissions that its agent handler Lee Pennington had gone to one CIA burglar's home, McCord's, on the night McCord was arrested, and helped Mrs McCord burn documents proving McCord's CIA status. CIA insiders had laughed about the fire causing smoke damage to the lounge-room ceiling.

It's also noteworthy that O'Connor as a senior lawyer is not attacking the Democrat establishment and media per se and says the rightist press is no better when doing "investigative" reports. Rightists, he says, merely have fewer writers and outlets. His beef is about today's "investigative" journalism ethos, where mere reporters take on the role of prosecutor, judge and jury to deny their targets any form of natural justice – and deny their readers access to whatever facts undermine the reporter's case. (The ABC's persecution of Cardinal Pell is a case in point). He even instances a *Post* editorial claiming that Watergate court cases, where claims are properly tested, are inferior to what the press dishes up: *"Courts are a capricious venue for arguments about history."* Unlike its reporters, the *Post* would claim. #

PART SIX

GRUMPY THOUGHTS FROM A GRUMPY OLD COOT

Chef Pascoe's roadkill à la mode with a dash of musk

4 January 2022

Despite 60 years of journalistic lunches, including a Big Mac from a Soviet GRU operative in Canberra, I've only enjoyed one really posh feed. That was in 1990 and my host was Tim Marcus Clark, CEO of the Bank of South Australia.

The intimate dining room was under an atrium as if the whole tower had been designed around it. Marcus Clark was feuding with his board and with Premier John Bannon about his wayward lending, so he wanted a puff piece from me in *Business Review Weekly*.

I kept getting distracted by the long scar under his chin – some assailant had cut his throat from ear to ear a few years earlier. A few months after my lunch the bank collapsed with $3 billion of dud loans, taking down Marcus Clark, Premier Bannon and much of SA. (The bank lost $700 million just on one deal, the Remm Myer Centre development in Rundle Mall).

I'm trying to imagine a scenario involving an equally posh lunch for top people at Melbourne University but I don't know how these lunches really go. I'll just do my clunky best. The menu is leftover wombat road-kill. To find out why, you'll have to read on.

I'm imagining a Vice-Chancellor, Dr Masculine, hosting Tesla guy Elon Musk and offering him a prestigious Enterprise Professorship.

Elon: Hi Dr Masculine!

Dr Masculine: Hi Elon! Make yourself at home on the sofa. The sofa is on *stolen Wurundjeri land of the Kulin Nation, and we pay our respects to Elders past, present and emerging. Sovereignty was never ceded.*

Elon: Hey I thought you owned the campus. The rent to these Kulins must cost a bomb.

Dr Masculine: It's complicated, but our Law Society students are leading the way with their "Pay the Rent" campaign. It wants me to pay rent especially to the Kulin Nation.

Elon: Say, why don't I lend you some lawyers and merchant bankers? I bet they can tailor something win-win tax-positive with the Kulin Embassy.

Dr Masculine: Thanks, *our chancellor's a barrister,* he can follow that up. But to change the subject, congrats on being so rich.

Elon: Oh, I'm comfortable. I get by.

Dr Masculine (coyly): Keep this under your hat, but as for me, I'm *Australia's best paid vice-chancellor* – $1.5 million last time around!

Elon: Wow, I'm impressed! The President of Princeton only gets a *million US* and the president of Yale only gets *$US1.16 million.*

Dr Masculine: They don't have the prestige we enjoy here in Dan Andrew's Victoria. But let's cut to the chase. We offer you a coveted Honorary Enterprise Professorship for building the trillion-dollar Tesla company and launching space rockets and other business stuff.

Elon: But isn't Melbourne University famously anti-capitalist? [Pulls out smart phone and googles]. The university says here that capitalism's *"death agonies will likely generate many wild quests for salvation through vulgar resource exploitation"* and:

> We should reconceive and replot our exit from capitalist mo-
> dernity, not as retrenchment to misery, but as quest for a new
> human plentitude. Freed from the diktak of capitalist growth,

and its straitened materialism, our species could discover fresh forms of realisation in things without 'value', at least as presently conceived. A post-accumulative political economy is the premise for a new urban modernity ...

Dr Masculine (blushing): It should be diktat, not 'diktak', and we Cambridge people say "plenitude" not "plentitude". But anyway pay no attention. That's just Professor Brendon Gleeson, director of our Melbourne Sustainable Society Institute. He's such a lovable rascal! His colleague, Sam Alexander, even co-authored a book with Rupert Read from Extinction Rebellion who advocated: *"It is just-about conceivable that this civilisation might survive by adopting an extremely disciplined eco-fascism."* Actually Brendan *bugged out of the Institute last September*, and on 6 December I got my pro-vice chancellor Mark to *sack everyone else there.*

Elon: So the Sustainable Institute wasn't sustainable?

Dr Masculine: Yeah no. (quoting his press release):

The closure of MSSI does not diminish the University's deep commitment to a sustainable society and to addressing the challenges of climate change.

Now Elon, about our Enterprise Professorship offer ...

Elon: Sounds good. Who got the previous one?

Dr Masculine: Oh, that was famous Aboriginal businessman Bruce Pascoe in September last year. *Enterprise appointments are highly selective to ensure appointees bring distinctive knowledge and skills that would be otherwise unavailable to the institution. Professorial-level Enterprise appointments are highly distinguished positions.* You'll have heard about Bruce and his *Dark Emu* story in Palo Alto I'm sure. Bruce's pre-contact forebears were agriculturalists living in stone villages of 1000 – early McMansions – and they began baking bread in 118,000BC.

Elon: Sounds good. What tribe's Bruce from?

Dr Masculine: Well mainly Yuin, Bunurong and Tasmanian. But he's also said he's *Wiradjuri, Punniler Panner, Koori, a descendant of the Ballarat and Geelong Aboriginal communities, and from a tribe bordering the Wathaurong of Geelong and Colac Victoria, along with a South Australian Aboriginal connection.* He discovered he was Aboriginal at the age of 30 – no, make that 18, – no, make that 9, when he was *speaking the Wathaurong language with his family.*

Elon: You've convinced me. And now tell me about his business successes.

Dr Masculine: Well there's been three main companies. You can google it on that *excellent Quadrant Online site.* He and his registered charity, Black Duck Foods, have been producing flour from native grass seeds for the past decade.

Elon: How many million tonnes so far?

Dr Masculine: Actually none is being offered on the Black Duck website yet. There also his Gurundgi Munjie company which ASIC is striking off, and he's a director of Twofold Aboriginal Corporation, Eden.

Elon: How's that one going?

Dr Masculine (googling): Well the auditor last March said:

Material Uncertainty Related to Going Concern.

We draw attention to Note 1 in the financial report, which indicates that the Corporation incurred a net loss of $466,107 during the year ended June 30, 2020, and, as of that date, the Corporation's current liabilities exceeded its current assets by

$542,937. These events or conditions, along with other mat-ters set forth in Note 1, indicate that a material uncertainty exists that may cast significant doubt on the Corporation's ability to continue as a going concern. Our opinion is not modified in respect of this matter.

But if you ask me, some government agency or pal under some pretext is bound to throw Twofold Aboriginal Corporation a million or two to get it viable again.

Elon: So all A-OK at Twofold Bay. Man, I could learn a lot from this Pascoe fellow about running a successful enterprise.

Dr Masculine (chortling): Well, Elon, as a special surprise he's right here and he's cooking our lunch today!

Elon (amazed): So what's he cooking for us?

Dr Masculine: It's his culinary specialty – roadkill! And here he is to tell you all about it.

Enter Bruce Pascoe wearing a chef's toque, and holding his new book *Country: Future Fire, Future Farming*. He opens it to his Chapter 4, "Future Farming – kangaroos and emus", and reads to Elon:

There is another avenue of protein collection we might con-sider. Every morning in East Gippsland the road toll becomes apparent, with carcasses of wallabies, kangaroos, possums and wombats every kilometre or so. In this district it is not uncommon to find kangaroos and wallabies with broken legs as the result of being hit by a car.

I will never forget finding one huge injured male by following his moans of agony. And I will certainly never forget the look he turned on me when I arrived with my gun. He knew ex-actly what was about to happen, and was ready. [Who knew Bruce was a kangaroo-whisperer?]

We harvest these animals with our cars, so why not use their bounty instead of allowing their carcasses to bloat? If we are going to be meat eaters, and there are good arguments for some meat in our diet, then let us be economical about our harvest ... Animals killed like this almost always die suddenly, without the meat-toughening release of adrenaline into their system.

Why don't we have patrol vans with people licensed to inspect roadkill and harvest anything left that is fit for human consumption or could be made into dog food? A simple temperature probe is almost all that is required. Older carcasses could be moved further off the highway so that eagles and crows were not tempted to feed too close to the road. Stringent health and refrigeration rules could be set in place so that we don't waste any resources. Harvesting that meat and the kangaroo and emu stock in our paddocks would mean we could afford to graze fewer hard-hoofed animals. (Kindle, p. 75 of 235).

Dr Masculine: The book shows great wisdom. No wonder National Museum Australia was *proud to be its co-publisher.*

Elon: (to Bruce eagerly): So what's for lunch?

Bruce: Wombat back legs! A truck hit it near my farm at Gipsy Point. I scraped it off the Mallacoota-Genoa Road. The head got squashed, but the hindquarters were pristine and the wombat didn't have time to release any meat-toughening adrenaline. I stuck a simple temperature probe up its arse and it had hardly begun to bloat. I separated the legs with an axe and they've been in my car fridge, involving stringent health rules, all the way down here to Melbourne University. You're in for a fine dining experience and what's more, wombat roadkill cuisine involves much fewer planet-killing CO_2 emissions than steak and lamb chops. I intend to sell any of today's leftovers to chefs in Lygon Street and the Paris end of Collins St.

(Enter waiters, exposing the wombat legs under silver salvers. Dr Masculine, Elon Musk and Bruce Pascoe tuck in, using saucers to spit out bits of gravel.)

Elon (to Dr Masculine): I really don't feel worthy to stand alongside your Enterprise Professor in Indigenous Agriculture, but I'm deeply grateful to accept your Honorary Enterprise Professorship.

Pascoe: *Koongadgee gobatarda* – that's goodbye and thanks in my native Wathaurong tongue.

Dr Masculine (to Elon): Allow me to phone you up an Uber to Tulla'. We've got a tight budget here, you'll understand. #

Eddie Mabo's secret politics

10 March 2022

How outrageous to suggest that Eddie Koiko Mabo was a card-carrying member of the Communist Party of Australia! For starters, that would suggest that Australian Communists precipitated the subsequent takeover of the 2.5 million square kilometres or the third of this continent now under native title.

In any event, Eddie Mabo repeatedly denied he was a CPA ticket-holder. He wouldn't have lied about that, surely?

We know Senator Arthur Gietzelt AO, Bob Hawke's one-time Minister for Veterans Affairs, was a secret CPA member despite all sorts of denials, but he was a politician, after all, and even trousered $14,500 in libel damages from the ABC in 1976 for calling him a Red. The late Stuart Macintyre in his CPA history, *The Party* (2022), outs Gietzelt but that was already old news.[10]

Eddie Mabo, in contrast, was such a good chap that Sir Ronald Wilson at the Human Rights Commission in 1992 awarded him posthumously a Human Rights Medal for his work for Aboriginal rights and justice. The next year, my favourite newspaper, *The Australian*, awarded him their Australian of the Year title. James Cook University, now notorious for its persecution of honest Barrier Reef scholar, Peter Ridd, in 2008 christened its Townsville library the Eddie Koiko Mabo Library. Astronomers have named a star Koiko after Mabo, and in 2017 the Mint issued a 50-cent coin with his smiling portrait.

Well, brace yourselves. Eddie Mabo was indeed a CPA ticket-

---

[10] Stuart Macintyre, *The Party: The Communist Party of Australia from heyday to reckoning*, Allen & Unwin, 2022.

holder. The Mint might as well re-issue its Mabo 50-cents with added hammer and sickle logo. Seeing that Mabo was definitely a CPA member (Townsville branch) in 1964 during the party's Soviet-worshipping era, the Mint could switch the coin's wording from "Right Wrongs, Write Yes for Aborigines!" to a Cyrillic version.

This little essay is not about the pros and cons of the High Court's 1992 Mabo land-rights decision, nor about whether there was anything villainous about the Communist Party doing a united-front job with oppressed Aborigines. I'm just putting stuff on the public record so Eddie Mabo's Communist Party membership can be included in the materials copiously dished out to preschoolers, primary and high schoolers and starry-eyed undergrads at universities (who all might consider Communism a good thing). I hope Mabo's greatest fan, the ABC, will amend its Mabo material after a close study of my essay.

My source for the Mabo revelation is the same Macintyre history, *The Party*. He writes (p. 468) with my emphasis:

> *John Nolan, a member of the Queensland state committee [of the pro-China breakaway outfit CPA – Marxist-Leninist], subsequently formed a branch in Townsville and tried to entice Eddie Mabo **across from the CPA branch there.***

I'm not surprised Mr Nolan failed to win over Mabo to his splinter party's brain-numbing mumbo-jumbo about rights and wrongs of the China-Soviet split, e.g., "Such differences are the cause of great concern to all here who desire to uphold the purity of our proletarian science."

How did Macintyre know that Eddie Mabo was in that CPA branch? His relevant footnote is "minutes of meeting of Townsville

ANTHEM OF THE UNWOKE

branch of CPA (M-L), n.d. [1964]" which looks kosher to me.[11] There's no further info from Macintyre about how long Mabo had been card-carrying pre-1964 and how long thereafter. It was clearly a significant span of years.

Now let's turn to Eddie's story, straight from the horse's mouth in *Edward Koiki Mabo, His Life & Struggle for Land Rights*, by Professor Noel Loos (James Cook University) and Koiki Mabo (University of Queensland Press 1996). The Foreword is by Marcia Langton, who writes that, thanks to Mabo, "Australia is a more honourable nation" and "The decision was a 'watershed' having 'an impact like no other legal event in Australia since Federation."

The book consists of Loos' tape-recordings of Mabo between 1984 and Mabo's death from cancer in January 1992, four months before the decade-long native title case was decided. The book in turn became the "bible" for a Blackfella Films episode in *First Australians* (2008) by Rachel Perkins, daughter of late Aboriginal Affairs Department head Charles Perkins. Melbourne University Press followed up with hard- and soft-cover coffee table books, a paperback reader, "and a well-produced study book for use in schools". Four years later, Perkins directed a full bio-epic on Mabo for the ABC.

Loos writes that he was having meals with Mabo during a Canberra academic conference and urged him to recount his life on tape.

---

[11] When the mainstream party folded in 1991, it generously bequeathed both $3 million in assets (today's equivalent, $6 million) and tonnes of its long-secret meeting records to scholars and archivists – Macintyre being of that genre. Party members in Victoria had already folded their branch in 1984 and tipped its cash into a new Socialist Forum, this Party money funding later Prime Minister Julia Gillard's part-time salary as administrator/clerk and "Stiletto Specialist" from 1984-87.

This he did, without interruption, for some time. We then developed a dialogue in which I asked him to elaborate on some aspects of his story and, in the process, more of his story unfolded, but it was still very much work in progress when he died. Because of his unique place in Australia's history, I have edited the tapes to express his perspective of his life in his own words and minimised, as much as possible, my contribution to the dialogue.

… It is my attempt to complete the autobiography we set out to create. As a result, we have this remarkable, if incomplete, life story of possibly the most important indigenous Australian in Australia's history.

Loos sums up:

At the time, the 1960s, many of the union leaders in Townsville who supported Koiki were members of the Communist Party: Eddie Heilbronn, Bill Timms, Bill Irving and Fred Thompson. In one way this was fortunate as the Communist Party had demonstrated a formal commitment to Aboriginal advancement reaching back to 1931 and affirmed in 1943. This had clearly been accepted at branch level in Townsville...

Mabo considered his understanding of mainland politics was largely derived from his involvement with the trade union movement, but initially he didn't even know what 'Communism' or 'Communist' meant.

Loos writes (my emphases), "I asked Koiki if he had ever thought of joining the Communist Party."

Mabo: *No. It was like the Labor Party. **I never ever joined it**. I don't know why. I got nominated [for the Labor Party] a couple of times, and I wanted to join the Labor Party while I* *was down at the Harbour Board. Then someone said, "You've got to have a good record and no police convictions." Well, I haven't got any police convictions anyway. They said, "... You've got to know three or four members of the Labor Party who would make recommendations for you to join." And I said, "Oh, no. Forget it." I didn't know any other members then. I didn't continue on with it.*

The quote above could read as Mabo's deflection of the original question about Communist Party membership. The Labor Party did not admit Communist Party ticket-holders. Mabo found himself being abused as a "black Commo".

"Although some attached this label to him, he said he was never tempted to become a member," Loos wrote in 1984.

I'm no psychiatrist, but while reading the tape transcripts I kept wondering if Mabo was required by the Party to conceal his membership, but being a basically truthful man, he compensated by being disarmingly frank about his intimate ties with Communists and their Townsville branch.

Mabo hero-worshipped his Communist mentors in Townsville, especially "old Communist" Eddie Heilbronn. He would hang around Townsville's "tree of knowledge" – an almond tree between the Post Office and the SGIO – to enjoy Heilbronn's stump oratory. He told the tape-recorder:

I never ever heard of Communist people before; I never heard of them, never read anything about them. The state elections were coming up and Eddie Heilbronn somehow nominated himself as a candidate. He was giving a speech and I stood by and listened to it. And I picked up something. He really got me, you know. I was sort of mesmerised by the way he spoke. And I got attracted to that, and then when I saw him again down at the Harbour Board, I used to ask him a lot of questions.

Mabo repeatedly explains that he got to know Communists as friends, only later discovering they were Communists. "But it didn't make any difference to me," Mabo said, "because I saw them as the kind of people that I could rely on for any advice."

Mabo paid dearly for his curiosity by the "almond tree of knowledge". Several Harbour Board anti-Communists spotted him there and snitched to the bosses. This got Mabo transferred to lower pay on a sledge-hammer gang. His Communist friends would give him advice but made it clear he had to fight his own battles. He took this to heart: "The Communist Party had a long history of involvement with Aboriginal people. They were the first white political party to offer them support in their struggle for justice."

In the mid-1960s Mabo and a Queensland Aborigine, Dick Hoolihan, were invited on to the Townsville Labour Council and enjoyed its conferences, he said.

Mabo: *I even went to the Communist conference. The Queensland Communist Party would have their conference and they would ask us to go, me and Dick Hoolihan. I think that was the starting off point of my political involvement in organisations.*

Does that strike you as a rather sophisticated "starting off point"? It certainly does to me.

Mabo said the National Party [i.e. CP/Lib] government was keeping him under surveillance, viewing his group's activism, such as its black community school and inter-racial seminars as Communist fronts. He thought the police were tapping their phones and warning off supporters such as the local clergy.

For certain, the Australian Security Intelligence Agency (ASIO) was keeping Mabo under surveillance. Perhaps the police were also involved.

Loos asked Mabo if he had ever attended Communist Party meetings.

I did. I went to a conference. There was a news crew, television, I think. The first time we had television back in 1966, I think, or '67. Or '68.

I was still down the Harbour Board when we had the Inter-Racial Seminar [in 1967]. It was after that, after the Inter-Racial Seminar, that I got invited to attend a conference. I wanted to hear their State President. I believed he was a very good speaker who couldn't repeat the same word twice. And I got attracted there because I admire people who can talk on the spot in front of huge crowds of people.

Anyway, I went along to it. Me and Dick Hoolihan sat in the background and I really admired that man. Anyway, while he was talking, there was a camera crew working. And of course I didn't know that we were detected as well. We were picked up by the camera. And of course that night the news flash went on television and someone from the Harbour Board picked it up. And about a week later – the Vietnam War was on at that time too – someone called me a Viet Cong. 'You're a Viet Cong.' 'What are you talking about? What do you mean?' He said, 'I saw you on television yesterday.'

Macintyre publishes in *The Party* an ASIO photo of Mabo at the 1965 conference of the North Queensland District Communist Party. ASIO was always particularly interested in undercover CPA members, as distinct from overt members.

His Communist sympathies – or probably his actual Party

membership – riled his wife Netta who, as a teacher's aide, became the breadwinner when he was between jobs. Mabo says:

Netta's attitude was much the same as the church-influenced people. I learnt at that time the difference between the Communist Party and the Labor Party and the Liberals and the Country Party, and that Queensland was governed by a coalition of both the Liberals and the National Party, the Country Party. And because she was constantly being brainwashed, maybe during her childhood days, against Communism – either through the church or somewhere along the line anyway – she developed a very bad attitude towards them, towards Communists. And she threatened me at one stage.

She said, 'If you don't get out of it, I'm going to leave.' I had to get out of the Advancement League and all the organisations that I was getting involved in, or she was going to leave. And then I tried my hardest and then eventually I convinced her that we've got no one to turn to. The moderate political or-ganisations won't listen to our pleas. We've got to have white support. You know, we're very much in need of it and we should grab any hand that comes to us.

And she eventually took it in and said welcome to people like [CPA member] Fred Thompson and [co-traveller or member] Frank Bishop. They would come in at any time and she would welcome them. I eventually convinced her.

Loos suggested to Mabo that it must have been a long step for Netta from her Islander village outside Halifax, which itself was a backwater near Ingham, to becoming aware of the political com-plexities of the world. "Yes. That's right. Even for me too it was a big step from that little island in the Strait."

275

He quit the Harbour Board in 1967 and became a gardener at James Cook University for eight years to 1975. He impressed the academics, who encouraged his self-education and from there the seeds of the Mabo land rights claim were sown. His university gardening job also helped pay off their mortgage. Loos asked him:

Loos: It wasn't bought by the Communist Party as someone once said?

Mabo: Oh, no. (We both laughed). #

The dog days of the Biden administration

15 February 2022

Tolerance and inclusiveness can be good things in government, but the Biden administration is starting to resemble the court of Caligula. Last month it appointed the gender-fluid engineer Sam Brinton (pronoun "they") to the Office of Nuclear Energy (budget $US1.6 billion). His role is deputy assistant secretary, second-in-charge of nuclear waste issues.

Brinton boasts of his after-hours participation in the BDSM "Pup" cult/fetish. He role-plays as handler and sex partner of a novice impersonating a dog, who commonly wears a tail anchored per rectum and is punished for making literal messes on the carpet.

Brinton's hobby is consensual and doesn't break any laws, in the US anyway. It can become dangerous – one Australian-born "Pup" (unconnected to Brinton) died in Seattle in 2018 as a result of silicone injections to create an over-size, dog-like scrotum and testicles.

The appointment has not attracted much publicity. The Democrat-friendly press's job is to shield Biden from criticism, and anyway the detail is beyond any limit of explicitness. I'm setting it out because it's necessary here. The fullest accounts are in *The Conservative American* blog.

In an elaborate description of the pup cult in *Metro Weekly*, a gay journal five years back, Sam Brinton, then 27, was photographed as handler to a Pup called Nubi, 24, who wore a leather puppy mask.

One of the hardest things about being a handler is that I've honestly had people ask, "Wait, you have sex with animals?"

Sam says. "They believe it's abusive, that it's taking advantage of someone who may not be acting up to a level of human responsibility ... The other misperception is that I have some really messed up background, like, did I have some horrible childhood trauma that made me like to have sex with animals."

Brinton's website has a video where he describes how, as a youth, his Southern Baptist missionary parents in Perry, Iowa (pop 7000), subjected him to painful conversion therapy including ice, heat, and electric shocks through his fingertips to divert him from gay culture. He claims he went to the third floor of their building to jump off and his mother told him there she would love him again if he would only change.

However, he has also told college kids fanciful tales about how he was a nuclear adviser to Trump and shoe-shopping consultant to Michelle Obama. His critics claim his stories about parental "conversion therapy" might also have fanciful elements, notwithstanding his submissions about it in 2014 to the United Nations Committee Against Torture.

Brinton is further insulated as a stalwart of "The Trevor Project", billed as the world's largest suicide prevention and crisis intervention group for LGBTQ youngsters.

He has a further role as a drag queen "Sister Ray Dee O'Active" in Washington's Sisters of Perpetual Indulgence, where he bills himself as "the slutty one" who studied "nuclear fabulousity" at MIT. At one point, he crowdfunded to buy and wear a pair of Manolo stilettos for the red carpet at the Oscars.

The *MetroWeekly* article continues,

The diversity within the community also extends to opinions about mixing puppy play with sex. For some, puppy play is completely independent of sex. For others, it's part of the fuller experience.

An alternative arrangement works best for Sam [Brinton] and Pup Nubi.

"I actually have trouble when we transition from pup play to having sex," Sam explains. "Like, 'No, I can't have you whimper like that when we're having sex,' because I don't want to mix that world. It's interesting, because he doesn't have to come out of pup mode to have me f–k him. I personally have to bring him out of pup perception for me. But then I'm still treating him as a submissive to me ..."

Pup "Bragi", 23, maintains, "Even the humping, it's not really a sexual thing, it's just part of the play". Brinton is quoted,

'I tell people that if you're going to be a good handler, you have to listen well. I can hear when Pup needs something faster, because of the difference in the grunts or the moans.'

Sam also says that watching a pup's eyes, his interactions with people, and his reaction time to certain commands can signal whether a pup needs to take a rest or break for water. "A handler should know that even if he's not whimpering for water, you know this is the time for something that he needs."

Brinton emphasises benign elements: "My headspace is equivalent to the mom who sees her kid in danger, or the dad who wants to teach his son how to play football. It's the concept of the teacher and nurturer ... My job is to make sure that while he's in headspace, I'm keeping him safe ..."

His self-bio says,

Sam has worn his stilettos to Congress to advise legislators about nuclear policy and to the White House where he advised President Obama and Michelle Obama on LGBT issues. He shows young men and women everywhere he goes that they can be who they are and gives them courage. Once, while he was walking around Disney World in 6 inch stilettos with his boyfriend, a young gay boy saw Sam with his boyfriend and started crying. He told his mother, "It's true, Mom. WE can be our own princess here ..." He works for other LGBT young people to have a similar opportunity to live genuinely and gladly as he does.

He evangelises about his persona to college students and the wide world. In his own website words:

No school is too small or remote. I mean it. I do request a fee which is all inclusive (hotel, flight, speaking fee, everything). If that is a problem PLEASE don't make it the reason we don't speak. I can and have worked with every budget under the sun. The message is important. Not the money. I might even be able to do a tour nearby which will help with getting multiple schools in one trip.

He has certainly garnered positive press, such as a piece in the official MIT press last May under the headline *Sam Brinton Saves the World*, which said that, apart from being "a champion for LGBTQ rights", his goal at MIT was "to save the world from nuclear waste related environmental disaster." He complained that some nuclear engineering students suggested he had got into the course only through winning a "diversity" fellowship.

A piece in *National Pulse* describes Brinton's "Kink 101" session at the University of Nebraska. The illustration shows him in a dress standing over three kneeling males with leather bondage-style dog masks on their heads.

One student in the audience for a Brinton talk at Rensselaer Polytechnic campus told the campus journal, "I enjoyed every second of the event. He has given these kinds of talks at Rensselaer in the past, and I hope they continue into the future."

The Biden appointment is a conundrum in the post-Christian stage of American left-liberalism. Brinton has the necessary qualifications and experience in nuclear waste handling – academically he earned Masters from MIT in both Nuclear Engineering and "TPP" involving "societal challenges through research and education at the intersection of technology and policy". My sampling of his previous nuclear work suggests he is good at his nuclear-waste job. Plus, he's no candidate for Chinese or Russian blackmail as he's proud and public about his fetishes.

But senior US officials need to be respected by their foreign counterparts in negotiations and treaties. A lipsticked gender-fluid US negotiator with a BDSM-leather fetish for doggy role-plays might not be accorded full respect by the nuclear experts of Xi Jinping, Putin or the Saudis.

Thought-provoking comments at American Conservative include

Daniel Baker: A lot of very talented people have been really, really weird. Gebhard von Blucher, the guy who kicked Napoleon's butt at Waterloo, thought he was pregnant with an elephant. George Patton, the general most feared and respected by the Germans in World War II, believed he was reincarnated. John Nash, a Nobel laureate in mathematics, was a schizophrenic who suffered from delusions that he was the Emperor of Antarctica. If [Brinton] knows his stuff, the weirdness of his bedroom antics is of no import to anyone but him and his playmates.

RBH: You may not care about sexual politics, but sexual politics cares about you. Like normalizing trans ideology in elementary schools and drag queens reading to children at public libraries – this sort of thing is coming to the public square, to an institution near you. If you object in any way, you'll be considered the problem. Neutrality was nice while it lasted, but that's not what time it is.

Steve Frank: You need the TRUST of the people you are trying to lead. That requires character. Would you TRUST this freak to babysit your young child even if he claimed to be an "expert" in child care?

JonF311: People need to keep their kinks private. Brinton's apparent openness about his shenanigans is what rules him out of bounds for any position of public trust.

Samton912: Sam Brinton is the face of evil, a pure disgusting evil that pretends it is simply another flavor of ice cream. Perhaps it is, but it is arsenic ice cream.

temp anon: Should he be fired? Publicly shamed? Forced into some sort of mental hospital/conversion therapy? Barred from government? Jailed?

Lila Rajiva: Ordinary heterosexual people do "yucky" things all day long, which really do no physical harm to anyone else, whatever the morality or immorality. They would look as ridiculous if they were held up to the public gaze. There are many more body blows being delivered to the Christian community by people inside it, including its leaders. Jerry Falwell Jr's public cavortings, minus a puppy mask, are every bit as ridiculous as Brinton's and much more damaging.

Thomas R: Is this guy the most qualified person in America? I kind of doubt it. I'm not saying his kinks helped get him the job, but I doubt they were super-exhaustive in finding the "best person."

Sean the Elder: Both DoD [Department of Defence] and the Department of Energy [DoE] have Reliability Programs for all personal intricately involved in the handling of nuclear materials. In DOE, it is called the "Human Reliability Program." According to DOE, "The HRP is a security and safety reliability program designed to ensure that individuals who occupy positions affording access to certain materials, nuclear explosive devices, facilities, and programs meet the highest standards of reliability and physical and mental suitability." I am familiar with the DoD "Personal Reliability Program" (I conducted a few audits associated with it) and they were pretty strict. If you got into a bar fight, you got pulled out and did not get access to nuclear material. If you took cold medicine without prior approval, you got pulled out and denied access to nuclear materials. If you had any incident with the police, you got pulled out. You don't take chances with nukes. Apparently, anything goes now. But five years ago, there is no way in Hell that this guy would have ever gotten a clearance or had been able to maintain [Reliability] status.

The ABC online news used to run its hit-jobs on Trump under the banner, "Trump's America". This dog material would fit nicely under an ABC banner, "Biden's America." #